Governance and Governmentality for Projects

This research-based book takes an organization-wide perspective to describe the governance and governmentality for projects in organizations. Governance of projects defines and directs the ways managers of projects, programs, and project portfolios carry out their work. Governmentality is the way the managers of these managers present themselves to those they lead.

Governance and Governmentality for Projects begins by introducing existing theories, models, and paradigms for governance and governmentality. It then develops a chronological framework of how governance and governmentality for projects is enabled in organizations, how it subsequently unfolds in organizations of different types and sectors, and the consequences of different governance approaches for project results, trust, control, and ethical issues in projects. Special emphasis is given to the link between corporate governance and the governance of projects, programs, and project portfolios. Three real-life case studies exemplify the research findings described in the book.

Through its structure, this book describes the development of governance and governmentality in the realm of projects from its organizational origins, via observable practices, to expected consequences of different implementations. Aimed at academics, postgraduate students in business and management, reflective practitioners, standards or policy developers, those in governance roles, and others in need of detailed knowledge of the spectrum of project-related governance in organizations, this book will help develop a comprehensive understanding of the theoretical and practical underpinnings of the subject, their interaction, and implications for implementation. This allows for understanding and developing of both generic and idiosyncratic governance structures, such as those needed in project-based organizations.

Ralf Müller is Professor of Project Management at BI Norwegian Business School, Norway.

Routledge Studies in Corporate Governance

1 **Corporate Governance Around the World**
Ahmed Naciri

2 **Behaviour and Rationality in Corporate Governance**
Oliver Marnet

3 **The Value Creating Board**
Corporate governance and organizational behaviour
Edited by Morten Huse

4 **Corporate Governance and Resource Security in China**
The transformation of China's global resources companies
Xinting Jia and Roman Tomasic

5 **Internal and External Aspects of Corporate Governance**
Ahmed Naciri

6 **Green Business, Green Values, and Sustainability**
Edited by Christos N. Pitelis, Jack Keenan and Vicky Pryce

7 **Credit Rating Governance**
Global credit gatekeepers
Ahmed Naciri

8 **Mergers and Acquisitions and Executive Compensation**
Virginia Bodolica and Martin Spraggon

9 **Governance and Governmentality for Projects**
Enablers, Practices, and Consequences
Edited by Ralf Müller

Governance and Governmentality for Projects
Enablers, Practices, and Consequences

Edited by Ralf Müller

NEW YORK AND LONDON

First published 2017
by Routledge
711 Third Avenue, New York, NY 10017

and by Routledge
2 Park Square, Milton Park, Abingdon, Oxon OX14 4RN

Routledge is an imprint of the Taylor & Francis Group, an informa business

© 2017 Taylor & Francis

The right of the editor to be identified as the author of the editorial material, and of the authors for their individual chapters, has been asserted in accordance with sections 77 and 78 of the Copyright, Designs and Patents Act 1988.

All rights reserved. No part of this book may be reprinted or reproduced or utilised in any form or by any electronic, mechanical, or other means, now known or hereafter invented, including photocopying and recording, or in any information storage or retrieval system, without permission in writing from the publishers.

Trademark notice: Product or corporate names may be trademarks or registered trademarks, and are used only for identification and explanation without intent to infringe.

Library of Congress Cataloging-in-Publication Data
Names: Müller, Ralf, 1957– editor.
Title: Governance and governmentality for projects: enablers, practices, and consequences / edited by Ralf Müller.
Description: New York: Routledge, 2016. | Series: Routledge studies in corporate governance; 9 | Includes bibliographical references and index.
Identifiers: LCCN 2016016857 | ISBN 9781138926356 (hardback: alk. paper) | ISBN 9781315683294 (ebook)
Subjects: LCSH: Corporate governance. | Project management.
Classification: LCC HD2741 .G686 2016 | DDC 658.4/04—dc23
LC record available at https://lccn.loc.gov/2016016857

ISBN: 978-1-138-92635-6 (hbk)
ISBN: 978-1-315-68329-4 (ebk)

Typeset in Sabon
by Apex CoVantage, LLC

Contents

List of Tables	vii
List of Figures	ix
About the Editor	xi
About the Contributors	xiii

1 Introduction   1
RALF MÜLLER

2 Organizational Project Governance   11
RALF MÜLLER

PART I
Concepts, Theories, and Models   25

3 Governance Theories   27
RALF MÜLLER

4 Governance Models and Paradigms   36
RALF MÜLLER

5 Governance Institutions   51
RALF MÜLLER, ERLING S. ANDERSEN, OLE JONNY KLAKEGG, AND
GRO HOLST VOLDEN

PART II
Organizational Enablers for Organizational Project
Governance and Governmentality   67

6 Tactical Organizational Enablers   69
RALF MÜLLER

7 Strategic Organizational Enablers   88
RALF MÜLLER

vi *Contents*

PART III
Practices in the Private and Public Sector 105

  8 Private Sector Practices 107
    RALF MÜLLER

  9 Governance in Public Projects: The Norwegian Case 129
    OLE JONNY KLAKEGG AND GRO HOLST VOLDEN

PART IV
Consequences for and of Governance 157

10 Governance and Project Success 159
    ROBERT JOSLIN

11 Governance Mechanisms in Projects 173
    RALF MÜLLER

12 Project Governance and Project Ethics 181
    RALF MÜLLER AND ØYVIND KVALNES

PART V
Cases of Organizational Project Governance 195

13 The Sugarloaf Alliance Case Study 197
    BEVERLEY LLOYD-WALKER AND DEREK WALKER

14 Governance at the Front-End: Managing the Clash of
    Objectives in Project Organizations 221
    SHANKAR SANKARAN AND CHRISTOPHER BIESENTHAL

15 Governance and Governmentality at Tasly Pharmaceuticals 238
    DAN LI

    Index 249

Tables

2.1	Comparison of Governance Practices at Corporate and Project Level	17
2.2	Linking Governance Paradigms to Governance Principles	19
2.3	Linking Project Governance to Governance Principles	20
4.1	Governance Paradigm Questionnaire	49
6.1	Organizational Enablers in the Project-Related Literature	75
6.2	Organizational Enablers by Institutional Theory Categories	81
6.3	Interaction of Organizational Enablers	83
7.1	Organizational Enablers, Their Factors, and Mechanisms	93
8.1	Relationship between Strategic and Tactical Practices	126
10.1	Success Dimensions from Khan et al. (2013)	172
12.1	Organizational Measures to Address Types of Ethical Issues	189

Figures

2.1	Governance Principles across Governance Levels	19
4.1	The Four Governance Paradigms	42
4.2	Governance Paradigms Mean by Country	44
4.3	Governance Paradigms Mean by Project Size	45
4.4	Governance Paradigms Mean by Project Type	45
5.1	The Structure–Collaboration Model, after Turner & Müller (2004)	60
7.1	Enabler Profiles of Organizations of Different Sizes	99
7.2	Enabler Profiles of Organizations at Four Levels of Success	101
8.1	Governance Profiles of Organizations at Three Levels of Project Success	122
8.2	Governance Profiles of Organizations at Three Levels of Organizational Success	123
9.1	Content of the Norwegian Governance Framework for Major Public Projects	138
9.2	Stochastic Cost Estimation: Definition of Key Terms	139
10.1	Governance Paradigms and Their Influence on the Comprehensiveness of a Methodology	164
10.2	Impact of Governance on Project Success	168
12.1	Types of Ethical Issues by Project Governance Paradigm	186
12.2	Correlations of Ethical Issues and Success with Project Governance Dimensions	187
15.1	The Project Management Office	240

About the Editor

Ralf Müller, DBA, MBA, is Professor of Project Management at BI Norwegian Business School. He lectures and researches in leadership, organizational project governance and management, and research methods. He is the recipient of the 2015 PMI Research Achievement Award and the 2012 IPMA Research Award.

About the Contributors

Erling S. Andersen is Professor emeritus of project management at BI Norwegian Business School, Oslo, Norway. He has been a visiting professor at the University of Tokyo, Japan and Nanyang Technological University, Singapore. He is honorary professor at the University of Southern Denmark. His book, *Goal Directed Project Management*, has been translated into ten languages.

Christopher Biesenthal, PhD, is a Senior Lecturer at the School of the Built Environment at the University of Technology, Sydney. His general areas of interest are project governance and project strategy, especially in regards to the underlying practices that constitute both concepts.

Gro Holst Volden is Research Director of the Concept Research Program at NTNU, Trondheim in Norway. Her research is in project evaluation, cost-benefit analysis, and investment decisions. Prior to her academic career, she was in the consultancy business and in state administration. She is President of the Norwegian Evaluation Society.

Robert Joslin, PhD, PgMP®, PMP®, CEng, has served as portfolio/project/ program academic researcher, lecturer and management consultant in telecom, banking, (re)insurance, manufacturing and direct marketing, whilst working for McKinsey & Co, Logica and his own consulting company. He has published papers and book chapters and presented at research conferences, including winning the 2015 EURAM best conference paper award.

Ole Jonny Klakegg, MSc, PhD, is Professor in Project Management at NTNU University, Norway, in combination with R&D Director at WSP Norway. Throughout his 26-year career, he has alternated between teaching and research at the university and working as a consultant in project management. He has experience from a large number of major projects in the public and private sector in Norway. His research interests include governance of projects, front-end management of projects, and management of risk and uncertainty.

xiv *About the Contributors*

Øyvind Kvalnes, PhD, is an associate professor at BI Norwegian Business School. His research interests are in business ethics, leadership, moral psychology, communication climate, and the philosophy of projects. His PhD is from the University of Oslo, with the dissertation titled *Living with Moral Luck* (1998).

Dan Li is Director of the Project Management Center at Tasly Pharmaceutical Group in China. She holds an MBA degree and is Senior Economist, Senior Engineer, and IPMP B level certified. She is the Sixth Committee member of the China Project Management Research Committee (PMRC). Her accolades include the 2015 Top 10 PMO Director in China Award and the 2006 IPMA International Project Management Award.

Beverley Lloyd-Walker, PhD, is a researcher based in two Research Centres within the School of Property, Construction and Project Management at RMIT University, Melbourne. Since commencing her academic career over 25 years ago, her research has covered several areas within project management, including careers, collaborative procurement arrangements, and ethics.

Shankar Sankaran, PhD, is a Professor of Organizational Project Management at the University of Technology Sydney in Australia, where he teaches advanced level subjects in a Master of Project Management Program. He teaches project governance and supervises doctoral students conducting research in aspects of organizational project management, including project governance.

Derek Walker, PhD, MSc, and Emeritus Professor RMIT University, commenced his academic career after various PM roles in the UK, Canada, and Australia. He was Professor of Project Management at the School of Property, Construction and Project Management. He actively pursues academic research into organizational learning, collaboration, leadership, and innovation.

1 Introduction

Ralf Müller

This is a research-based book on governance and governmentality in the realm of projects, or organizational project governance, as we call it in the remainder of the book. Our aim is to provide the reader with a chronological framework of project-related governance and governmentality as it unfolds in organizations and how this framework links into corporate governance.

The book starts with a brief theoretical underpinning of governance and then builds a framework for organizational project governance. The framework starts with the organizational prerequisites and drivers for the establishment of governance structures for projects in organizations. This is followed by the strategic and tactical governance practices applied in the private and public sectors today and the impact of these practices on organizational and project success. The framework finishes with the outline of some of the consequences, in terms of issues and behaviors, seen in projects and organizations applying the different governance approaches shown in this book.

The book is written for academics, postgraduate students, reflective practitioners, standards or policy developers, those in governance roles, and others in need of a detailed knowledge of the spectrum of project-related governance in organizations. The reader learns not only about the practices and approaches to governance and governmentality, but also about the theoretical implications that stem from the research findings. Therefore, it is a source for both those in search of different practices and those in search of understanding. To that end, it is a "why and what" book, and not a "how to" book. For the latter the reader is referred to the large number of consultant books on the market. For the former this book will be a source of many new insights and perspectives.

The Dawn of a New Perspective

Project management has a proud history of one-time, unique undertakings, carried out as standalone endeavors outside the day-to-day operations of organizations, or as standalone organizations limited in lifetime by the duration of the project. This view has changed in recent decades

2 *Ralf Müller*

as projects and project management became more and more the business model for the delivery of products or services to customers internal and external to the organization, with ever-smaller undertakings being named projects. The emergence of portfolio management showed how projects could become the operations of an organization. More recently, the boundaries between operations and projects became blurred even more with the popularity of agile and Scrum methods, which make it hard to identify where the repetitive processes claimed for operations end and the unique processes claimed for projects start. Given the success of these approaches, these developments were a positive for the world of projects and their management.

Is the same true for the governance of projects? Not really. Biesenthal and Wilden (2014) found the first mention of governance in academic project management journals was around the end of the last century, after which it started to increase exponentially, especially from about 2005. Research in project-related governance commenced from a contract perspective and then moved into the specific structures of different project types, such those for large capital projects (e.g., Miller & Hobbs, 2005) or projects in specific industries, such as NASA (Shenhar et al., 2005), construction (e.g., Pryke, 2005), public sector projects (e.g., Klakegg, Williams, & Magnussen, 2008), the governance of interfirm projects (Ruuska, Ahola, Artto, Locatelli, & Mancini, 2011), or the governance and governmentality of Olympics projects (Clegg, Pitsis, Rura-Polley, & Marosszeky, 2002).

Similarly, the focus broadened from individual projects to organizational project settings; for example, with the identification of different organizational structures, contingent on project size and number of customers in an organization (Turner & Keegan, 1999), or the importance of a balance between project, program, and portfolio thinking for organizational success (Blomquist & Müller, 2006). Recent years have shown the emergence of more fundamental questions around the nature of governance per se and its embeddedness in the organizational context (e.g., Ahola, Ruuska, Artto, & Kujala, 2013; Müller, 2009; Too & Weaver, 2014). The most recent studies look into the prerequisites for governance, such as the organizational enablers for project governance (Müller, Shao, & Pemsel, 2016).

From early on, the theoretical base of many of these publications followed the traditional corporate governance theories, such as transaction cost economics (e.g., Reve & Levitt, 1984; Winch, 1989) or agency theory (e.g., Bergen, Dutta, & Walker, 1992). Thus, the theoretical base of project governance was strongly influenced by corporate-level governance theories. However, a similar link in the understanding of the governance function or its underlying principles is missing. The literature on governance in projects largely ignores the link between, or the embeddedness of, project-related governance and corporate governance (for a discussion of this, see Chapter 2).

This gap is addressed in this book. The parts on enablers, practices, and consequences discuss their particular contribution to corporate governance through their contribution to the four *good governance principles* defined by the Organization for Economic Co-operation and Development (OECD) in its report by the Business Sector Advisory Group on Corporate Governance (Millstein, Albert, Cadbury, Feddersen, & Tateisi, 1998). Through this, we show the integration of project-related governance into organizational project governance and its embeddedness in corporate governance. This is further described in Chapter 2.

Positioning Governance

The literature used in this book is mainly of an academic nature, as we build on empirical research and sound theoretical contributions. However, some practitioner literature should also be mentioned, as it is representative of the wide variety of governance approaches. In Chapter 2 we present the two general approaches to governance, which are the non-prescriptive, principle-based approach and the prescriptive, rule-based approach. Both are exemplified in the popular guidelines.

A non-prescriptive, principle-based approach is described in the Guide to Governance of Project Management by the Association for Project Management (APM) (APM, 2004). Their guide addresses the area where corporate governance overlaps with projects and seeks to guide board-level directors in addressing portfolio direction, project sponsorship, project management effectiveness and efficiency, as well as disclosure and reporting. To accomplish this, the guide provides eleven principles for the governance of project management (APM, 2004, p. 6):

1 The board has overall responsibility for governance of project management.
2 The roles, responsibilities and performance criteria for the governance of project management are clearly defined.
3 Disciplined governance arrangements, supported by appropriate methods and controls, are applied throughout the project life cycle.
4 A coherent and supportive relationship is demonstrated between the overall business strategy and the project portfolio.
5 All projects have an approved plan containing authorisation points at which the business case is reviewed and approved. Decisions made at authorisation points are recorded and communicated.
6 Members of delegated authorisation bodies have sufficient representation, competence, authority and resources to enable them to make appropriate decisions.
7 The project business case is supported by relevant and realistic information that provides a reliable basis for making authorisation decisions.

4 *Ralf Müller*

8   The board or its delegated agents decide when independent scrutiny of projects and project management systems is required, and implement such scrutiny accordingly.

9   There are clearly defined criteria for reporting project status and for the escalation of risks and issues to the levels required by the organisation.

10 The organisation fosters a culture of improvement and of frank internal disclosure of project information.

11 Project stakeholders are engaged at a level that is commensurate with their importance to the organisation and in a manner that fosters trust.

This principles-based guide does not suggest a particular process. It does not assume governance to be the rigid application of a methodology, but the flexible and intelligent application of the above principles. The guide also refers to the UK Listing Authority's Combined Code, 2003, and the Sarbanes-Oxley Act, 2002.

A prescriptive, rule-based guide can be found in the Project Management Institute's (PMI) Practice Guide for Governance of Portfolios, Programs, and Projects (PMI, 2016). This practice guide provides detailed processes and activities at different organizational levels, such as portfolios, programs, and projects. It distinguishes between governance elements, such as governing bodies (boards and executive committees), governance roles and authorities (for organizational leaders, steering committees, sponsors, portfolio managers), governance domains and functions (such as alignment, risk, performance, and communications; oversight, control, integration, and decision making), and portfolios, programs, and projects (to optimize investments; deliver outcomes and business value; create a unique product, service, or result) (PMI, 2016, p. 5). The guide provides in-depth guidance on processes, responsibility assignment matrices, framework, and their implementation.

A slightly different approach is chosen by the ISO Standard for Project, Programme and Portfolio Management—Guidance on Governance. At the time of writing, this guide was still under development, and reference can only be made to a draft version that the author is currently reviewing. It describes the context and guidelines for the governance of projects, programs, and portfolios. The draft standard provides guidance on the elements, responsibilities, and activities in governance. At each level of project, program, and portfolio management, it addresses the governing body, as well as responsibilities of governance in taking forward the organizational values, addressing policies, risk, decision making, sustainability, statutory requirements, and reporting. To that end, the draft version lends itself to a more principles-based approach to governance.

The three examples above show some variety in the approaches to governance, but also differences in the understanding of governance per se. While the ISO Draft Standard links governance closely to the organizational value system and responsibilities, just as in this book (and in Müller, 2009), the APM guide mainly addresses the board of directors' principles, and the PMI guide focuses on the activity level with detailed processes, tasks, and tools. To that end, the three publications complement each other and, taken together, offer a broad scope of governance approaches from which practitioners can draw.

Both the PMI guide and the Draft ISO Standard emphasize the differences between management and governance. Governance is associated with key words, such as authorizing, defining, directing, monitoring, etc., whereas management is described as working within the limitations set by governance and with key words such as implementing, communicating, selecting, and optimizing. Too and Weaver (2014, p. 1385) describe the difference as:

> *The governance system defines the structures used by the organization, allocates rights and responsibilities within those structures and requires assurance that management is operating effectively and properly within the defined structures. The role of management is to manage the organization within the framework defined by the governance system; this applies particularly to the governance and management of projects.*

In this book we use a similar distinction. Management is a goal-oriented activity, whereas governance defines the framework (including the limitations) within which management is executed. For example, achieving a project's objective through the partnership of several organizations is a management activity, but the definition of the types of contracts that are acceptable for any of the organizations is a governance task. Or even more broadly: driving from Norway to a holiday resort in the south of France is a management activity, while the maximum speed at which we are allowed to drive, the tolls we have to pay for the motorways, etc. are governance responsibilities of various institutions in the countries we pass through and are independent of our goal-oriented task, namely, the holiday tour.

The use of terms varies significantly throughout the literature. For example, "governance principles" are described by some writers and institutions as: change culture, leading change, envisioning and communicating a better future, adding value, learning from experience, adapting to change, or managing by stages. However, strictly speaking, these are management tasks, not governance principles.

We mentioned above that governance is the framework within which management tasks, such as those described, are executed. Governance is established based on governance principles, which are the fundamental norms, rules, or values that are desirable and guide the establishment of governance practices (see Chapter 2). Governance principles are different from management principles, as the former typically underpin the ways in which management is steered, and thus provide norms, rules, and values for setting up a framework to steer management, whereas management principles refer to the organization of work and the people used to execute work. Examples can be found in the governance principles of corporations, such as General Electric (General Electric Company, 2016), which refer to principles such as role, size, and selection of board members, which translates to role, size, and selection of steering group members in projects, programs, or portfolios. This is different from management principles, such as those defined by Henry Fayol (2016), which refer to ways in which work execution is organized, such as through division of work, centralization of power for work-related decision making, processes for ordering material, remuneration of workers etc. This translates to principles of organization of work within a project. Hence, governance has a different perspective and builds its practices on a different set of principles.

Governance practices are the "lived" practices of governance in an organization, which include, but are not limited to, the totality of governance structures, processes, policies, etc. implemented across organizational levels, such as projects, programs, or portfolios. Governance structures define the means by which governance tasks, their coordination, and their supervision are directed toward the achievement of governance objectives.

Governance objectives are the particular goals or values that should be accomplished through governance. The nature of governance objectives is often different from that of management objectives, as the former are typically long-term and often independent of the goals of a management task. Moreover, governance objectives may be difficult to measure, as they may include aspects such as ethics, religion, or other value systems that do not always lend themselves to a rationality exercised thorough measurement. Thus, governance objectives may differ from management objectives by not necessarily being SMART (specific, measurable, achievable, relevant, time-bound).

Organizations may define their particular governance objectives (e.g., maximizing wealth of shareholders), which may be different for the levels of projects, programs, and portfolios. These are not governance principles, but governance objectives or values, whose implementation is governed through governance principles. Chapter 2 provides an introduction to governance principles and defines the governance principles used in this book to link corporate governance with organizational project governance.

The Architecture of the Book

The book is divided into five parts. It starts by laying the theoretical foundation for the rest of the book, which is followed by the organizational enablers for governance. This leads to governance practices, and subsequently to the consequences of different governance practices. The book concludes with three exemplary cases of governance.

Introduction 7

Part 1 addresses the concepts, theories, and models for governance and governmentality in organizational project governance. Here:

Chapter 2 introduces and defines the concept of organizational project governance and governmentality. It clarifies the underlying assumptions and perspectives taken in this book. A major part of this chapter is the description of the four governance principles that link governance across hierarchies and to corporate governance. This is complemented by the concept of governmentality, which presents the human side of governing and continues a governance approach from one level to the next.

Chapter 3 introduces and provides a repository for the most popular governance theories used throughout the book. These are shareholder theory, stakeholder theory, agency theory, stewardship theory, and transaction cost economics. These theories will be frequently referred to in the different chapters.

Chapter 4 provides examples of models of organizational project governance. This exemplifies the breadth of existing models and their different underlying ontologies. This is followed by the introduction of the four governance paradigms, which will be used in many of the studies described in the rest of the book.

Chapter 5 describes the roles and responsibilities of the most popular governance institutions found in organizational project governance in the private and public sectors. This includes the board of directors, program and portfolio management, as well as project management offices (PMO), sponsor, owner, and project steering groups. Special emphasis is given to the communication between the steering group and the project manager.

Part 2 describes the organizational enablers for organizational project governance and governmentality. Here:

Chapter 6 addresses the operational-level characteristics, which allow organizations to establish organizational project governance and governmentality. The chapter starts by describing the concept of organizational enabler and its application to existing literature and empirical studies. The results provide for a tactical perspective on the establishment of organizational project governance. The conditions for the establishment, as well as the nature, of the particular enablers is described for each of the levels of project governance, governance of projects, and governmentality.

Chapter 7 extends the discussion to a strategic perspective by addressing the organization-wide enablers for governance and governmentality for projects. This provides for those particular enablers that crossover multiple governance levels. The chapter outlines best practices by showing

8 *Ralf Müller*

the presence and strength of these enablers in companies with different levels of success. The chapter finishes by theorizing on the role of enablers for organizational project governance, their development over time, as well as their contribution to the four governance principles.

Part 3 describes the variety of practices in organizational project governance and governmentality. Here:

Chapter 8 addresses the private sector practices, by outlining first the tactical practices, structured by project governance (i.e. the governance of a single project), governance of projects (i.e. the governance of groups of projects), and governmentality (i.e. the ways those in governing positions interact with those that are governed). This is followed by the strategic practice, which leads to a multidimensional framework for capturing and visualizing strategic, organization-level practices of governance and governmentality.

Chapter 9 addresses governance in the public sector. The authors highlight the use of governance frameworks implemented to secure successful investment projects. The Norwegian governance scheme is used as an example for the successful application of a governance framework to large state-funded investment projects.

Part 4 describes some of the consequences that result from different governance approaches. Here:

Chapter 10 addresses the direct and indirect relationships between governance and project success, as well as between project methodology and success. Results from empirical studies show which governance paradigms are more conducive to project success. The chapter shows how governance acts as an enabler to achieving success if aligned to the environmental factors.

Chapter 11 addresses the application of trust and control as governance mechanisms in projects. It starts by outlining how trust and control regulate different aspects of governance. This is followed by a discussion of the different mixes of trust and control found in different governance approaches.

Chapter 12 addresses the relationship between project governance structures and associated ethical issues. It shows the types and frequencies of ethical issues in projects and their variations across different governance approaches, as well as the measures organizations take to avoid or mitigate the occurrence of ethical issues. This chapter concludes by theorizing on the role of governance paradigms with respect to ethical issues in projects, and on the conditions for a possible causality where governance determines the consequences described in this section of the book.

Introduction 9

Part 5 provides four exemplary case studies, which are used by the authors of the chapters to describe some of their findings. The chapters may also be used as examples for implementation of governance in private or public sector organizations.

Chapter 13 describes a public-benefit project, which was delivered by the Sugarloaf Pipeline Alliance during a period of prolonged drought. The chapter outlines the governance approach for this public sector project, which allowed the project to deliver the original stated outcome on budget and ahead of schedule. At the same time, it ensured the safety of staff, satisfaction of affected communities, reinstatement of flora and fauna, and an overall environmental net gain.

Chapter 14 describes the ethical issues that occurred in two project organizations in Australia. The issues were primarily driven by internal conflicts caused by each party's self-interest, which became apparent in their concerns regarding how decisions taken in the interest of the organization could affect each of them personally. The authors' suggested solution is to adopt governance practices to minimize 'interface' problems.

Chapter 15 describes the successful transformation of Tasly Pharmaceuticals in China from a functional organization to a project-based organization. The case outlines how governance and governmentality were used to set up the structures, work with people and their concerns, balance roles and functions between line and matrix organizations, as well as handle the conflicts that arose between functional departments and project departments. It shows how a PMO transformed an organization through careful governance.

References

Ahola, T., Ruuska, I., Artto, K., & Kujala, J. (2013). What Is Project Governance and What are Its Origins? *International Journal of Project Management*, 32(8), 1321–1332. doi:10.1016/j.ijproman.2013.09.005

APM. (2004). *Directing Change: A Guide to Governance of Project Management*. High Wycombe, UK: Association for Project Management.

Bergen, M., Dutta, S., & Walker, O. C. (1992). Agency Relationships in Marketing: A Review of the Implications and Applications of Agency and Related Theories. *Journal of Marketing*, 56(3), 1.

Biesenthal, C., & Wilden, R. (2014). Multi-Level Project Governance: Trends and Opportunities. *International Journal of Project Management*, 32(8), 1291–1308. doi:10.1016/j.ijproman.2014.06.005

Blomquist, T., & Müller, R. (2006). *Middle Managers in Program and Portfolio Management: Practice, Roles and Responsibilities*. Newton Square, PA: Project Management Institute.

Clegg, S. R., Pitsis, T. S., Rura-Polley, T., & Marosszeky, M. (2002). Governmentality Matters: Designing an Alliance Culture of Inter-Organizational Colaboration for Managing Projects. *Organization Studies*, 23(3), 317–337.

10 *Ralf Müller*

Fayol, H. (2016). Henry Fayol's 14 Principles of Management. *Academia*. Retrieved March 23, 2016, from https://www.academia.edu/384009/Henry_Fayols_14_principles_in_Management

General Electric Company. (2016). Governance Principles. Retrieved March 23, 2016, from https://www.ge.com/sites/default/files/GE_governance_principles.pdf

Klakegg, O. J., Williams, T., Magnussen, O. M., & Glasspool, H. (2008). Governance Frameworks for Public Project Development and Estimation. *Project Management Journal*, *39*(Supplement), S27–S42.

Miller, R., & Hobbs, B. (2005). Governance Regimes for Large Projects. *Project Management Journal*, *36*(3), 42–51.

Millstein, I. M., Albert, M., Cadbury, A., Feddersen, D., & Tateisi, N. (1998). *Improving Competitiveness and Access to Capital in Global Markets*. Paris, France: OECD Publications.

Müller, R. (2009). *Project Governance*. Aldershot, UK: Gower Publishing.

Müller, R., Shao, J., & Pemsel, S. (2016). *Organizational Enablers for Project Governance*. Newtown Square, PA: Project Management Institute.

PMI. (2016). *Governance of Portfolios, Programs, and Projects: A Practice Guide*. Newtown Square, PA: Project Management Institute.

Pryke, S. D. (2005). Towards a Social Network Theory of Project Governance. *Construction Management and Economics*, *23*(9), 927–939.

Reve, T., & Levitt, R. E. (1984). Organization and Governance in Construction. *International Journal of Project Management*, *2*(1), 17–25. doi:10.1016/0263-7863(84)90054-1

Ruuska, I., Ahola, T., Artto, K., Locatelli, G., & Mancini, M. (2011). A New Governance Approach for Multi-Firm Projects: Lessons from Olkiluoto 3 and Flamanville 3 Nuclear Power Plant Projects. *International Journal of Project Management*, *29*(6), 647–660. doi:10.1016/j.ijproman.2010.10.001

Shenhar, A., Dvir, D., Milosevic, D., Mulenburg, J., Patanakul, P., Reilly, R., Ryan, M., Sage, A., Sauser, B., Srivannaboon, S., Stefanovic, J., & Thamhain, H. (2005). Toward a NASA-Specific Project Management Framework. *Engineering Management Journal*, *17*(4), 8–16.

Too, E. G., & Weaver, P. (2014). The Management of Project Management: A Conceptual Framework for Project Governance. *International Journal of Project Management*, *32*(8), 1382–1394. doi:10.1016/j.ijproman.2013.07.006

Turner, J. R., & Keegan, A. (1999). The Versatile Project-Based Organization: Governance and Operational Control. *European Management Journal*, *17*(3), 296–309.

Winch, G. M. (1989). The Construction Firm and the Construction Project: A Transaction Cost Approach. *Construction Management and Economics*, *7*(4), 331–345.

2 Organizational Project Governance

Ralf Müller

This chapter introduces organizational project governance and the related concepts, perspectives, and underlying assumptions used in this book. We start by defining projects as temporary organizations in need of governance. Then, the focus turns to the concept of governance and its definition, as well as the four principles of good corporate governance, which will pervade the rest of the book. Subsequently, we compare some corporate level governance practices with those in temporary organizations, and then define the three levels of governance, which are: the project, groups of projects (such as programs and portfolios), and the board. We conclude this chapter with the concept of governmentality as the human side of governing, which links the governance approaches at the various levels in the organization.

Projects as Temporary Organizations in Need of Governance

Projects are different things to different people. Depending on the perspective taken, projects can be understood, for example, as processes or tasks when taking an operations perspective, as team endeavors when taking a psychology perspective, as implementation of a methodology when taking a management theory perspective, and so forth. Along with the differences in perspectives, we would expect differences in governance, as an operations perspective toward a process would lead to a different governance than a psychology perspective toward a team endeavor. In other words, whenever we talk about governance we must first clarify the perspective we are taking toward the governed object in order to ensure a fit between the governance approach and our understanding of the nature of what is being governed.

In this book, we take an organizational theory perspective, in which we perceive a project as a temporary organization. A project is then a *temporary organization, to which resources are assigned to undertake a unique, novel, and transient endeavor managing the inherent uncertainty and need for integration in order to deliver beneficial objectives of change* (Turner & Müller, 2003, p. 7).

12 Ralf Müller

This view allows us to look at projects as standalone, autonomous, or even sovereign organizational entities, which individually and collectively need to be governed in order to contribute in the most beneficial way to the objectives of the wider organization (e.g., the corporation). This perspective is different from more internal views of projects as temporary organizations, such as those of Lundin and Söderholm (1995), who outlined the internal processes, phases, and dependencies of the temporary organization. This is important for the understanding of what goes on when working within temporary organizations. In this book, we complement this with an outside view, an organization-wide perspective, and understand projects as temporary organizations, functioning as building blocks for the business of a wider organization or corporation. From this corporation-wide perspective, projects are temporary organizations to fulfill the production function. They act as: (1) agencies for change; (2) agencies to manage risk, and by doing this; (3) utilize resources in a productive manner. These temporary organizations are managed by a project manager, who acts as the chief executive officer (CEO) of the temporary organization. He or she serves as an agent to a principal, which is typically the owner or sponsor of the project (Turner & Müller, 2003).

Looking at projects as temporary organizations has several advantages. For example, temporary organizations include help and aid missions, as well as other mission-like endeavors, which are not always defined as projects, but—when defined as temporary organizations—would fall under similar governance schemes as projects. Another advantage is that it makes the entire literature on organizational governance relevant for projects. To that end, projects, practitioners, and academics can make use of a large and relevant body of knowledge, which allows them to leverage, instead of reinvent for projects, what has been developed on governance in the field of organizational theory for several decades.

In the remainder of the book we use the term *project* as defined above, and thus imply a temporary organization perspective. Similarly, we use the term *organization* when we mean the corporation, a division in a corporation, a department, work group, or other organizational entity as defined within a corporation.

The Concept of Governance

Along with the large body of knowledge on governance comes a multitude of definitions. Corporate-level governance is often defined as the means by which organizations are directed and their managers held accountable for conduct and performance (OECD, 2001), by defining the objectives of the organization, providing the means to achieve those objectives, and controlling progress (OECD, 2004). Among the more detailed definitions are at least three different streams of definitions that can be identified as:

- *Governance as a system of controls*: these definitions center around governance as a system or collection of control structures and mechanisms

Organizational Project Governance 13

to direct and control organizations, including related responsibilities, such as the need to balance economic and social objectives, as well as individual and communal goals (Cadbury, 1992; Larcker & Tayan, 2011).

- *Governance as processes*: these definitions focus on the role of processes through which organizations are directed and controlled (OECD, 2001) and made responsive to the rights and wishes of their stakeholders (Demb & Neubauer, 1992).
- *Governance as relationships*: these definitions stress the role of governance in defining the relationships among the various stakeholders, which can be internal or external to the organization, the rights, responsibilities and relationships of the different participants in the organization, including external auditors, regulators, or other legitimate stakeholders (Monks & Minow, 1995; OECD, 2001).

Within these streams, the approaches to governance vary considerably. By taking the example of corporate governance orientation, or the *raison d'être* of the corporation, we see that it can fall anywhere on a spectrum of approaches, which range from being solely in place to generate shareholder return to one that tries to balance and satisfy the diverse requirements of a multitude of stakeholder groups (of which the shareholders are one group), and the many stages in between these extremes (Clarke, 1998; Davis, Schoorman, & Donaldson, 1997; Jensen & Meckling, 1976). Hence the definition of governance should not be confused with its contents.

The broadness of the definitions above mirrors the breadth of scope of governance at the corporate level. However, this broadness of definitions has been criticized for supporting the recent corporate scandals through a too narrow focus at the top of the organization (Naciri, 2010). This book addresses this criticism by looking at lower levels of governance, where similar governance principles apply, but within a smaller scope. Hence, in this book, we look at a small fraction of governance in a corporation, that of governance of projects. We only engage with those parts of corporate governance that touch upon the work of projects. Readers interested in learning more about the wider scope of corporate governance are recommend to have a look at Clarke (2004, 2007).

A question often raised is whether project governance lies within or outside corporate governance. Existing literature on corporate governance implies that corporate governance comprises all activities in an organization, which includes its projects. Moreover, if projects with external organizations were outside the corporate governance of each of the contracting parties, then we would have to admit that project-based organizations (i.e., corporations that make their business through projects) almost completely work outside their own governance system. This cannot be in the interest of the shareholders and stakeholders of the organization and would even make corporate governance obsolete. Rather than that, we view all project-related governance as a subset of corporate governance, which includes both

14 *Ralf Müller*

projects within the organization as well as projects with external, contracted partners, customers, clients, etc. The contractual obligations signed with these external partners constitute the lowest common denominator of the different corporate governance systems that come together through a given contract. To that end, if an organization accepts contractual terms that are not in line with its corporate governance policies, it implicitly extends its own governance policies for the given contract.

One aspect that is often overlooked is the relationship of governance with the value system of the organization. This has been raised as an issue at both the corporate (Naciri, 2010) and the project level of governance (Müller, 2009). Examples include the role of governance in defining whether the organization values people following the processes or individual heroism in achieving its objectives, as can be seen by the level of freedom granted and the type of control applied to managers in doing their work (Chapter 4). Given this, we term the governance of projects, programs, portfolios, and the totality of all projects as organizational project governance and define it as:

> *Organizational project governance coexists within the corporate governance framework and is the means by which individual projects, groups of projects (such as programs or portfolios), and the totality of all projects in an organization are directed and controlled and managers are held accountable for the conduct and performance of them.*
>
> *Governance provides the value system, structures, processes, and policies that foster transparency, accountability, responsibility, and fairness to allow projects to achieve organizational objectives and foster implementation that is in the best interest of all stakeholders, internal and external, and the corporation itself.*

The above definition implies a linkage of organizational project governance with corporate governance through the four principles of good governance. These were defined by the Business Sector Advisory Group on Corporate Governance to the OECD (Organization for Economic Co-operation and Development), also known as the Millstein Report (Millstein, Albert, Cadbury, Feddersen, & Tateisi, 1998). They outline the continuous evolution of governance practices to meet changing conditions, through a necessary and ongoing process of adapting, refining, and adjusting governance. This does not allow for single universal models or static final structures that every corporation should emulate. However, the authors of the report identify a few fundamental parameters, of which some are relevant also at the project level. These include the importance of shareholders, but also responsiveness to the demands and expectations of other stakeholders, transparency and oversight of management, and voluntary adaptation and evolution of governance boards.

Principles of Good Governance

The Millstein Report outlines four principles of good governance, which are transparency, accountability, responsibility, and fairness. Aras and Crowther (2010) refer to them as the four practice principles of good corporate governance. These principles (also referred to as approaches or standards) pervade good governance at all levels of the organization and are almost universally used in corporate and public governance policies. As governance at each level in the organizational hierarchy contributes to the four principles, they link governance across levels and thereby also link governance related to projects with corporate governance. The principles are phrased in corporation-wide terms in the original report, and here interpreted in the context of projects as temporary organizations:

Transparency is concerned with investors' (such as project sponsors') and other stakeholders' confidence in the overall efficiency of the undertaking, which depends on the disclosure of accurate, timely information about project and organizational performance. To be of value, this information should be clear, consistent, and comparable. Governance institutions (e.g., steering groups, program or portfolio managers) should require this information and should also collaborate in the development of clear, consistent, and comparable standards for disclosure of information, as well as encourage ongoing improvements in both disclosure techniques and formats, for example, through better technology or disclosure of new relevant information.

Accountability is concerned with the clarity of roles, rights, and responsibilities of the major participants (such as project manager, sponsor, program and portfolio manager) for governance to be effective. In a project setting, the steering group is positioned to hold the project manager accountable to the project sponsor for achieving project objectives, while the steering group itself is accountable to their management for accomplishing the project's business case. The steering group's oversight of the project manager reduces the divergence between project and sponsor's interests, thus it minimizes the agency problem described later on in this volume. Accountability ensures the organization's ability to achieve its objectives by use of audits and by naming the particular roles (and the individuals in these roles) and their specific deliverables or contributions to the project.

Responsibility is concerned with keeping the standards of professional societies when pursuing project or organizational objectives. This includes that governance institutions ensure that individuals, teams, and organizations abide by the laws of their society and work in conjunction with accepted professional standards. This also includes the support and encouragement for education and training of organizational members.

16 *Ralf Müller*

Fairness is concerned with equal and fair treatment of employees, suppliers, contractors, etc., for example, in contracting or hiring. It also includes protection against illegal actions, as well as a general awareness that contractual relationships are enforceable.

In the following chapters of this book, we outline the specific contributions that organizational project governance makes to the four governance principles. Through this, we link project-related governance to corporate governance, which allows us to see projects and organizations in a holistic and more realistic manner. This overcomes the weakness of those studies in project-related governance that ignore the insights from research in corporate governance.

Comparison of Corporate-Level and Project-Level Governance Practices

So far, we have presented our perspective toward organizational project governance and assumed that the governance of projects as temporary organizations can be compared with governance of the more permanent organizations. To assess the viability of this assumption, we take a look at governance practices at both the corporate and the project level. We use the report by Shearman and Sterling (2012) on the general governance practices of the largest US public companies as a basis to compare corporate governance with governance practices of projects as temporary organizations. Table 2.1 summarizes the findings.

With the perspective of projects as temporary organizations, we imply that the project manager is the CEO and the steering committee is the board of directors of the temporary organization (Turner & Müller, 2003). Items 1 to 3 address the board's respective steering group accountabilities and responsibilities. We see clear similarities, of course, in the respective scope. Like in item 3, the scope of strategy for the CEO is the corporation and for the project manager it is the project. Items 4 and 5 address the differences in governance approaches. Rule-based approaches enforce a "comply or get punished" approach, whereas principle-based approaches imply a "comply or report" approach (these are further described in Chapter 1). Here, we also see similarities between the levels of governance, as shown by the rule-based approaches, which often emphasize processes and particular tasks and techniques, like those of OPM3 from the Project Management Institute (PMI, 2013), versus the principle-based approaches, such as that of the Association for Project Management (APM, 2004) for project governance. Items 6 to 9 refer to practices in separating accountabilities, for instance, the separation of the CEO and chairman of the board role at the corporate level is mirrored by the separation of steering group chairman and project manager,

Organizational Project Governance 17

Table 2.1 Comparison of Governance Practices at Corporate and Project Level

Item	Governance Practice	Corporate Governance	Project Governance
1	Accountability to shareholders for performance	Chairman of the Board	Chairman of Steering Committee
2	Responsibility for strategy and policy making	Board members	Steering Committee members (for the project)
3	Ensuring conformance of management with strategy and policies	Chief Executive Officer	Project Manager
4	Prescriptive rule-based approaches	e.g., US	"Bottom-up" approaches to project governance, e.g., MSP, or control-based governance as defined by PMI
5	Non-prescriptive principle-based	e.g., UK	"Top-down" approaches to project governance, such as APM's Guide to governance of project management
6	Separation of CEO and Chairman of the Board's roles	27% of companies; only 10% have a related policy	Most of the time in projects
7	Time-limited CEO contracts	unknown	Given by the nature of the temporary organizations
8	Minimum number of non-executive directors serving on the board	75% at minimum	Sometimes
9	A senior non-executive director	15% of companies	Sometimes

which is common practice in projects. Time-limited contracts occur naturally for project managers, due to the time limitation of their temporary organization. The last two items refer to board members from outside the organization. In temporary organizations this depends on the nature of the project and appears more often in larger projects or customer delivery projects. Altogether, Table 2.1 shows a substantial commonality in the governance setup at corporate and project levels. We take this as sufficient

18   *Ralf Müller*

evidence that governance at the project level can be linked to and leverage insights from governance at the corporate level.

Organizational Project Governance

Despite the similarities in structure as shown above, there is growing awareness that the contents of governance vary by hierarchical level in the organization. In projects, this means that governance content differs in at least at three levels: the project, groups of projects (e.g., programs or portfolios), and the board of directors, which looks at the totality of projects in the organization (e.g., Biesenthal & Wilden, 2014; Müller, 2009; Turner, 2009). Therefore, in organizational project governance, we distinguish between project governance, governance of projects, and board level governance of projects.

Project governance refers to the governance of a single project. It is typically executed by a steering group, which directs and controls the project manager. This group often appoints the project manager, defines the scope, means (e.g., the methodology) and ends (e.g., objectives) of the project, and provides the resources to accomplish the objectives. It also defines the scope and frequency of reporting, reviews, audits, and so forth.

Governance of projects refers to the governance of groups of projects, such as programs or portfolios of projects. The contents of governance are here merely concerned with the standardization of governance across the projects in a program or in a portfolio. This includes decisions on the number and type of project management methodologies that can be used in the organization, the transparency and comparability of project performance and results measures in reporting, questions of resource sharing across projects, or prioritization of projects, to name a few. This is mainly executed by senior managers whose position gives them the required authority to fulfill these tasks.

Board-level governance of projects refers to the project-related governance at the board of directors. Fundamental decisions on the organization's relationship with projects are made here, such as the extent to which the organization uses projects as building blocks for its business, the establishment of project management offices (PMOs), or the balance in hiring permanent versus temporary project managers.

Detailed descriptions of governance practices at these levels can be found in Chapters 8 and 9. The following chapters in this book outline the contribution of each of those levels to the four governance principles. They describe the contributions of project governance, governance of projects, and board-level governance of projects to corporate governance.

Figure 2.1 summarizes the discussion on governance levels and their contribution to corporate governance through the four governance principles.

This leads to the question of how governance of projects and project governance link to the four governance principles. This is addressed as a series of questions that should be answerable by project managers in well-governed settings. Table 2.2 shows the questions that should be asked at

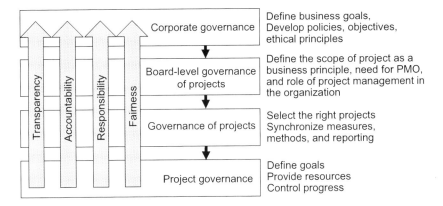

Figure 2.1 Governance Principles across Governance Levels

Table 2.2 Linking Governance Paradigms to Governance Principles

	Organizational Project Governance Practice	*Governance Principles*			
		Transparency	*Accountability*	*Responsibility*	*Fairness*
Governance of projects	Shareholder versus stakeholder orientation	What is the role of the organization in the market?	What results are we committed to deliver?	What does management do to accomplish the results?	Do we conduct our work in an ethical way?
	Outcome versus behavior control	What do we expect project managers and teams to accomplish?	Are the performance measures linked to strategic objectives?	Who will control and judge performance?	Do we measure and control performance of projects and teams in a fair way?
	Policies	Do we have standardized reporting using comparable measures?	Are the performance measures linked to strategic goals?	Do we select the right projects, project managers, and teams?	Do we have appropriate power balances in the organization?

the level of governance of projects to check for the accomplishment of the four governance principles. The column on organizational project governance practices refers to the dimensions of the project governance paradigms, which are explained in detail in Chapter 4.

20   *Ralf Müller*

Table 2.3 Linking Project Governance to Governance Principles

Organiza-tional Project Governance Practice	Corporate Governance Principles			
	Transparency	*Accountability*	*Responsibility*	*Fairness*
Steering Group	Are appropriate communication structures in place? Are the status and performance of the projects transparent?	Who is accountable for the project's strategic results and who for tactical performance?	Do sponsor and project manager interact for the achievement of strategic and tactical objectives?	Is there a shared understanding of the balance in prioritizing tactical and strategic objectives?
Methodology	Is a project management methodology used and known to the required parties?	Are the sponsor's accountabilities to higher management defined and known by the project manager?	Are responsibilities and roles in the project defined and communicated?	Is the project management methodology lived in an ethical way and in accordance with organizational policies?

(row label spanning table: Project Governance)

Table 2.3 shows the link between project governance and the four governance principles through a series of questions. These questions should be answerable by a project manager in well-governed projects.

Questions that remain unanswered indicate areas for further clarification by the governance institutions.

Governmentality

So far, we have looked solely at governance, which Foucault (1991) refers to as the governing of "things" (like organizations) or the "science" of governing. To reflect corporate reality we need to complement this with the governing of people, or the "art" of governance, which is known as governmentality (Foucault, 1991). The need for a complementary view can be explained by analogy to a computer system, which only becomes useful when the hardware (the governing of things—governance) is complemented by software (the governing of the user—governmentality).

Governmentality is defined as *the mentalities, rationalities, and ways of interaction, chosen by those in governance roles to implement, maintain, and change the governance structure.* The term governmentality comes from the words governance and mentality (a characteristic way of thinking). As a concept, it reflects the particular approaches (mentalities) that governors have toward those they govern and, with them, the mentality in executing their governance task. The term was coined in 1957 by the French semiologist Roland Barthes (Barthes, 2013) when he described the ways in which political governments present themselves to the public and the ways in which this steers the inferences that the public draws. Using the example of a government's media appearance, he showed how, through symbols and signals, the interpretations and inferences the public draws are impacted. Moreover, he showed how the relationship between the government and the public, as well as the social relationship within the public, are formed through the governance's appearance (Barthes, 2013). Thus, governmentality can be seen as the discourses by which governors control and manage relations with the rest of the world (Grieve, 2014).

Despite its emergence in 1957, the concept of governmentality became well known only 20 years later, when the French philosopher Michel Foucault used it in his studies and his lectures at the Collège de France. Foucault used governmentality as a concept in his studies on power and neoliberalism, where he reduced the scope of the original concept to the needs of his study themes and focused merely on "active consent and subjugation of subjects, rather than their oppression, domination or external control" (Clegg, Pitsis, Rura-Polley, & Marosszeky, 2002, p. 317). Governmentality in its original sense is a broader concept than that used by Foucault and can be applied to a wide array of situations. In this book we use its original conceptualization by Barthes.

The relationship between governance and governmentality is explained by Foucault in his 1978 lectures, where he presents governance as a layered concept. He uses the example of three layers: the individual and his or her self-governance, which he connects with morality; followed by the governance of the family and its connection in governance with economics; and finally the governance of the state, connected to yet another type of governance. Governmentality is here seen as the link between the layers, or "the essential continuity of one type with the other" (Foucault, 1991, p. 91). In analogy with that, we apply the concept of governance to the layers of project governance, governance of projects, and board-level governance of projects, and the concept of governmentality as the link between these governance levels. We follow earlier suggestions that governance should always be discussed together with its associated governmentality, as only this complementarity provides for an integrated view of the governance task (Müller, Pemsel, & Shao, 2014).

We mentioned that in everyday work, governmentality reflects the way a particular approach to governance gets implemented (Clegg, Pitsis, Rura-Polley, & Marosszeky, 2002) by addressing the human side of governing. It is the way a governance institution and its members (such as a steering group) present themselves to those they govern (i.e., a project). This presentation reveals their attitude toward the people they govern and sets the "tone" for the interaction between and among them. Therefore, Lemke (2007) described governmentality as an ideological mechanism that presents governors (i.e., political leaders) as the origin of social relations.

While governance defines the structures, policies, processes, roles, accountabilities, and responsibilities, it does not define how governance is implemented in the daily work of an organization. This is done through governmentality. An example in the project context is that governance provides the project management methodology for a project, while governmentality regulates how the use of this methodology is enforced. This enforcement can be done, for example, through *authoritative* approaches, by penalizing project managers for not using it; or *liberal* approaches, by outlining the methodology's benefits for the organization and possible incentives for the project managers; or *neoliberal* approaches, by setting and influencing values that the members of an organization share and respect, and thus follow (Clegg et al., 2002; Dean, 2010; Foucault, 1991).

These differences in governmentality surface, for example, in the ways organizations control their employees. More authoritative governmentality is often associated with enforcing strict process compliance, supported by surveillance and control methods that allow the capture and recording of people's behavior and the punishment of any misbehavior. This approach is often found in high-risk industries, in order to enforce the use of a proven and trusted process and reduce possible human errors. Examples include civil airline pilots or firefighters, who have to follow their process to ensure safety for consumers and themselves. We address this form of behavior control in more detail in the chapter on governance paradigms (Chapter 4) and governmentality practices (Chapter 8).

Liberal approaches to governmentality emphasize the benefits, such as organizational results, incentives, or other benefits, resulting from a certain behavior or accomplishment of a particular objective. This approach suggests, but does not strictly enforce, a certain behavior by appealing to the rationality of the governed. Examples include the processes in new product development teams, where proven processes are recommended, but can be circumvented if necessary. These organizations often exercise control by controlling the outcome of work in form of meeting pre-established objectives, rather than strictly following a process.

The neoliberal forms of governmentality seek to influence the self-regulation and self-reflection of individuals, so that they can correct and control their own behavior in line with their society's values. This is done by setting and referring to a set of values and beliefs that the members of an organization or society share (Clegg et al., 2002; Villadsen, 2010). Miller and Rose (1990, pp. 14–15) describe how practicing neoliberal governmentality reduces the need for direct observation and personal contact, because "contemporary 'governmentality' accords a crucial role to 'action at a distance', that is to say, to mechanisms which promise to shape the economic or social conduct of diverse and institutionally distinct persons and agencies without shattering their formally distinct or 'autonomous' character." By aspiring to the collective interests of the people within a group or organization, neoliberal governmentality shapes, but does not necessarily determine, the actions of individuals (Clegg, 1994; Clegg et al., 2002).

This chapter provided the definitions and underlying assumptions of the rest of the book. In the next chapter, we start with the timely development of governance and governmentality by addressing the organizational enablers that allow for both to develop.

References

APM. (2004). *Directing Change: A Guide to Governance of Project Management*. High Wycombe, UK: Association for Project Management.

Aras, G., & Crowther, D. (2010). Corporate Social Responsibility: A Broader View of Corporate Governance. In G. Aras & D. Crowther (Eds.), *A Handbook of Corporate Governance and Social Responsibility* (pp. 265–280). Farnham, UK: Gower Publishing Limited.

Barthes, R. (2013). *Mythologies*. New York, NY: Hill & Wang.

Biesenthal, C., & Wilden, R. (2014). Multi-Level Project Governance: Trends and Opportunities. *International Journal of Project Management*, 32(8), 1291–1308. doi:10.1016/j.ijproman.2014.06.005

Cadbury. (1992). *The Financial Aspects of Corporate Governance*. London, UK: Gee (a division of Professional Publishing Ltd.).

Clarke, T. (1998). The Stakeholder Corporation: A Business Philosophy for the Information Age. *Long Range Planning*, 31(2), 182–194. doi:10.1016/S0024–6301 (98)00002–8

Clarke, T. (2004). *Theories of Corporate Governance* (T. Clarke, Ed.). Milton Park, UK: Routledge, UK.

Clarke, T. (2007). *International Corporate Governance*. Milton Park, UK: Routledge.

Clegg, S. R. (1994). Weber and Foucault: Social Theory for the Study of Organizations. *Organization*, 1(1), 149–178.

Clegg, S. R., Pitsis, T. S., Rura-Polley, T., & Marosszeky, M. (2002). Governmentality Matters: Designing an Alliance Culture of Inter-Organizational Colaboration for Managing Projects. *Organization Studies*, 23(3), 317–337.

Davis, J. H., Schoorman, F. D., & Donaldson, L. (1997). Toward a Stewardship Theory of Management. *Academy of Management Review*, 22(1), 20–47.

Dean, M. (2010). *Governmentality: Power and Rule in Modern Society* (2nd ed.). London, UK: SAGE Publications Ltd.

Demb, A., & Neubauer, F. (1992). *The Corporate Board: Confronting the Paradoxes*. New York, NY: Oxford University Press.

Foucault, M. (1991). Governmentality. In G. Burchel, C. Gordon, & P. Miller (Eds.), *The Foucault Effect* (pp. 87–104). Chicago: University of Chcago Press.

Grieve, G. P. (2014). Government Map II. Governmentality. Retrieved from http://www.gpgrieve.org/3maps/gmap2.html

Jensen, M. C., & Meckling, W. H. (1976). Theory of the Firm: Managerial Behavior, Agency Costs, and Ownership Structure. *Journal of Financial Economics*, 3(4), 305–360.

24 *Ralf Müller*

Larcker, D., & Tayan, B. (2011). *Corporate Governance Matters*. Upper Saddle River, NJ: Pearson Education Inc.

Lemke, T. (2007). An Indigestible Meal? Foucault, Governmentality and State Theory. *Distinktion: Scandinavian Journal of Social Theory*, *8*(2), 43–64.

Lundin, R. A., & Söderholm, A. (1995). A Theory of the Temporary Organization. *Scandinavian Journal of Management*, *11*(4), 437–455.

Miller, P., & Rose, N. (1990). *Governing economic life. Economy and Society*, *19*(1), 1–31. doi:10.1080/03085149000000001.

Millstein, I. M., Albert, M., Cadbury, A., Feddersen, D., & Tateisi, N. (1998). *Improving Competitiveness and Access to Capital in Global Markets*. Paris, France: OECD Publications.

Monks, A. A. G., & Minow, N. (1995). *Corporate Governance* (4th ed.). Chichester, UK: Wiley & Sons Ltd.

Müller, R. (2009). *Project Governance*. Aldershot, UK: Gower Publishing.

Müller, R., Pemsel, S., & Shao, J. (2014). Organizational Enablers for Governance and Governmentality of Projects: A Literature Review. *International Journal of Project Management*, *32*(8), 1309–1320. doi:10.1016/j.ijproman.2014.03.007.

Naciri, A. (2010). *Internal and External Aspects of Corporate Governance*. Milton Park, UK: Routledge.

OECD. (2001). *Governance in the 21st Century*. Paris, France: OECD Publishing. Retrieved from http://www.oecd.org/futures/17394484.pdf

OECD. (2004). *OECD Principles of Corporate Governance 2004*. Paris, France: OECD Publishing. doi:10.1787/9789264015999-en

PMI. (2013). *Organizational Project Management Maturity Model (OPM3) Knowledge Foundation*. Newtown Square, PA: Project Management Institute.

Shearman & Sterling. (2012). *Corporate Governance of the Largest US Public Companies: General Governance Practices*. Shearman & Sterling LLP.

Turner, J. R. (2009). *The Handbook of Project-Based Management* (3rd ed.). London, UK: McGraw-Hill.

Turner, J. R., & Müller, R. (2003). On the Nature of the Project as a Temporary Organization. *International Journal of Project Management*, *21*(1), 1–7.

Villadsen, K. (2010). Governmentality. In M. Tadajewski, P. Maclaran, E. Person, & M. Parker (Eds.), *Key Concepts in Critical Management Studies* (pp. 125–129). Thousand Oaks, CA: SAGE Publications Inc.

Part I

Concepts, Theories, and Models

This part presents the concepts, theories, and models underlying the chapters in this book.

The concepts of organizational project governance and governmentality are defined and presented in Chapter 2. The governance theories referred to in the rest of the book are introduced in Chapter 3.

The theoretical perspective is then taken forward to a variety of models and paradigms of organizational project governance in Chapter 4. The most popular governance institutions found in organizational project governance are presented in Chapter 5.

This part lays the theoretical foundation for the chapters to come.

3 Governance Theories

Ralf Müller

This chapter presents some of the most popular theories on governance. We start with two organizational theories, namely, shareholder theory and stakeholder theory. These corporate governance theories underscore the *raison d'être* of the organization and its intended role in the market. We then turn to three behavior-related governance theories, which are agency theory, stewardship theory, and transaction cost economics.

The theories described in this chapter have a long history of development and are used in many different situations. A comprehensive description would go beyond the scope of this chapter. Therefore, we only provide an introductory level of description, to the extent that the application of these theories can be better understood in the remaining chapters. For more detailed descriptions we refer to Thomas Clarke's (2004b) edited volume *Theories of Corporate Governance*, as well as the references given below.

Shareholder Theory of the Firm

Shareholder theory is a corporate governance theory which assumes that a corporation exists in order to maximize the wealth of its owners, the shareholders (Friedman, 1970). This is typically achieved through profit maximization. Thus, the objective of maximizing shareholder wealth, or in other words, maximizing shareholders' return on investment (ROI) or maximizing share price, governs all policies and actions in the corporation. It is underpinned by the maxim of the financial industry, which claims that *the price of a share of stock today fully reflects the market's best estimate of the value of all future profits and growth that will accrue to that company* (Blair, 2004, p. 174). This governance orientation is often associated with North American governance principles and the Chicago School of Law and Economics. It manifests itself in the Michigan Supreme Court agreement that:

> *A business corporation is organized and carried on primarily for the profit of the stockholders. The powers of the directors are to be employed for that end. The discretion of directors is to be exercised in the choice of means to attain that end, and does not extend to a change*

28   *Ralf Müller*

> *in the end itself, to the reduction of profits, or to the nondistribution of profits among stockholders in order to devote them to other purposes.*
>
> (cited by Allen, 1992, p. 268)

A shareholder orientation in corporate governance implies an organizational value system that prioritizes the interests of shareholders over those of other stakeholders. This often results in a narrowed focus, such as mainly on quantitative financial results, at the expense of the more qualitative objectives, such as employee wellbeing, ethical standards, and good relationships with the society in which the corporation exists. Proponents of this governance approach often refer to the need to focus managers' attention toward a single 'bottom line' result in order to achieve corporate and shareholder objectives. They also refer to the difficulties in managing a more diverse set of stakeholders in alternative governance structures, which risk too much diversification and thus a loss of focus on the needs of the prioritized stakeholder group, the shareholders.

In shareholder-oriented governance structures, the managers (including the board of directors) are regarded as agents of the shareholders (Clarke, 2004a). Jensen and Meckling (1976) identified some of the problems arising between managers and owners in shareholder-oriented governance and described it in their agency theory, which is described later in this chapter. Shareholder theory thus represents the corporate governance approach, and agency theory explains the behavior of people working within a shareholder-oriented governance approach. This requires structures (such as contracts, processes, and policies) to assure managerial action is always in the best interests of the shareholders.

Shareholder theory is the most popular perspective in corporate governance studies. This is also reflected in the project management literature. Examples include Turner (1998), who stated that projects in the private sector are undertaken to add value to the sponsoring organization, which ultimately increases their share value. Blomquist and Müller (2006) found that portfolio managers in project-oriented companies often take a shareholder theory perspective when deciding on the acceptance of projects.

Stakeholder Theory of the Firm

Stakeholder theory is a corporate governance theory, where the *raison d'être* of the corporation is to offer products and services to establish a market that would otherwise not exist. In this market are numerous stakeholder groups, all of which need to be served in order to keep the market alive. Allen (1992, p. 271) puts it as:

> *Surely contributors of capital (stockholders and bondholders) must be assured a rate of return sufficient to induce them to contribute their capital to the enterprise. But the corporation has other purposes of perhaps equal dignity: the satisfaction of consumer wants, the provision of*

> *meaningful employment opportunities, and the making of a contribution to the public life of its communities. Resolving the often conflicting claims of these various corporate constituencies calls for judgment, indeed calls for wisdom, by the board of directors of the corporation. But in this view no single constituency's interest may significantly exclude others from fair consideration by the board.*

Hence, stakeholder theory assumes that many different stakeholder groups exist simultaneously. Examples include shareholders, customers, employees and their families, suppliers, the local community, environmental groups, etc. The requirements stemming from these groups are often diverse and the corporation must balance these requirements in order to stay in the market or even maintain its market's existence. The growing importance of corporate social responsibility and its related social objectives for organizations recently contributed to the growing popularity of this theory and shifted the balance from merely economical measures to a more balanced set of economical and social measures of corporate performance (Aras & Crowther, 2010). Naciri (2010, p. 12) goes as far to say that it

> *is currently more commonly believed that corporations should exist to create wealth for the whole society. Accordingly, the aim of corporate governance mechanisms and the responsibility of corporate directors are undergoing a certain shift in their purposes, and companies are more and more expected to work for a broader goal that may include shareholders' wealth maximization.*

The stakeholder theory's basic tenet is, therefore, that organizations' objective is to balance the conflicting interests and claims of the different stakeholder groups, which includes traditional financial objectives over an extended period of time, as well as other objectives, such as corporate social performance objectives, like their reputation, attractiveness as an employer, and the generation of goodwill from the society they are embedded in. This is a wider horizon than in companies that adapt a shareholder orientation, which typically prioritizes short-term financial results.

The corporation's stakeholders are all those who gain or lose something through the actions of the organization. This may include not only closely linked groups, such as employees and suppliers, but also communities, industries, and society as a whole. Stakeholder theory takes into account the quality of relationships between the corporation and its stakeholder groups. Proponents of this approach claim that it allows the organization to achieve concerted productivity gains by coordinating corporate knowledge and activities across company boundaries. Examples include the combination of knowledge and productivity, gained through technological cross-fertilization and mutual gains in form of good relationships and employee stock options in the Silicon Valley (Clarke, 2004a).

30 *Ralf Müller*

Managers in stakeholder-oriented governance structures can be seen as either agents or stewards. To that end, both agency and stewardship theory apply as an explanation for managers' behavior. We start with agency theory in the next section and then continue with stewardship theory.

Agency Theory

Agency theory is grounded in economics and assumes individuals to be rational and self-serving. It can be traced back to Adam Smith's classical work *The Wealth of Nations* (Smith, 1776, 2013), where he stated:

> *The directors of companies, being the managers of other people's money rather than their own, cannot well be expected to watch over it with the same anxious vigilance with which (they) watch over their own.*

The original form of agency theory used this perspective to describe the relationship between owners (shareholders) and managers of a firm (Jensen & Meckling, 1976). From there, the theory has developed into a grant theory, which explains more generally the relationship between one or more principal(s) and one or more agent(s) (Davis, Schoorman, & Donaldson, 1997). It builds on the axiom that ownership of a task (by an agent) must be separated from the control of a task (by a principal). This separation leads to a potential principal–agent conflict because of the different interests of the two parties. It arises because the principal depends on the agent to undertake some action on the principal's behalf, and the principal does not know whether the agent always acts in the principal's interest (Bergen, Dutta, & Walker, 1992; Jensen, 2000), especially when both are self-interested, utility-maximizing parties. Utility maximization by one party may be supported through lack of information by the other party, thus resulting in an information imbalance between principal and agent.

In project settings, this refers to situations where the project owner (as principal) is in conflict with the project manager (as agent) because the latter is better informed about the project and its status than the former and may use this information for his or her own advantage. Attempts to resolve this conflict comprise measures such as additional control structures, where the principal can gain better insight into what the agent is doing or obtain the same level of information as the agent, as well as measures to align the objectives of both parties, such as incentive systems and contracts that foster behavior of agents that is in the best interests of the principal. All these measures add undesired agency costs to the project or transaction. Agency costs, therefore, tend to be minimized to a level where the project owner feels comfortable with the quality and quantity of information about the project and its manager (Turner & Müller, 2004).

The critique of agency theory is mainly along the lines of its inherent investor view, narrow economic view, and its underlying assumption that humans are primarily motivated by financial gains (Barney & Hesterly, 1996).

Stewardship Theory

Stewardship theory is grounded in psychology and sociology and proposes that people behave in a pro-organizational, collectivistic, and trustworthy manner, because this behavior leads to higher utility than the self-serving and opportunistic behaviors described by agency theory. The behavior of stewards is collective because they seek to attain the objectives of their organization:

> *Stewardship theory defines situations in which managers are not moti-vated by individual goals, but rather are stewards whose motives are aligned with the objectives of their principals.*
>
> (Davis et al., 1997, p. 21)

Stewardship theory explains individuals' behavior in terms of principal–steward relationships, where the steward is steered by high levels of identification and commitment to the organization, and motivated by intrinsic factors, such as the work itself, which leads to prioritization of collectivistic goals over individual goals. Davis et al. (1997) associate stewardship theory's psychological underpinnings with the higher levels of Maslow's (1970) hierarchy of needs and agency theory with the respective lower levels. Stewards are seen as using personal power and value involvement-oriented situations (Davis et al., 1997). In project-related governance settings this lends naturally to a preference for being controlled by results or outcomes rather than just 'following the process' (Müller & Lecoeuvre, 2014).

Hernandez (2012) investigated the psychology underlying stewardship behavior. He traces it back to individuals' need for control of their own behavior and the meaning derived from this behavior. He concludes that stewards and their organizations benefit from stewardship behavior because a "stewardship governance approach facilitates a sense of psychological ownership rather than material ownership" (Hernandez, 2012, p. 182).

Compared with agency theory, stewardship theory is relatively young and is yet to establish itself and its theoretical contribution relative to other governance theories. This is shown by the higher popularity of agency theory and transaction cost economics (TCE) (Williamson, 1975, 1985) in governance studies. However, stewardship theory is gaining increased momentum, especially in studies on more contemporary settings, such as in Franck and Jungwirth's (2003) work on the governance of open source development projects. The relationship between agency and stewardship theory is seen differently in different industries. A literature review by Cares et al. (2006) showed a preference for agency theory in governance studies in for-profit organizations, while its appropriateness for the not-for-profit sector was questioned. Contrarily, they see stewardship theory as potentially appropriate for not-for-profit organizations. Sundaramurthy and Lewis (2003) propose that modern enterprises need a simultaneity of both agency theory-type control structures and stewardship theory-type collaborative structures,

32 *Ralf Müller*

where the relative importance of one practice over the other is determined by the organization's history. In this scenario, organizations that are successful with their control orientation will remain, while those with less success will enter into a self-reinforcing downward circle. For contexts that are characterized by diversity and shareholder involvement, they recommend more stewardship-type approaches, which balance collaboration and control, done by encouraging people's trust in human capabilities, distrust in human limitations, and task-related cognitive conflict among governance actors.

This is taken further by authors who perceive agency and stewardship theories as being the opposite endpoints of a continuum or a swinging pendulum. They propose that any state in between these endpoints of pure agency or pure stewardship can be reached in corporate reality (Clarke, 2004a; Hernandez, 2012; Müller & Lecoeuvre, 2014). Here, an individual's locus of self-definition helps to locate their position on the continuum, where an individualistic focus tends toward agency, relational locus toward balanced, and collectivistic locus toward stewardship approaches (Hernandez, 2012).

Transaction Cost Economics

TCE addresses the administrative costs in transactions such as projects. Transaction costs are here seen as the economic equivalent to friction in physical systems, which stems from the complexity of the relationship between buyers and sellers in the market and the incompleteness of contracts between them. TCE shares some commonalities with agency theory, such as its origin in economics and its aim to avoid opportunistic behavior or deviations from agreed-upon terms. However, TCE takes a different perspective than agency theory. While the latter takes a dyadic perspective toward the principal–agent problem, TCE takes the perspective of overall costs for negotiating and possibly renegotiating contracts, as well as controlling and enforcing their execution.

Williamson's seminal 1975 work addresses the classical question of whether a firm should 'make' a product or 'buy' it in the market. A 'make' provides for better control of 'fit for purpose' or lowering of maladaptation costs. However, this is balanced by generally higher management costs. A 'buy' typically provides for lower prices through economies of scale and price competition in the market, which may be balanced by a lower fit for purpose. Williamson (1975) outlines that transaction costs are contingent on three main dimensions:

- The degree of *asset specificity*, which describes the extent an object in a transaction (or deliverable of a project) is specific or unique to the individual transaction (or project) and cannot be redeployed in future or other transactions. This is the strongest indicator for transaction costs.

Governance Theories   33

- The degree of *uncertainty*, which is a combination of:

  a   the lack of communication or conscious supply of false and misleading signals
  b   the general uncertainty in human behavior
  c   the general risk of the undertaking

- The *frequency* of the transaction, where repetitive routine transactions require no specialized governance structures, whereas unique transactions demand very specific governance structures.

The higher the first two and the lower the third dimensions, the higher the transaction costs will be. Several variations of these dimensions are found, such as that by Adler, Scherer, Barton and Katerberg (1998), who propose that high levels of asset specificity, uncertainty, and contract incompleteness lead to 'make' decisions, whereas low levels lead to 'buy' decisions.

TCE views an organization or project as a network of contracts, with the overall aim of adjusting the economics of governance efforts to the characteristics of a transaction, such as a project.

In his later work, Williamson (1985, p. 387) generalizes this as:

> *Transaction costs are economized by assigning transactions (which differ in their attributes) to governance structures (the adaptive capacities and associated costs of which differ) in a discriminating way.*

Thus, TCE proposes that organizations adapt their governance structures, such as contracts, to minimize transaction costs. For example, a fixed-price, fixed-date delivery contract for a project or component requires different governance and control structures than a time and material or cost-reimbursement contract (Müller & Turner, 2005)

TCE's success as a governance theory is not without criticism. Skeptics' arguments center around the crudeness and simplicity of its models, its underdeveloped trade-offs, severe measurement problems, and too many degrees of freedom (Williamson, 1985). Despite these critiques it is the foremost governance theory and used frequently for the study of marketing phenomena, such as joint projects between independent firms in buyer–seller relationships.

This chapter has provided an introduction to the most popular governance theories. Their application in conceptual and empirical context will be described in the later chapters.

References

Adler, T. R., Scherer, R. F., Barton, S. L., & Katerberg, R. (1998). An Empirical Test of Transaction Cost Theory: Validating Contract Typology. *Journal of Applied Management Studies*, 7(2), 185–200.

34 *Ralf Müller*

Allen, W. T. (1992). Our Schizophrenic Conception of the Business Corporation. *Cardozo Law Review, 14*(2), 261–281.

Aras, G., & Crowther, D. (2010). Corporate Social Responsibility: A Broader View of Corporate Governance. In G. Aras & D. Crowther (Eds.), *A Handbook of Corporate Governance and Social Responsibility* (pp. 265–280). Farnham, UK: Gower Publishing Limited.

Barney, J. B., & Hesterly, W. (1996). Organizational Economics: Understanding the Relationship between Organizations and Economic Analysis. In S. R. Clegg, C. Hardy, & W. R. Nord (Eds.), *Handbook of Organization Studies* (pp. 115–147). London, UK: Sage Publications.

Bergen, M., Dutta, S., & Walker, O. C. (1992). Agency Relationships in Marketing: A Review of the Implications and Applications of Agency and Related Theories. *Journal of Marketing, 56*(3), 1.

Blair, M. M. (2004). Ownership and Control: Rethinking Corporate Governance for the Twenty-First Century. In T. Clarke (Ed.), *Theories of Corporate Governance: The Philosophical Foundations of Corporate Governance* (pp. 174–188). New York, NY: Routledge.

Blomquist, T., & Müller, R. (2006). *Middle Managers in Program and Portfolio Management: Practice, Roles and Responsibilities.* Newton Square: Project Management Institute.

Cares, R., Du Bois, C., Jegers, M., De Gieter, S., Schepers, C., & Pepermans, R. (2006). Principlal-Agent Relationships on the Stewardship-Agency Axis. *Nonprofit Management & Leadership, 17*(1), 25–47.

Clarke, T. (2004a). The Stakeholder Corporation: A Business Philosophy for the Information Age. In *Theories of Corporate Governance: The Philosophical Foundations of Corporate Governance* (pp. 189–201). London, UK: Routledge.

Clarke, T. (2004b). *Theories of Corporate Governance* (T. Clarke, Ed.). Milton Park, UK: Routledge.

Davis, J. H., Schoorman, F. D., & Donaldson, L. (1997). Toward a Stewardship Theory of Management. *Academy of Management Review, 22*(1), 20–47.

Franck, E., & Jungwirth, C. (2003). Reconciling Rent-Seekers and Donators—The Governance Structure of Open Source. *Journal of Management & Governance, 7*(4), 401–421.

Friedman, M. (1970). The Social Responsibility of Businesses is to Increase Its Profits. *The New York Times Magazine,* September 13, 1970. Retrieved October 9, 2013, from http://www.colorado.edu/studentgroups/libertarians/issues/friedman-soc-resp-business.html

Hernandez, M. (2012). Toward an Understanding of the Psychology of Stewardship. *Academy of Management Review, 37*(2), 172–193. doi:10.5465/amr.2010.0363

Jensen, M. C. (2000). *A Theory of the Firm: Governance, Residual Claims, and Organizational Forms.* Cambridge: Harvard University Press.

Jensen, M. C., & Meckling, W. H. (1976). Theory of the Firm: Managerial Behavior, Agency Costs, and Ownership Structure. *Journal of Financial Economics, 3*(4), 305–360.

Maslow, A. H. (1970). *Motivation and Personality.* New York, NY: Harper & Row.

Müller, R., & Lecoeuvre, L. (2014). Operationalizing Governance Categories of Projects. *International Journal of Project Management, 32*(8), 1346–1357. doi:dx.doi.org/10.1016/j.ijproman.2014.04.005

Müller, R., & Turner, J. R. (2005). The Impact of Principal-Agent Relationship and Contract Type on Communication between Project Owner and Manager. *International Journal of Project Management*, 23(5), 398–403.

Naciri, A. (2010). *Internal and External Aspects of Corporate Governance*. Milton Park, UK: Routledge.

Smith, A. (1776/2013). *The Wealth of Nations. Bibliomania*. Retrieved from http://www.bibliomania.com/2/1/65/112/frameset.html

Sundaramurthy, C., & Lewis, M. (2003). Control and Collaboration: Paradoxes of Governance. *Academy of Management Review*, 28(3), 397–415.

Turner, J. R. (1998). *The Versatile Project Based Organization: Historical Perspectives on Future Research*. Henley Reearch Centre: Henley Management Centre.

Turner, J. R., & Müller, R. (2004). Communication and Co-Operation on Projects Between the Project Owner as Principal and the Project Manager as Agent. *European Management Journal*, 22(3), 327–336.

Williamson, O. E. (1975). *Markets and Hierarchies: Analysis and Antitrust Implications*. New York, NY: Collier Macmillan, Canada, Ltd.

Williamson, O. E. (1985). *The Economic Institutions of Capitalism*. New York, NY: The Free Press.

4 Governance Models and Paradigms

Ralf Müller

This chapter addresses the models for organizational project governance and extends these into project governance paradigms. We start by giving a short overview of the most popular models for organizational project governance and their different ontological origins. We then build a model that combines the theories addressed in the previous chapter to build an organization-wide project governance model. By combining the theories, we identify four project governance paradigms, which are used in the remaining chapters of the book.

Models of Organizational Project Governance

The models described below represent governance as a system, using general rules and concepts. Hence, they are abstract simplifications of an aspect of the world, such as governance, based on a particular ontology, with the aim to support knowledge and communication about the subject. The models are examples of the multitude of ontological and theoretical perspectives that may underlie governance models. To that end, they emphasize different aspects of governance, such as the process and roles of governance, elements that make up a governance regime, organizational embeddedness, or organizational project governance.

Process Models

An example of a process- and roles-based model is that by Turner (2009). By taking a process perspective, it identifies three processes and the associated roles and their relationships for the governance of projects. The model is described as three concentric circles of governance processes. The innermost circle refers to the governance activities closest to the project. These are defining objectives, providing the means to achieve those objectives, and monitoring progress. This inner process circle is governed by a process at the intermediate circle, which addresses the needs and requirements for the intended project deliverables and the project results. The related activities include defining client needs, desired outcome (i.e., deliverable), desired output (i.e., achievement of business case), required process, delivered output, and delivered outcome. This process circle is governed by an outer circle, which describes the process of interaction between client manager, sponsor, steward project manager, and project owner (see also Chapter 5 for a detailed description of this interaction).

The model defines a minimum of four governance roles:

- *Sponsor*—this role identifies and justifies the need for the project and its benefits (e.g., the project's business case). In addition, it is the ambassador role of the project, convincing others that the project is needed and helping acquire the required resources. This role often holds the budget for the project.
- *Steward*—this role works in conjunction with the sponsor to define the project output (e.g., its deliverable) and the benefit that it can bring; often done by a senior manager from a technical department.
- *Project Manager*—this role defines and manages the process for successful project delivery, as well as its monitoring and control mechanisms.
- *Owner or Business Change Manager*—this role ensures that the project's deliverables are used as intended and provide the planned benefits. This role starts after the project has delivered its product or service and is either fulfilled by the owner or delegated to a business change manager.

In terms of contribution to the four governance principles, this model supports transparency by linking the role of steward (pre-project) with that of the project manager (project execution) and that of the owner and business change manager (post-project execution). This is done through a common set of business objectives and project objectives that are defined early on, which follows the project from the initial idea to the creation of business benefits. The clearly defined roles provide for accountability and responsibility in task execution, which, together with transparency, lay the ground for at least some level of fairness.

Governance and Governmentality-Based Models

An example for a governance and governmentality-based model is that by Walker, Segon, and Rowlinson (2008). This model balances governance and governmentality in the form of hard factors (governance) and soft factors (governmentality).

Hard factors refer to the structures, rules, and regulations used to systematically identify accountabilities and discharge the responsibilities for the delivery of project objectives. This includes elements such as organizational design as well as a way to structure transparency, accountabilities, and responsibilities. It also includes policies and procedures, work processes, regulations, and codes of practices to clarify responsibilities and accountabilities, as well as legal requirements, audits, reporting, performance measures, and stakeholder disclosure to address all four governance principles.

Soft factors (named governmentality in this book) are represented in the form of people's interaction with the governance structure, the way they interpret and enforce regulatory frameworks, as well as their relationship with one another. This includes the workplace and organizational culture, the leadership style employed by management and their use of power, as well as motivation and behavioral aspects. This is seen in relation to the resources and knowledge that are needed as well as possible collaborations or networks.

This model proposes a balance of governance and governmentality through trust and credibility between actors, which builds on clear accountabilities and transparency, paired with known responsibilities and the required fairness.

Nested Models

Too and Weaver (2014) suggest a three-layered, nested model of organizational project governance. At the lowest level is a project delivery system (including project management) executed by middle and front-line managers, which is nested in a management system at the next higher level, the executive level. This, in turn, is nested in a governance system at the board of directors' level. The model emphasizes the mutual dependency of the governance and management systems for good organizational results. Here, the governance system defines the structures, rights and responsibilities, and the requirements to ensure effective work in these structures, while management executes its role within this framework.

The model reduces governance to two main functions:

1 Decisions on which projects to approve, fund, and support. This includes communication with management about the strategic framework to select the 'right' projects and programs, mechanisms for effective use of resources, rules, and procedures, as well as rights and responsibilities of project participants.
2 Oversight and assurance, accomplished through agreement with and possible modification of the strategic plan, the alignment of projects with it, and the project's specific contribution to this plan. This includes the monitoring of performance, the stewardship of resources, and communication with stakeholders.

Too and Weaver suggest that good project governance is achieved through the optimization of the balance between four organizational elements, which are: (1) portfolio management (which focuses on selecting the 'right' projects and programs); (2) project sponsorship (which links the executive level

Governance Models and Paradigms 39

and project/program level with a focus on delivering value); (3) PMOs (for oversight and strategic reporting); and (4) projects and programs (whose effective management is a measure of the effectiveness of the governance system).

Layered Models

The layered governance model by Müller (2009) explains the interfaces of the governance levels of projects, programs, portfolios, and board of directors through institutional, agency, and stewardship theories, as well as transaction cost economics.

At the level of projects, the model defines instances of governance, such as a steering group meeting, as an event where a governor, such as the steering group, acts as an agent to the stakeholders and the public by being accountable for the project's legitimacy (including the fairness principle) and responsible for its professional execution and transparency of its performance. At the same time, the governor (i.e., steering group) is a principal for the project manager. This project manager acts as an agent or steward contingent on the governor's view of the governed. This has implications for the governance mechanisms applied. Steering groups who look at their project managers from a predominantly agency theory perspective accord the role of agent to the project manager and tend to foster monitoring and control as the governance mechanism. Contrarily, steering groups that foster mainly stewardship approaches tend to use trust as their main governance mechanism. Hence, agency and stewardship theories describe the dyadic and situational relationship between the governor (steering group) and governed (project manager) at a particular moment in time. Transaction cost economics explains the governor's view of the entire governance life cycle (in addition to the project objectives as such), and the emphasis on reducing unnecessary transaction costs. For more details on these theories, see Chapter 3.

The layered model proposes that the same principle applies to the interface between the steering group (as agent/steward) and portfolio management (as principal), as well as between portfolio management (as agent/steward) and the board of directors (as principal). A special role is taken by the PMO. Those in a consulting and training role would act as agents or stewards for higher levels of management, such as steering groups or program/portfolio managers, and act as principals for the project managers in their domain. Those PMOs who provide project management services will be agents/stewards for the steering committees, as described above.

The models described above exemplify the diversity of models for organizational project governance. Decisions on the selection of a particular model should take into account the scope (project or organization wide), the subject of modeling (such as the process, tasks, organizational elements, or relationships and behaviors), and the need for a link to corporate governance (such as through agency or stewardship theory).

Governance Paradigms

A paradigm is a particular thinking pattern. In the context of governance this refers to thinking patterns in the execution of governance. Examples include the expectation by a steering group in shareholder-oriented governance structures that project managers are sensitive to financial goals and try to maximize return on investment for shareholders, or steering groups in stakeholder-oriented governance structures who expect their project managers to attract further stakeholder groups for their project's product by possibly adding value to it.

We now describe a model of four governance paradigms, which were conceptually developed by Müller (2009) and operationalized by Müller & Lecoeuvre (2014). Since then, the paradigms have been used in a number of studies addressing a diverse set of research questions (for example, in Aubry, Müller, & Glückler, 2012; Müller, Turner, Andersen, Shao, & Kvalnes, 2014; Rosario Bernardo, 2015). They are also used in several chapters of this book.

The four paradigms link corporate governance with organizational project governance through an overlay of two dimensions: the corporate governance orientation and the control structures in a project's parent organization.

The corporate governance orientation builds on Clarke's (1998) and Hernandez's (2012) models, which show a corporation's governance orientation on a continuum from shareholder to stakeholder orientation. Hernandez uses the example of a pendulum that swings between shareholder and stakeholder orientation and addresses the question whether the organizational unit that governs a project is more shareholder or more stakeholder oriented. A predominantly shareholder orientation indicates a governance orientation in line with shareholder theory, where the requirement to maximize shareholder wealth is prioritized relative to the requirements of other stakeholders. A predominantly stakeholder orientation indicates governance approaches in line with stakeholder theory, which aims at serving a wider spectrum of stakeholders, of which shareholders are but one, and the balancing of the diverse set of requirements from the different stakeholder groups (Clarke, 1998; Davis, Schoorman, & Donaldson, 1997).

Dimensions to measure both shareholder-to-stakeholder orientation and behavior versus outcome control were taken from the literature by identifying subject areas that overlap in the corporate and project governance literature and, thus, those corporate governance dimensions that 'reach through' from the corporate level to the project level. The questionnaire is provided in the Appendix in the form of seven-point semantic differential scales.

The measurement dimensions for shareholder versus stakeholder orientation are described below in the form of their ranges, with each of them starting from a more shareholder orientation (the former) to a more stakeholder orientation (the latter):

- *Decision making* addresses whether decisions are governed by the need to maximize shareholder wealth (Jensen, 2010), or to satisfy a variety of stakeholder groups (Donaldson & Preston, 1995).

- *Remuneration* addresses whether (project) managers' remuneration should be tied to corporate (project) performance as per Benito and Conyon (1999) or not, as suggested by Jones (1995).
- *Legitimacy* is a "generalized perception or assumption that the actions of an entity are desirable, proper, or appropriate within some socially constructed system of norms, values, beliefs, and definitions" (Suchman, 1995, p. 574). This ranges from legitimizing the primacy of maximizing shareholder wealth as a governance principle (Jensen, 2010; Merino, Mayper, & Tolleson, 2010) to legitimizing the diversity of stakeholder interests as a moral basis for management and their actions (Charreaux & Desbrières, 2001; Donaldson & Preston, 1995).
- *Financial objectives*, which range from prioritizing the importance of financial objectives, such as company profits, over social responsibilities of a firm (Friedman, 1970) to prioritizing manager–stakeholder relationships because of their significant direct and indirect impact on the firm's results (Berman, Wicks, Kotha, & Jones, 1999).
- *Long-term objectives* addresses whether profitability is seen as the organization's long-term objective (Friedman, 1970), or long-term survival, and its satisfaction of the diversity of objectives of stakeholder groups (Freeman, Wicks, & Parmar, 2004).

The second dimension of the paradigm model addresses the way the governing institution controls the project and its manager. Building on that, it models organizational control structures as ranging from controlling outcomes, such as reaching agreed upon objectives, to controlling behavior, such as following a given process.

Related measurement dimensions for the outcome versus behavior control continuum are listed below. Again, the list shows the ranges of each measurement dimension, starting from a merely behavior control perspective (the former) and ending with a merely outcome control perspective (the latter):

- *Process versus outcome orientation.* This addresses whether organizations prioritize controlling people's behavior by fostering process and procedure compliance or prioritize controlling people's work outcome by de-emphasizing the role of formal processes and procedures (Ouchi, 1980).
- *Level of control.* This ranges from exercising tight control by use of sophisticated control systems to loose control using informal relationships (e.g., Brown & Eisenhardt, 1997; Mintzberg, 1985; Ouchi & Maguire, 1975).
- *Adherence to job description.* The nature of the job role determines the appropriateness of mere behavior control (i.e., through the adherence to job descriptions) or outcome control (i.e., trusting people to define their appropriate on-the-job behavior themselves) (Eisenhardt, 1985). Clarity of job description is here linked to organizational and project success (Belout, 1998; Tsui, 1987).

42 Ralf Müller

- *Role of support institutions.* This addresses the institutionalization of practices in organizations. Approaches range from habitualization of work practices by enforcing compliance at the task or project level (Scott, 2014) to the establishment of organizational units that institutionalize at the more strategic level the ways business objectives are accomplished (Hobbs & Aubry, 2007).
- *Compliance expectations.* This addresses process and methodology compliance versus self-leadership to execute tasks/projects. While some writers link process compliance to organizational and project success (Jaafari, 2003; Schwaber, 2004), others prioritize self-management due to the intrinsic motivational values (Manz, 1986).

Figure 4.1 shows the four governance paradigms as the overlay of the two main dimensions: shareholder versus stakeholder orientation and behavior versus outcome control. They are: Conformist, Flexible Economist, Versatile Artist, and Agile Pragmatist.

A *conformist* paradigm is characterized by a shareholder orientation in governance and a behavior control focus. Process and methodology compliance are emphasized as the governance means to secure highest return on investment for shareholders. The underlying assumption is that efficiency is maximized by trusting the process over the capabilities of individuals. This paradigm is often found in organizations with a homogenous set of a few or relatively simple projects. Examples include product or service development organizations, where project management is a minor subset and side task.

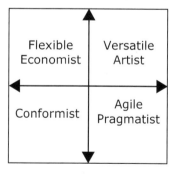

Figure 4.1 The Four Governance Paradigms

Institutions such as PMOs are rarely found in these organizations, due to the low priority these organizations assign to project management.

A *flexible economist* paradigm is characterized by a shareholder orientation combined with an outcome control focus. Governance here aims for a flexible application of the most effective project management methods, tools, techniques, and management approaches for the project to yield the highest possible return on investment for the organization's shareholders. PMOs can provide relevant training and support of project managers in using tools and techniques. This requires highly professional project managers who can select and adjust processes and methodologies to minimize costs and efforts. These organizations often see project management as one of their core competences, and they have well-trained and sometimes certified project managers. In addition, these organizations often have PMOs in place to support project managers through consulting and training.

A *versatile artist* paradigm is characterized by a stakeholder orientation in combination with outcome control. Versatility is needed to balance the diverse set of, often conflicting, requirements from the various stakeholder groups. These organizations often employ the most senior and experienced project managers, who tailor or newly develop their methodologies and work practices in accordance with project needs. Project management is seen as a core competence of the organization, and the project managers are well-trained or certified by professional institutions. These organizations often use PMOs for business and operational purposes, whereby they link the strategic levels of the organization, such as portfolio management, with tactical and operational levels, such as in projects.

An *agile pragmatist* paradigm is characterized by a stakeholder orientation combined with behavior control. This paradigm emphasizes process compliance, as found in the current stream of agile methods in project management, which aim for a time-phased delivery of functionalities, such as in IT projects. The balance of the diversity in stakeholder requirements is addressed by the project sponsor, who decides on the prioritization of functions to be implemented or user needs, often in accordance with their value for the business. This paradigm allows for flexibility for changes in scope or other changing requirements from project stakeholders.

The four paradigms are mutually exclusive at the corporate level, as a corporation is typically clear on its approach to corporate governance and the ways in which it controls its employees. However, the paradigms are not mutually exclusive at the lower levels of the corporation. Contingent on an organizational unit's particular contribution to the strategic goals, the paradigm can vary. For example, maintenance departments in a corporation may be directed to maximize profits and follow defined processes (a conformist paradigm), whereas development departments may have to balance the requirements of different user groups of their future product and are controlled by level of innovation (a versatile artist paradigm).

The paradigm model was tested through a worldwide survey with 478 responses by checking its validation of existing patterns (see Müller & Lecoeuvre, 2014 for more details). Patterns tested included country patterns, such as those shown in Figure 4.2, which supports findings from corporate governance that English-speaking countries tend to employ shareholder-oriented governance. The figure shows all English-speaking countries using on average more shareholder than stakeholder approaches, of which all except Australia prefer on average to control behavior. Some countries, such as Sweden, are almost exclusively represented in the sample through large corporations, which speaks for its shareholder orientation, whereas others, such as Lithuania and Norway, are represented by many small organizations. Small organizations in small countries are likely to maintain and extend their network of business partners through more entrepreneurial approaches to business, which focus on long-term business through value creation for customers rather than short-term profit generation for the owners.

Figure 4.3 confirms the pattern that larger projects are more often governed by strict shareholder orientation and process compliance, such as in large infrastructure projects (described in Chapter 9). This is complemented by small projects, which are on average governed through a stakeholder orientation combined with outcome control. The figure shows an almost linear relationship between project size and governance paradigm changes. Starting at a versatile artist paradigm for small projects, the increase in project budget increases the strength of the conformist paradigm.

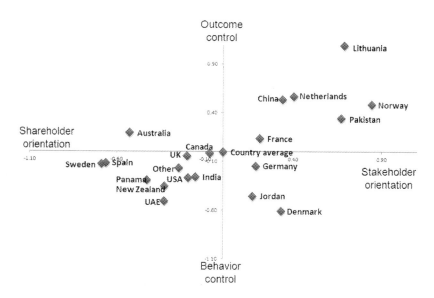

Figure 4.2 Governance Paradigms Mean by Country

Governance Models and Paradigms 45

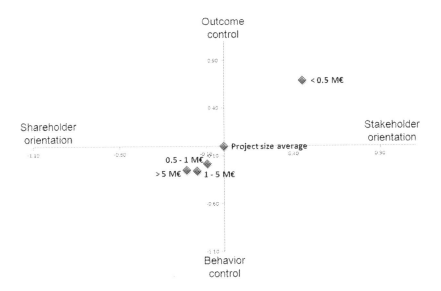

Figure 4.3 Governance Paradigms Mean by Project Size

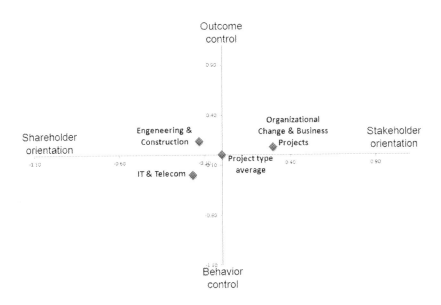

Figure 4.4 Governance Paradigms Mean by Project Type

Figure 4.4 shows the average paradigm by sector. The IT and telecom industries are shown as relatively more process oriented than other industries, which is also reflected in the popularity of agile, lean, and other process-focused methodologies, which are required due to the abstract nature of

46 *Ralf Müller*

the project deliverables. This is less of an issue in engineering and construction, where existing physical products (e.g., buildings) and standards often reduce the risks of misunderstanding at the requirements definition stage, so the focus in governance can shift to more outcome control. Both industries prefer on average a shareholder-oriented governance, which may be explained through the size of the firms in these industries. This is different with organizational change and business projects. Relative to the other industries, these companies often also employ smaller consulting companies for these types of projects, which are then on average governed by a stakeholder orientation and outcome control.

The four governance paradigms are used in several studies described in this book. Therefore, we have devoted more space for a detailed discussion of these than of other models. Still, a more comprehensive description will be outside the scope of this chapter. These details can be obtained from the publications referenced above.

This chapter has shown the variety of models and perspectives present by introducing some exemplary models for organizational project governance. We then discussed the model for governance paradigms, which links governance at the corporate level with governance at the project level.

References

Aubry, M., Müller, R., & Glückler, J. (2012). *Governance and Communities of PMOs*. Newton Square, PA: Project Management Institute.

Belout, A. (1998). Effects of Human Resource Management on Project Effectiveness and Success: Toward a New Conceptual Framework. *International Journal of Project Management*, 16(1), 21–26. doi:10.1016/S0263-7863(97)00011-2

Benito, A., & Conyon, M. J. (1999). The Governance of Directors ' Pay : Evidence from UK Companies. *Journal of Management and Governance*, 3(2), 117–136.

Berman, S. L., Wicks, A. C., Kotha, S., & Jones, T. M. (1999). Does Stakeholder Orientation Matter? The Relationship between Stakeholder Management Models and Firm Financial Performance. *Academy of Management Journal*, 42(5), 488–506.

Brown, S., & Eisenhardt, K. M. (1997). The Art of Continuous Change: Linking Complexity Theory and Time-Paced Evolution in Relentlessly Shifting Organizations. *Administrative Science Quarterly*, 42(1), 1–34.

Charreaux, G., & Desbrières, P. (2001). Corporate Governance: Stakeholder Value Versus Shareholder Value. *Journal of Management and Governance*, 5(2), 107–128.

Clarke, T. (1998). The Stakeholder Corporation: A Business Philosophy for the Information Age. *Long Range Planning*, 31(2), 182–194. doi:10.1016/S0024-6301(98)00002-8

Davis, J. H., Schoorman, F. D., & Donaldson, L. (1997). Toward a Stewardship Theory of Management. *Academy of Management Review*, 22(1), 20–47.

Donaldson, T., & Preston, L. E. (1995). The Stakeholder Theory of the Corporation: Concepts, Evidence, and Implications. *Academy of Management Review*, 20(1), 65–91.

Eisenhardt, K. M. (1985). Control: Organizational and Economic Approaches *. *Management Science*, 31(2), 134–149.

Freeman, R. E., Wicks, A. C., & Parmar, B. (2004). Stakeholder Theory and "The Corporate Objective Revisited." *Organization Science*, 15(3), 364–369. doi:10.1287/orsc.1040.0066

Friedman, M. (1970). The Social Responsibility of Businesses Is to Increase its Profits. *The New York Times Magazine*, September 13, 1970. Retrieved October 9, 2013, from http://www.colorado.edu/studentgroups/libertarians/issues/friedman-soc-resp-business.html

Hernandez, M. (2012). Toward an Understanding of the Psychology of Stewardship. *Academy of Management Review*, 37(2), 172–193. doi:10.5465/amr.2010.0363

Hobbs, B., & Aubry, M. (2007). A Multi-Phase Research Program Investigating Project Management Offices (PMOs): The Results of Phase 1. *Project Management Journal*, 38(1), 74–86.

Jaafari, A. (2003). Project Management in the Age of Complexity and Change. *Project Management Journal*, 34(4), 47–57.

Jensen, M. C. (2010). Value Maximization, Stakeholder Theory, and the Corporate Objective Function. *Journal of Applied Corporate Finance*, 22(1), 32–42. doi:10.1111/j.1745-6622.2010.00259.x

Jones, T. M. (1995). Instrumental Stakeholder Theory: A Synthesis of Ethics and Economics. *The Academy of Management Review*, 20(2), 404. doi:10.2307/258852

Manz, C. C. (1986). Self-Leadership: Toward an Expanded Theory of Self-Influence Processes in Organizations. *Academy of Management Review*, 11(3), 585. doi:10.2307/258312

Merino, B. D., Mayper, A. G., & Tolleson, T. D. (2010). Neoliberalism, Deregulation and Sarbanes-Oxley: The Legitimation of a Failed Corporate Governance Model. *Accounting, Auditing & Accountability Journal*, 23(6), 774–792. doi:10.1108/09513571011065871

Mintzberg, H. (1985). Of Strategies, Deliberate and Emergent. *Strategic Management Journal*, 6(June 1984), 257–272.

Müller, R. (2009). *Project Governance*. Aldershot, UK: Gower Publishing.

Müller, R., & Lecoeuvre, L. (2014). Operationalizing Governance Categories of Projects. *International Journal of Project Management*, 32(8), 1346–1357. doi:dx.doi.org/10.1016/ j.ijproman.2014.04.005

Müller, R., Turner, J. R., Andersen, E. S., Shao, J., & Kvalnes, Ø. (2014). Ethics, Trust and Governance in Temporary Organizations. *Project Management Journal*, 45(4), 39–54.

Ouchi, W. G. (1980). Markets, Bureaucracies and Clans. *Administrative Science Quarterly*, 25, 129–141.

Ouchi, W. G., & Maguire, M. A. (1975). Organizational Control: Two Functions. *Administrative Science Quarterly*, 20(4), 559–569.

Rosario Bernardo, M. (2015). *Project Management Indicators for Enhancing the Governance of Projects*. Unpublished PhD thesis, Lille, France: SKEMA Business School.

Schwaber, K. (2004). *Agile Project Management with SCRUM*. Redmont, WA: Microsoft Press.

Scott, W. R. (2014). *Institutions and Organizations* (4th ed.). London, UK: SAGE Publication Ltd., UK.

48 *Ralf Müller*

Suchman, M. C. (1995). Managing Legitimacy: Strategic and InstitutionalApproaches. *Academy of Management Review*, 20(3), 571–610.

Too, E. G., & Weaver, P. (2014). The Management of Project Management: A Conceptual Framework for Project Governance. *International Journal of Project Management*, 32(8), 1382–1394. doi:10.1016/j.ijproman.2013.07.006

Tsui, A. S. (1987). Defining the Activities and Effectiveness of the Human Resource Department: A Multiple Constituency Approach. *Human Resource Management*, 26(1), 35–69. doi:10.1002/hrm.3930260104

Turner, J. R. (2009). *The Handbook of Project-Based Management* (3rd ed.). London, UK: McGraw-Hill.

Walker, D. H. T., Segon, M., & Rowlinson, S. (2008). Business Ethics and Corporate Citizenship. In D. H. T. Walker & S. Rowlinson (Eds.), *Procurement Systems—A Cross Industry Project Management Perspective* (pp. 101–139). Abdingdon, Oxon, UK: Taylor and Francis.

Appendix: Governance Paradigm Questionnaire

Table 4.1 Governance Paradigm Questionnaire

In my organization . . .

. . . decisions are made in the best interest of the shareholders and owners of the organization and their Return on Investment (RoI)	0 0 0 0 0 0 0	. . . decisions are made in the best interest of the wider stakeholder community (incl. shareholder, employees, local communities, etc.)
. . . the remuneration system includes stock options for employees and similar incentives that foster shareholder RoI thinking	0 0 0 0 0 0 0	. . . the remuneration system provides incentives for community, environmental, humanitarian, or other non-profit activities outside and/or inside the organization
. . . prevails an image that profitability determines the legitimacy of actions (including projects)	0 0 0 0 0 0 0	. . . prevails an image that wider social and ethical interests determine the legitimacy of actions (including projects)
. . . I am sometimes asked to sacrifice stakeholder satisfaction for the achievement of financial objectives	0 0 0 0 0 0 0	. . . I am sometimes asked to sacrifice the achievement of financial objectives for improvement of stakeholder satisfaction
. . . the long-term objective is to maximize value for the owners of the organization	0 0 0 0 0 0 0	. . . the long-term objective is to maximize value for society

The management philosophy in my organization favors . . .

. . . a strong emphasis on always getting personnel to follow the formally laid down procedures	0 0 0 0 0 0 0	. . . a strong emphasis on getting things done even if it means disregarding formal procedures
. . . tight formal control of most operations by means of sophisticated control and information systems	0 0 0 0 0 0 0	. . . loose, informal control; heavy dependence on informal relationships and the norm of cooperation for getting things done

(Continued)

Table 4.1 (Continued)

. . . a strong emphasis on getting personnel to adhere closely to formal job descriptions	0 0 0 0 0 0 0	. . . a strong emphasis to let the requirements of the situation and the individual's personality define proper on-job behavior
. . . support institutions (like a PMO) should ensure compliance with the organization's project management methodology	0 0 0 0 0 0 0	. . . support institutions (like a PMO) should collect performance data in order to identify skills and knowledge gaps
. . . prioritization of methodology compliance over people's own experiences in doing their work	0 0 0 0 0 0 0	. . . prioritization of people's own experiences in doing their work over methodology compliance

5 Governance Institutions

Ralf Müller, Erling S. Andersen, Ole Jonny Klakegg, and Gro Holst Volden

This chapter describes the most popular governance institutions found among a large variety of institutions in the private and public sector. We start by presenting the 'organizational building blocks' that are used for the various approaches to organizational project governance. With institutions or, more specifically, organizational institutions, we mean an organized body of people (full-time, part-time, dedicated, or virtual) with a specific purpose in the governance of projects.

The chapter addresses the most popular organizational institutions that are involved in the governance of projects. As there are numerous institutions that fulfill some sort of governance role for projects, such as the many national, safety, industry, and professional regulation bodies in, for example, the pharmaceutical or automobile industries, we have to be selective in the number of institutions to address. Therefore, we focus on those institutions that are most common, are closest to the project, and most directly influence projects. For the governance of projects, we address the board of directors, program and portfolio management, as well as project management offices (PMOs). For project governance, we address the project owner and the project steering group, as well as the communication between the steering group and the project manager. The roles and focus areas of other governance institutions can be found in the respective industry literature. The chapter concludes with a summary of the contributions these institutions make to the four governance principles.

Institutions for the Governance of Projects

Institutions for the governance of projects are those organizational entities whose activities influence more than a single project. Their work addresses groups of projects, such as the board of directors' activities concerning the entirety of projects in a company, or groups of projects like those in programs or portfolios of projects. In doing this, these institutions bridge the objectives of the organization with corporate and business unit-wide practices.

52 Ralf Müller et al.

Board of Directors

Boards of directors decide on the nature of the business and the extent that this business is executed through projects. This includes decisions on the nature of project work and its governance in organizations (Müller, 2011; Turner, 2009). The Tasly Pharmaceuticals case described in Chapter 15 is an example of a board of directors' decision to transform a process-oriented company into a project-oriented one. This was done through a strategic PMO, which was set up to develop and implement the transformation process and subsequently perform the long-term governance of all projects in the organization.

Along with the board's decisions on the extent to which work is done through projects in an organization comes the decision on the nature and extent of project-related governance. This includes decisions on the establishment of a PMO, its mission and scope of accountability and responsibility, as well as decisions on the employment of project managers versus procurement of temporary project management services from the market, the level of seniority, and so forth.

Being the highest project-related governance body within the organizational hierarchy, the board of directors must also govern the project-based part of the organization by setting its objectives, providing the means to achieve those objectives, and defining the ways progress is measured and reported. For example, during the time when one of the authors (Ralf Müller) was the Worldwide Director of PMO and Project Management at NCR Corporation's Teradata Business Unit, the board of directors set two major objectives for him and his organization: a) reduce the number of projects at risk by 20% annually, and b) reduce the amount of revenue at risk by 20% annually. 'At risk' was defined as all the 'red' projects in the business unit's portfolio of major projects (i.e., those over US $5,000,000 in customer revenue). Portfolio reporting was done on a monthly basis and classified the major projects into green, when percent cost and schedule variance were less than 5% over plan, yellow when they were between 5% and 15%, and red in cases of more than 15% plan deviation. Additional qualitative measures were used for the same purpose, that is, identification of projects at risk, in order to devise remedies. Thus, the board of directors was always up to date on the status of major projects, their issues, and the amount of business at risk.

Portfolio Management and Program Management

Portfolios are groups of projects that require the same skill sets (Müller, 2009). Portfolio managers' role in the governance of projects lies mainly in setting the relative priority of projects, their visibility through portfolio reporting (see above), and their staffing through resources. Through this they significantly impact the scheduling of projects and their execution. Moreover, portfolio managers often sit in project steering groups where they, among others, decide on the direction of the project at hand and also get input on the quantity and quality of skills required in the future. With this information, they can develop, hire, or employ resources to ensure the required set of skills is available by the time it is needed.

Programs are groups of projects that share a common goal, which cannot be reached with just one project (Müller, 2009). Hence, a program sets the context for individual projects. The program manager acts as the owner or sponsor of each project in the program and takes on the related governance roles.

Turner and Keegan (2001) empirically developed a governance model that outlines the relationship between project, program, and portfolio managers. They call it the Broker–Steward Model. It consists of four roles: the client, the broker (program manager), the steward (portfolio manager), and the project manager. In this model, the client articulates the need for a product or service, which is then taken up by an entrepreneurial broker who maintains a seller–buyer relationship with the client. Triggered by the client needs, the broker involves the steward to put together the network of resources to deliver the project (i.e., ensure the right skills are available at the right place and time), while considering the long-term objectives of the supplying organization and the parallel projects in the organization, as well as their resources and skills needs. Once broker and steward agree on the execution of the project, the steward appoints a project manager for project execution.

The model shows the inherent conflict between the roles of broker (program manager) and steward (portfolio manager). While the entrepreneurial broker aims for maximization of business through exploration of business opportunities, the steward limits the execution of these opportunities to those that are in the best interest of the supplying organization, under special consideration of the relative importance of a given opportunity in light of all other opportunities and the existing resource and skills constraints. This raises a question of best practice: Is the relative dominance of the broker or steward role beneficial for the business of project-based parts of organizations? A related study by Blomquist and Müller (2006) showed that organizations often govern their project business in one of four ways:

- As *independent projects*, which neither share resources nor have a common goal.
- As *programs of projects*, where the main criteria for acceptance of a project into the portfolio is its contribution to a higher objective, typically one of a few strategic objectives of the organization. Here, the resources might not be shared across projects, but the goals are.
- As *portfolios of projects*, where the main criteria for acceptance of a project is its contribution to the productivity of existing resources. Here, skills are shared across projects, but not necessarily project objectives.

54 *Ralf Müller et al.*

- As *hybrids of program and portfolio* thinking, where the combination of shared resources and common objectives across projects is the main criteria for accepting projects.

The study showed that organizations with a hybrid form of governance of their project-based business perform significantly better than organizations with any of the other forms of governance. Organizations using the independent project approach scored lowest by reaching about 35% of the possible performance objectives. Those using program and portfolio approaches achieved approximately 50% of the possible performance objectives, and organizations with a hybrid approach accomplished more than 70% of the possible performance. Here, success was measured with a ten-question construct comprised of three questions each on project-, program-, and portfolio-level success, and one question on the overall success of the organization.

However, the results do not imply causation. We do not claim that a hybrid form of governance will automatically lead to better results, because it is possible that organizations with a high level of project performance can afford to set up a hybrid governance structure. Given the effects of governance maturity over the growth of organizations (as described in Müller, Shao, and Pemsel, 2016), it is likely that the size of the organization and the organization's business through projects has a major implication on this governance structure. As described in Chapters 6, 7, and 8, organizations apply different governance structures at different stages of growth. Small organizations apply project orientation, while medium-sized organizations (250–1,000 employees) often subordinate project tasks to the corporate production processes in order to maximize organizational efficiency. When organizations grow further, and the number of projects and skills needs in these projects also increase, they find a better balance between skills needs and resource utilization, which allows them to organize their business more and more as projects instead of a pure process organization.

Project Management Offices

Project management offices (PMOs) are organizational entities that address a large variety of governance tasks for projects. Monique Aubry from the University of Quebec in Montreal, Canada, has conducted an extensive research program on PMOs. Her studies showed the diversity in perspectives on PMO purpose, roles, and mandates (Aubry, Hobbs, & Müller, 2010). The program started by focusing on the functions of PMOs in the project context. These were, in order of decreasing frequency of use (Aubry et al., 2010, p. 304):

1. *Monitoring and controlling project performance.* This function is most often associated with PMOs. It contributes to the transparency principle

and control mechanism in governance by making the status of projects transparent to governing and managing entities.

2 *Development of project management competencies.* This is a knowledge governance task, where PMO members train and advise project managers (as well as others) in appropriate practices, new techniques, etc., in order to improve project performance.

3 *Development and implementation of standard methodologies.* This contributes to standardization in governance of projects as described above. It ensures a consistent usage of methodologies from an agreed upon pool of methodologies in an organization.

4 *Multi-project management.* This is a less often used function and refers to the coordination of projects, often by doing resource leveling and prioritization within a portfolio of projects.

5 *Strategic management.* Occasionally, PMOs are included in the strategic work, like development of the business, the staff and its skills, and the markets to target.

6 *Organizational learning.* Some PMOs are involved in organization-wide learning. This is predominantly related to lessons learned from projects and the dissemination of the learning throughout the organization. However, it can also include courses for all employees on the nature of project-based working, as is shown in Chapter 15 with the pharmaceutical company.

7 *Execute specialized tasks* for project managers, e.g., preparation of schedules. These are specialized PMOs who are called in for their particular service. In these cases the PMO is not a governance, but a service provider organization.

8 *Management of customer interfaces.* This is another management services function, where the PMO coordinates the interface between a buyer and a seller organization in a project.

9 *Recruit, select, evaluate, and determine salaries* for project managers. This is a further consulting role, where PMOs are called in for their subject matter expertise and not for their governance capabilities.

The list shows that the top three functions for PMOs relate to their governance role in organizations, and the less often used functions are services that are related to and draw on the specialized project knowledge of PMO members. These functions are not static, however. PMOs tend to be dynamic, mandate-driven entities, with about half of them being closed down after they have accomplished their mandate. The other half dynamically adapt to changing mandates over time. These changes in mandates are caused by a number of triggers, such as change in the organization's chief executive officer or the need for improvement in particular areas (e.g., portfolio management). Overall, the study on the forces that drive changes in PMOs showed that there are no patterns in triggers for changes, but rather a myriad of different causes, both internal and external to the organization. A further finding of this study was that PMO mandates often relate to solving issues in the following categories: portfolio management and methods, collaboration and accountability, project management maturity and performance, and work climate. PMOs typically address these issues successfully, so that some of the PMOs are closed down because of "mission accomplished," while others get a new mandate to solve the next issue (Aubry, Hobbs, Müller, & Blomquist, 2011).

The categories of issues listed above are indicators that the PMO is a tool for top management to implement governance structures at the level of groups of projects. The establishment of PMOs and the set up of their mandate is further described in Chapter 7 under strategic governance practices. The top three functions above are also further described in Chapter 6 as part of the tactical governance practices. Functions four to six are more management-related functions in support of the strategy, and functions seven to nine are specialized services provided by PMO members. Hence, the premier task of the PMO is tactical-level governance of projects.

Recent years have shown that larger organizations establish specialized PMOs. Popular specializations are by project types or geographies. Here, PMOs are established for selected functional organizations and their particular projects, such as for IT or Accounting, or for each business unit in a company. Some organizations establish PMOs to cover geographical areas, such as Europe or North America, to be closer to the projects and possibly to their customers. This has led to an increase in the number of PMOs, and with it the emergence of PMO hierarchies and network structures. These structures require yet another governance, that of multiple PMOs and the communities of project managers therein (Aubry, Müller, & Glückler, 2012).

These networks and hierarchies can range from two or three to several hundred PMOs. One of the Telecom organizations in these studies had more than 250 PMOs organized in a hierarchy, with a global PMO at the top, where methodologies, processes, etc. are developed. A worldwide PMO reports to the global PMO and has the mandate to deploy its developments. Regional PMOs report to the worldwide PMO and have country-level PMOs reporting to them. The governance of this hierarchy follows carefully developed mandates, which specify the task and goals at each hierarchical level, along with policies and processes that identify accountabilities and responsibilities for daily work with project managers, but also escalation processes and accountabilities in case of problems. The horizontal and vertical communication is done through a communication platform that allows for dissemination of information, methodologies, processes, policies, etc., but also for training, blogs, and ad-hoc chats of PMO members within their clearly defined scope of interaction. More network-oriented structures tend to be governed by a leading PMO, whose power is granted as a formal position or given by its expertise (Aubry et al., 2012).

The governance of these networks or hierarchies demands not only differentiation of tasks, as described above in terms of specific mandates, but also clear accountabilities and responsibilities of PMOs as network entities or hierarchical nodes. This is typically implemented through clear roles. Three roles in particular were identified in these studies:

- *Controlling*: these PMOs are typically in a higher hierarchical position than other PMOs. They are accountable for aggregate project results in line with the organization's strategy and the PMO objectives.
- *Serving*: these PMOs provide services for other PMOs and their clients, such as project management, recovery management, or planning services.
- *Partnering*: these PMOs take on tasks that cannot be accomplished through controlling nor through serving approaches. This includes knowledge management and dissemination, which requires collaborative working styles, or the maintenance of wider organizational networks for the identification of new business opportunities, development of staff, or solving of specific issues.

Most of the organizations show a mix of these roles in their PMO network. While a few are balanced across the roles, the vast majority shows a clear dominating role per PMO. This is most often the controlling role, often followed equally by serving and partnering roles (Aubry et al., 2012).

This supports the prior notion of PMOs as one of the primary governance institutions for projects. However, this does not mean that PMO members are the primary contact persons for project managers when they ask for help. A social network analysis showed that project managers tend to contact their peers, especially those they worked with before, when they are in need of knowledge on a project management subject. About 90% of this type of communication is in clusters of project managers, with very few exchanges across clusters (Müller, Glückler, Aubry, & Shao, 2013). Aubry et al. (2012) concluded their studies on the governance of PMO networks with a so-called Bagel Metaphor, where they showed that centrally located, top-level PMOs in a controlling role are circumvented in day-to-day communication by other PMOs. These other PMOs adopt more serving and partnering roles in their interaction and knowledge-sharing practices. Like in a bagel, there is an empty spot in the center of the PMO network. Hence, from a theory perspective, the governance of governance institutions underlies the same agency, steward, and transaction costs issues as described in Chapter 3.

The role of PMOs as governance institutions is not limited to projects but can extend to Program Management Offices and Portfolio Management Offices, with essentially the same mandate of ensuring the application of the most appropriate practices, as well as setting up governance structures within the scope of their sphere of action, such as programs or portfolios, respectively.

Institutions for Project Governance

Institutions for project governance are those organizational roles or entities that are accountable or responsible for the results of a single project—such as the project owner, who is concerned with the achievement of the particular business case for the project he or she owns, or a steering group, which is concerned with the delivery of a particular project within the scope of a contract between organizations. In doing this, these institutions bridge the objectives of their employing organization with those of the project.

Project Owner and Sponsor

The project owner is the organizational unit or individual who is accountable for the project on behalf of the parent organization. The owner is also ultimately responsible for the project's results, which includes the correct set up of the project's management and governance structure and its follow-up. The project owner represents the highest level of project management in a project, and is directly accountable for the project. The title underlines the relationship to the project, a sense of ownership, and, consequently, a sense of responsibility for it.

Project sponsors are those organizational entities or individuals who provide the financial or other resources to execute the project. In many industry projects, the owner and the sponsor are identical, like in a marketing department, where the marketing manager owns the development project for a new product and also holds the budget to run the project. However, this is not always the case. For example, aid projects are typically owned by the government of a country, while the funding comes from the World Bank. Here we have a clear split between owner and sponsor, which implies a simultaneous governance from both institutions. Here, the sponsoring institution takes more of a 'governance of projects' perspective in order to manage its portfolio of investment projects, whereas the country organization is more concerned with the day-to-day governance of the project. We now focus on the role of the project owner.

The project owner liaises between the project's parent organization and the project and thus relates to both organizations. Several studies have emphasized this duality of roles. Andersen (2012) suggests that the owner in its relation to the project organization is responsible for the accuracy of the project charter, approval of project plans, control of progress and results, and fostering a sense of team spirit in the project. The owner's relation with the parent organization includes responsibilities for the inclusion of the right people in the project, meeting the project's obligations, ensuring the project's priority in complying with the needs of the organization in the event of a resource shortfall or adverse internal politics, and ensuring timely decision making in the parent organization. Crawford et al. (2008) found a similar dual role of owners and called the roles project support and project governance. When owners take the perspective of the project toward its parent organization and help the project to get resources, decisions, and sign-offs by the parent or client organization, then the owner provides project support. When owners take the perspective of the parent organization toward the project and define goals, means, and ends of the project, then they provide project governance.

Helm and Remington (2005) studied the most desirable attributes of project owners. They found that most of the respondents to their questionnaire preferred attributes that relate to professional acumen and seniority. This includes appropriate seniority and power, political knowledge and savviness, ability to connect projects and strategy, as well as being courageous, motivational, partnering individuals, with good communication skills. The study also highlights a mistaken overemphasis in structure at the expense of too little focus on the behavioral attributes of good sponsorship. Andersen (2012) builds on these findings in his empirical study and identifies the need for owners to be active in socialization activities in the project, which should be directed by the project management work guidelines. He also emphasizes the need for close relationships between project owners and project managers for project success. The latter point was empirically proven by Turner and Müller (2004), who showed that projects with a high involvement of the project owner are more successful than those with a low involvement of the sponsor.

Turner and Müller (2004) studied 200 projects worldwide to investigate the relationship between project owner and manager. They identified two characteristic dimensions of this relationship. These dimensions relate to the level of project performance. In the most successful projects, the relationship between the two roles is characterized by high levels of collaboration and medium levels of structure. Here, collaboration is the level of shared understanding of the project objectives as well as the relational norms between the parties. The latter refers to the willingness of the parties to work together for the benefit of the project, which means that the achievement of project objectives is prioritized over the achievement of the respective roles' own organization. Structure is the extent of strictly following the methodology and the clarity of the roles of project owner and manager. The highest performing projects were of medium levels of structure, which is indicative of a balance in process compliance and flexibility in roles, where the project manager is authorized to run the project on a day-to-day basis and the owner interferes only when needed. Decreasing levels of project success were correlated with a decrease in measures at both dimensions. Figure 5.1 shows the relationship between structure, collaboration, and project success.

This has implications for the governance paradigms and resembles the practices, theories, and consequences described throughout this book. For example, Figure 5.1 indicates that too much or too little process orientation (e.g., by blindly following the methodology or having no methodology at all) may be detrimental to project performance. A certain level of structure is needed, just enough to reduce the project risks to a level that the owner is comfortable with (which reflects both transaction cost and agency theories) and to allow the project team and manager to be flexible enough in their roles to deal with unforeseen circumstances in the project. The collaboration

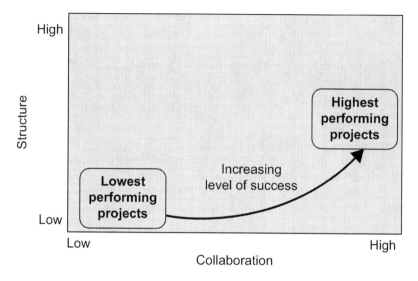

Figure 5.1 The Structure–Collaboration Model, after Turner & Müller (2004)

dimension relates to agency theory in a similar way. If the parties agree on the objectives and prioritize the accomplishment of the project over potential short-term gains and personal utility, then the agency problems and their associated costs are minimized. From a governance paradigm perspective, it can be assumed that the best performing projects will not be found at the extreme of behavior or outcome control, but at a reasonable equilibrium of both, as well as in more stakeholder-oriented governance paradigms, which de-emphasize control as a governance mechanism (as in agency theory) and emphasize trust instead.

Project Steering Groups

A steering group (or steering committee or project board) is the extension of the project owner role to a group. The advantage of this approach is the potential for more variety in input for better decision making, and also a balance of the workload across more, and potentially more knowledgeable, individuals in their specific areas. The Office of Government Commerce (OGC) in the UK proposes the Prince2 governance framework, which recommends that the Steering Group (or in their terms Project Board) is accountable to program or corporate management for the success (or failure) of the project (OGC, 2009, p. 21). Prince2 states that the owner is responsible for the business case and for chairing the steering group. The suggested composition of a steering group should include the owner, a project executive (typically a senior sponsoring manager), a senior user, and a senior supplier as representatives for their respective stakeholder groups, as well as others as required. The project manager reports to the steering group, but has no role in decision making. However, this is only a recommendation. In practice, organizations use a wide variety of different models. In the case of the pharmaceutical company described in Chapter 15, all members of the steering group are line mangers (department managers, directors, assistant vice presidents), and this composition seems to work for the company. That begs the question of when such a steering group is appropriate. Andersen (2008) highlights two circumstances in which steering groups staffed by line managers may be appropriate:

- When there is little or no familiarity with project work within the organization
- When the project involves several organizations

If the organization lacks experience in project work, it is particularly important to give the project and project manager the necessary support and respect. Setting up a steering group helps achieve these goals, and is better than delegating tasks to individuals. Since the steering group comprises the organization's senior line managers, it will be seen as an important entity, and its opinions will be taken seriously elsewhere in the organization.

If a project involves several organizations or enterprises, a steering group is essential; for example, when several companies collaborate on hardware and software development in a project. Issues connected with the project will obviously need to be dealt with by several executive managers, as many as there are companies in the alliance. Some decision making has to be done collectively, and a steering committee will be able to meet those demands.

This leads to the question of the accountabilities and responsibilities of the steering group. Formal standards like Prince2 (OGC, 2009) summarize them as:

- Be accountable for the project
- Provide unified direction
- Delegate effectively
- Facilitate cross-functional integration
- Commit resources
- Ensure effective decision making
- Support the project manager
- Ensure effective communication

Other organizations have compressed these tasks into a set of strategic management functions to be taken care of in every single project (Berntsen, 2004):

- Appoint and dismiss the project manager
- Define and follow up on project goals

62 Ralf Müller et al.

- Decide on management and implementation strategy
- Secure the necessary resources (competence, money, etc.)
- Perform strategic control actions and revisions

The above examples are exemplary for the varying level of formality in the accountabilities and responsibilities of steering groups. Hence, the scope of steering group work is contingent on the practices in an organization.

Research has outlined some issues with the steering group approach to governance. These center around low levels of effectiveness due to difficulties in conclusion finding, resulting in slow decision making and exaggerated investigation into peripheral issues. Moreover, they are sometimes seen as being too controlling and bureaucratic, as well as too far from where the real work is done. These challenges seem to be common in all sectors, not least in the public sector, where the stakeholders are many and highly diverse (Elonen & Artto, 2003).

Other Project Governance Groups

Depending on project type, size, industry, etc., there may be many more organizations involved in the governance of projects. Examples include quality committees who, as their title implies, are set up for quality assurance purposes. Other examples include advisory groups, which are established for their specific knowledge in a particular area. Common to these organizations is that they normally report to the project manager or steering group to improve decision making in project governance.

Linking Governance Institutions and Governance Principles

The institutions described in this chapter provide for a number of contributions to the four corporate governance principles. In other words, there are clear contributions from project(s)-level governance to corporate governance, which mark the link between these levels of governance. The list below is meant to be exemplary and in no way exhaustive, as the large variety of roles and mandates of the institutions for project(s)-level governance would open a very long discussion.

Transparency

All the institutions listed above contribute to better transparency of the projects, as well as the programs and portfolios of projects. At the individual project level, PMOs are often involved in auditing troubled projects and consulting with project managers in the ways to manage projects, which provides for transparency on the part of the practices applied in projects. Moreover, PMOs also collect performance data from projects and compile them into program- or portfolio-level reports, which provides for transparency of business results and level of goal accomplishment. This complements the work of steering groups, owners, and sponsors, who, through review meetings and periodic reporting, foster transparency from the business perspective and transparency of the overall risk of the project. Together, these institutions have the potential to provide a comprehensive overview of the status of individual projects and groups of projects, such as programs or portfolios. Research has shown that organizations with a high level of transparency in their project work achieve better portfolio-level results. Examples include organizations that make portfolio-level results accessible to their employees, as well as those that have transparent processes for project prioritization and resource assignment to projects (Müller, Martinsuo, & Blomquist, 2008). Writers like Nordberg (2011) or Larcker and Tayan (2011) describe easy access to corporate information as a "good practice" in corporate governance. This transparency at the level of governance of projects translates into better transparency for the board of directors. The latter plays a key role in enabling transparency by setting up portfolio and program management as governance structures of the project-based part of the business and establishing related reporting and information-sharing policies. It is worth noting that transparency can hardly be enforced through pressure and increased control. As described later in the chapters on the consequences of governance and governmentality, environments with too rigid control and reporting structures are characteristic of hidden (bad) information and incorrect reporting. Research in the private sector shows that rather than through excessive control, transparency should be instilled through an environment of mutual trust, where clear accountabilities and responsibilities contribute to transparency, and the fairness principle provides for ethical practices in a no-blame culture (Müller, Turner, Andersen, Shao, & Kvalnes, 2014). This is set up by the governors. The implications for the public sector are described in Chapter 9.

Accountability and Responsibility

Accountability and responsibility go hand in hand when establishing the above-mentioned governance institutions. Each institution becomes at least accountable to the role it reports to in the wider organization. Thus, practice-oriented PMOs are often accountable to the head of project management or their particular business unit, while business-oriented PMOs often report to the head of a business unit or the board of directors. The reports and review meetings mentioned in the transparency section above hereby serve as an indicator of the level of responsibility they have in doing their work, as well as the results of their engagements. However, responsibility also lies with those roles that PMOs report to. As described in the chapters on governance consequences, a PMO is not a panacea. When mid-career-level PMO managers are sent to consult on or audit projects with senior-level project managers, they may run into trouble. In fact, studies showed that improper

64   *Ralf Müller et al.*

or unrealistic advice from PMOs can cause serious ethical issues for projects and their managers (Müller et al., 2014). It is one of the responsibilities of managers of PMO managers to ensure an appropriate fit between consultant and consultee in PMO engagements.

In a similar vein, project owners, sponsors, steering groups, and program managers are accountable to their parent organization for the business results of the project they govern. This is often along the lines of the business case that underlies a project or program and its contribution to strategic objectives. Their responsibilities are in the proper objective definition of the project, set-up and follow-up of their projects, provision of required resources and acceptance of plans, deliverables, and project closure. All this must be accomplished within the confines of professionally and socially accepted means, such as state-of-the-art methodologies and techniques, as well practices in line with the laws, morals, and sustainability objectives of the society.

Portfolio managers are typically accountable to the board of directors or head of larger business units for selecting the 'right' projects for the organization. Thus, they are the point of accountability for effectiveness in doing projects (i.e., doing the right projects), whereas program and project managers are the point of accountability for efficiency in project and program delivery (i.e., doing projects right) (Blomquist & Müller, 2006). Their responsibilities include the professional (and transparent) set-up of portfolios, project selection criteria and processes, as well as objective achievement in line with professional, ethical, organizational, and societal standards.

The board of directors is accountable to the owners, shareholders, and stakeholders of the company for the organization's strategy and results. Responsibilities are wide-ranging and include, from a project perspective: the setting up the organization's strategy and the use of projects as a business principle to achieve this strategy, setting up the management and governance infrastructure (project managers, PMOs etc.), and the governance of its implementation.

Fairness

Contributions to the fairness principle in governance come from many different perspectives. These include avoiding inappropriate practices in terms of selecting, contracting, and ethically managing customers, suppliers, and employees. Other examples include the use of cultural sensitivity in assigning work to people, so that it does not infringe upon their religious, cultural, or personal value systems. There are numerous aspects that can be taken into account when it comes to fairness. However, morality and business ethics pervade all governance institutions. PMOs, which are often the governance institutions most intimately involved with a project, will have information about the business practices within the project and may address them when violation of moral principles, laws, or similar occurs. Project owners, sponsors, and steering groups will have insights into the selection and contracting practices for customers, consultants, and suppliers and can intervene when required. This is also the case at the program and portfolio level, where resource and business partner selection, contracting, and development take place. Finally, the board has the overall accountability for the practices in terms of fairness and the responsibility to establish a business that is ethically and professionally legitimate, as well as legally and societally acceptable.

The four sections above have provided some examples of the contribution of project-related governance institutions to corporate governance principles. To that end, these institutions link corporate governance with the governance of projects at the middle management level and project governance at the operational level.

This chapter has given an overview of the most popular governance institutions in organizational project governance. The extent to which these are used in the industry and the results related to their engagement are further described in Chapter 8.

References

Andersen, E. S. (2008). *Rethinking Project Management*. Harlow, UK: Pearson Education Ltd.

Andersen, E. S. (2012). Illuminating the Role of the Project Owner. *International Journal of Managing Projects in Business, 5*(1), 67–85. doi:10.1108/17538371211192900

Aubry, M., Hobbs, B., & Müller, R. (2010). Images of PMOs: Results from a Multi-Phase Research Program. In B. Sandrino-Arndt, R. L. Thomas, & L. Becker (Eds.), *Handbuch Project Management Office* (1st ed., pp. 301–321). Düsseldorf, Germany: Symposion Publishing.

Aubry, M., Hobbs, B., Müller, R., & Blomquist, T. (2011). *Identifying the Forces Driving Frequent Change in PMOs*. Newtown Square, PA: Project Management Institute.

Aubry, M., Müller, R., & Glückler, J. (2012). *Governance and Communities of PMOs*. Newton Square, PA: Project Management Institute.

Blomquist, T., & Müller, R. (2006). *Middle Managers in Program and Portfolio Management: Practice, Roles and Responsibilities*. Newton Square, PA: Project Management Institute.

Crawford, L., Cooke-Davies, T., Hobbs, B., Labuschagne, L., Remington, K., & Chen, P. (2008). Governance and Support in the Sponsoring of Projects and Programs. *Project Management Journal, 39*(Supplement), S43–S55.

Elonen, S., & Artto, K. (2003). Problems in Managing Internal Development Projects in Multi-Project Environments. *International Journal of Project Management, 21*(6), 395–402.

Helm, J., & Remington, K. (2005). Effective Project Sponsorship an Evaluation of the Role of the Executive Sponsor in Complex Infrastructure Projects by Senior Project Managers. *Project Management Journal, 36*(3), 51–61.

Larcker, D., & Tayan, B. (2011). *Corporate Governance Matters*. Upper Saddle River, NJ: Pearson Education Inc.

66 *Ralf Müller et al.*

Müller, R. (2009). *Project Governance*. Surrey: Gower Publishing.

Müller, R. (2011). Project Governance. In P. Morris, J. K. Pinto, & J. Söderlund (Eds.), *Oxford Handbook of Project Management* (pp. 297–320). Oxford, UK: Oxford University Press.

Müller, R., Glückler, J., Aubry, M., & Shao, J. (2013). Project Management Knowledge Flows in Networks of Project Managers and Project Management Offices: A Case Study in the Pharmaceutical Industry. *Project Management Journal, 44*(2), 4–19.

Müller, R., Martinsuo, M., & Blomquist, T. (2008). Project Portfolio Control and Portfolio Management in Different Contexts. *Project Management Journal, 39*(3), 28–42.

Müller, R., Shao, J., & Pemsel, S. (2016). *Organizational Enablers for Project Governance*. Newton Square, PA: Project Management Institute.

Müller, R., Turner, J. R., Andersen, E. S., Shao, J., & Kvalnes, Ø. (2014). Ethics, Trust and Governance in Temporary Organizations. *Project Management Journal, 45*(4), 39–54.

Nordberg, D. (2011). *Corporate Governance*. London, UK: SAGE Publication.

OGC. (2009). *Directing Successful Projects with Prince2*. London, UK: TSO.

Turner, J. R. (2009). *The Handbook of Project-Based Management* (3rd ed.). London, UK: McGraw-Hill.

Turner, J. R., & Keegan, A. (2001). Mechanisms of Governance in the Project-Based Organization: Roles of the Broker and Steward. *European Management Journal, 19*(3), 254–267. doi:10.1016/S0263-2373(01)00022-6

Turner, J. R., & Müller, R. (2004). Communication and Co-Operation on Projects Between the Project Owner as Principal and the Project Manager as Agent. *European Management Journal, 22*(3), 327–336.

Part II

Organizational Enablers for Organizational Project Governance and Governmentality

This part presents the organizational characteristics that give rise to organizational project governance and governmentality.

The part starts in Chapter 6 with the identification of operational-level prerequisites for the establishment of project-related governance and governmentality. This addresses the tactical level of project governance and governance of projects.

This is extended into the strategic enablers in Chapter 7. These are the organization-wide enablers that link across governance levels and with organizational success.

This part finishes by theorizing on the role of enablers for organizational project governance and governmentality. That includes their role, their development over time, as well as their contribution to the four governance principles.

6 Tactical Organizational Enablers

Ralf Müller

In this chapter, we address the operational-level characteristics that allow organizations to establish governance and governmentality in the realm of projects. We develop the concept of organizational enabler and report on the results of applying this concept to existing literature and to empirical studies. This helps to identify the distinct enablers at the levels of project governance, governance of projects, and governmentality. We thus develop a tactical perspective on how to establish governance for projects. The chapter finishes by theorizing on the role and interaction of the identified organizational enablers for governance of projects. This tactical perspective is complemented with a more strategic perspective in Chapter 7.

The Concept of Organizational Enablers

The factors or circumstances that allow organizational phenomena, such as governance, to emerge are typically referred to as organizational enablers. These are the antecedents of a phenomenon, without which the phenomenon would not exist, or at least not in the same way. The term organizational enabler is frequently used, but rarely defined or even investigated. The dictionary definition of 'enabler' is "a person or thing that makes something possible" (OxfordDictionaries, 2014). The Project Management Institute (PMI©) defines organizational enablers as "structural, cultural, technological, and human practices" that can be leveraged to support and sustain the implementation of strategic goals (PMI, 2013, p. 36). The healthcare literature goes further and defines an enabler as "one who gives power, strength, or competency sufficient for the purpose; one who renders efficient or capable" (Kjorlie Lee & Ventres, 1981, p. 506). These definitions range from describing enablers as facilitators to viewing them as amplifiers of certain effects.

A popular way of understanding organizational enablers, which combines the different definitions above, is as a combination of factors and mechanisms:

- *Factors*: the forces that give direction, such as accumulated knowledge in organizations to decide on a course of action or shape interest, such as in energy-saving programs, etc. (Dosi, 1982). These factors either

70 *Ralf Müller*

support or hinder a situation or action and thereby set the stage for enablers.

- *Mechanisms:* the means by which effects triggered by factors are produced, such as incentives, constraints, or feedbacks to steer certain actions in organizations (Dosi, 1982; Michailova & Foss, 2009).

In their study on sense-giving in organizations, Maitlis and Lawrence (2007) suggest that enablers are made up of two parts that coexist:

- *Process facilitators:* the idiosyncratic combination of policies, structures, practices, and routines that allow for results to emerge. This includes, for example, those particular combinations that support achievement of organizational Critical Success Factors (CSF) and the accomplishment of organizational objectives.
- *Discursive abilities:* an organizational actor's abilities to construct and articulate persuasive accounts of the world. This is the individual's cognitive combination of expertise, legitimacy, and opportunity, which allows for sense-making in organizations. It is conveyed and honed through social interaction and ideologies, as well as the actors' abilities to shape each other's interpretation of reality.

These elements of organizational enablers are highly context dependent because different contexts will give rise to different powers and allowances for the features underpinning enablers (Mesquita & Brush, 2008). The relationships between the elements underpinning enablers in organizations are not simple, however. An enabler in one context might not be an enabler in another context (Seddon, Calvert, & Yang, 2011), or at other points in time (Gulati, Sytch, & Tatarynowicz, 2012).

Through our studies we identified that organizational enablers are the interplay and coexistence of both structural and mental elements. Together they carry forward a phenomenon within a social structure (Müller, Pemsel, & Shao, 2014, 2015). Thus:

- Organizational structure provides for process facilitation through coexistence of organizational factors and mechanisms, whereby the factors support or hinder actions or situations, while being executed or amplified through the mechanisms.
- Social structure in an organization provides the basis for discourse, where discursive abilities of the organizational actors are supported or hindered through factors which, in turn, are executed or amplified through mechanisms.

Hence, organizational enablers consist of four elements, which are process facilitators and discursive abilities, with each element having its own factors and mechanisms.

- *Process facilitator factors* involve tangible characteristics, conditions, and variables directly impacting the effectiveness, efficiency, and viability of governance. Examples include the degree of customer involvement or formalization of procedures in project governance (Ahadi, 2004).
- *Process facilitator mechanisms* are the means to increase the likelihood of certain outcomes, such as through structures or rules. Examples include informal organizational routines, meetings, minutes of meetings, etc. (Prencipe & Tell, 2001).
- *Discursive ability factors* are the communicative and interactional characteristics that impact the mentality and attitudes of people, such as top management support or organizational culture (Ahadi, 2004).
- *Discursive ability mechanisms* are structures supportive of organizational sense-making and discourse, such as rules and regulations, synchronized communication structures, dedicated network structures, etc.

This model of organizational enablers is used in the following section.

Organizational Enablers for Governance and Governmentality in Projects

The following section on operational-level enablers is structured by project governance, governance of projects, and governmentality. Details of the conceptual and empirical studies underlying these findings can be found in Müller, Pemsel, and Shao (2014, 2015).

Organizational Enablers for Project Governance

Project governance is enabled through the next higher level of governance, which is the governance of projects. This level provides the required governance infrastructure, which ensures that the governance structures and frameworks suit the particular requirements of a project and its organizational context. This infrastructure comes to bear through structures that provide authority for its execution thus:

> *Organizational enablers for project governance are the authority to procure, implement, and execute governance frameworks, policies, and project-specific structures, as well as the presence of specialized project governance roles to oversee the execution of these frameworks.*

Governance frameworks are hereby understood as "an organized structure established as authoritative within the institution, comprising processes and rules established to ensure projects meet their purpose" (Klakegg, Williams, & Magnussen, 2009, p. 1). Hence frameworks, such as project management methodologies and their required infrastructure in the form of, for example, meetings and project-specific organizational structures, are

72 Ralf Müller

an organization's basic structures for executing projects which, in conjunction with organizational project governance policies (i.e., the principles that guide decision making for the achievement of rational outcomes), govern the management of individual projects. Governance is executed through institutions and roles for project governance, such as those of project sponsors, steering groups, or project management offices (PMOs).

The presence of the governance infrastructure in the form of governance frameworks, policies, institutions, roles, and the associated authority to implement them constitute the process facilitator factors of the organizational enabler. Mechanisms related to this factor include built-in flexibility in governance structures and frameworks, as well as idiosyncratic organizational structures that can be tailored for projects in order to meet business requirements (e.g., by project size or importance of clients).

Discursive abilities factors for project governance provide for sensemaking by individuals in the organization and include aligned objectives of the project, the project manager, and sponsor, as well as their synchronization with the organization's strategy. Mechanisms that support these factors are communication structures that allow for these alignments, plus the execution of further governance functions, such as goal setting, provision of resources, and control of progress.

This combination of structural and social factors and mechanisms provide for project governance to be established in an organization.

The contributions of these enablers to the four corporate governance principles are manifold. Most of the enablers contribute to several principles simultaneously. For example, governance frameworks, clear roles and responsibilities, and the presence of governance institutions, such as PMOs, contribute to transparency by clarifying processes, communicating goals and expectations, and providing sufficient visibility of the status of the project. These enablers also contribute to the responsibility principle by assigning roles to people working in projects, managing and governing projects, or having other stakeholder roles. Accountabilities are established through them by defining the goals and providing the means to accomplish those goals. Similarly, they also contribute to organizational policies and aligned objectives, and to the principles of fairness and ethical conduct. In summary, the project-level contribution to governance principles lies in enabling structure and transparency in the organization and execution of work.

Organizational Enablers for Governance of Projects

Governance of projects, such as in programs or portfolios of projects, is enabled through flexibility in the wider governance and structures of the organization. This is rooted in the unique requirements stemming from the nature of the particular programs or portfolios and the idiosyncrasies of their outputs and diversity of stakeholders, which requires a level of adaptation between the wider organization and the programs and portfolios. Of particular importance is the possibility to set up organizational structures that are specific for a program or a portfolio in order to allow for effectiveness in the selection of the right projects and efficiencies in managing the deliverables of the individual projects. At the same time, a common set of governance mechanisms must be maintained within these programs and portfolios, such as: transparency in project selection and results; similarities in reporting principles, to preserve accountability for the deliverables and responsibilities for the associated tasks; and adherence to the ethical standards of the organization. Hence,

> Organizational enablers for governance of projects are flexibility in corporate structures and ways of interactions, which allow for effectiveness in project selection and efficiency in project execution.

The process facilitator factors include flexibility in organization structures in order to adjust them to the varying needs of different programs and portfolios. They also include the selection and provision of governance frameworks to adjust governance to the various projects in the organization, while keeping up with the shared values and synchronized routines. Support provided by governance institutions and middle management in coordinating projects and solving their issues is another factor that facilitates the governance process. Mechanisms supporting these factors are the idiosyncratic structures derived from the needs of the programs and portfolios and application of the governance frameworks. Examples include governance institutions with flexible and changeable mandates, such as those for PMOs or steering committees, driven by the acute issues of a program or portfolio.

Discursive ability factors include cognitive aspects, such as the awareness of the organization-wide implications of doing business by projects, the roles and institutions that execute governance, and the related governance policies and goals. Mechanisms that support these factors are communication events and structures for sharing and synchronizing information across projects through meetings and other events, but are also organizational, such as the dynamic creation of new roles for the benefit of projects, PMOs, or related networks.

The contribution of the enablers for governance of projects to the corporate governance principles are mainly in the balancing of flexibility and standardization of work routines to a level that allows for appropriate governance. Contributions to transparency are in the selection and communication of appropriate governance frameworks, goals, and their levels of accomplishment. Contributions to accountability and responsibility can be found in the establishment of governance institutions (such as PMOs) and the adjustment of their mandates to the issues at hand, as well as the adjustment of organizational structures (and with it the roles and responsibilities of people) to the organization's types of portfolios of projects. Last but not least, policies and communication about the implications of doing business

74   *Ralf Müller*

by projects and the work in temporary organizations like projects, as well as the associated implications for performance measures and expectations, contribute to the principle of fairness in corporate governance.

Organizational Enablers for Governmentality

Organizational enablers for governmentality address the way the governance system (the combination of policies, institutions, and individuals) presents itself to the governed. It sets the tone for the interaction and provides the freedom for people to act. This ranges from very narrow, as in authoritative systems that enforce obeying the rules and strictly following the processes, to neoliberal approaches, which set the social context for people to make their own decisions and self-control their behavior. The literature shows three dimensions that an enabler for governmentality should address in the context of projects, in order to develop people toward greater levels of freedom (Lindkvist, 2004):

- *People's mindfulness of the wider organization.* This is important for developing the decision-making capabilities and the decision quality of individuals. It is fostered through individuals' awareness of organizational capabilities and their deliberate attempts to improve organizational results (as opposed to results of a single project), by building internal and external corporations or adapting existing structures to new upcoming opportunities.
- *People's self-responsibility.* This includes people's willingness to accept responsibility for the benefit of the organization, including responsibility for results, associated efforts, or entire projects.
- *People's self-organization within limits.* This includes people's acceptance of empowerment for and willingness to self-organize their work within and across projects.

Empirical studies show that these three mental predispositions work best in the context of liberal to neoliberal governmentality approaches that foster less clearly defined organizational structures, autonomous projects, decentralized work practices, and organizations that dynamically (re-)organize or change teams, roles, and structures. They also show that in companies with a strong project culture, 'thinking in projects' enables more liberal approaches to governmentality. Hence,

> *Organizational enablers for governmentality are the extent 'thinking in projects' pervades the organization and the extent to which individuals are mindful of the organization, self-responsible, and self-organizing to a degree that matches the goals of the corporation.*

Process facilitator factors for governmentality include organizational design and provision of resources and autonomy, which are granted by next higher-level management. Related mechanisms include flat organization structures,

Tactical Organizational Enablers 75

people's willingness for executing formal and informal roles simultaneously, and a general trust between the people and their governance structure.

Discursive ability factors include a central ideology of the organization, which provides a vehicle for communicating the organization's values, supported by a communication culture and a general awareness of people about the temporality of their work and the associated performance measures. Mechanisms supporting these factors include networking structures among people, synchronization of reporting and communication structures, and the support of knowledge exchange events.

Here again, the contributions to corporate governance principles are manifold. Contributions to transparency are accomplished through communicated organizational ideologies and structures. Contributions to accountability and responsibility lie in granting autonomy to projects and their managers, in terms of their roles, responsibilities, and scope of decision-making authority, as well as accountabilities for delivery. Contributions to the governance principle of fairness lie in allowing project managers and team members to develop to their own desired level of self-responsibility and self-organization, and to decide on the scope of executing both formal and informal roles simultaneously.

Table 6.1 summarizes the organizational enablers by their level and underlying process facilitators and discursive abilities, each with their respective factors and mechanisms. The table also shows some of the key references for the elements of the enablers.

Table 6.1 Organizational Enablers in the Project-Related Literature

	Organizational enablers for project governance *include the authority to procure, implement, and execute governance frameworks, policies, and project-specific structures, as well as the presence of specialized project governance roles to oversee the execution of these frameworks*	
	Process facilitators	*Discursive abilities*
Factors	Presence of • A governance infrastructure, such as governance roles in the organization (Miller & Hobbs, 2005) • Governance frameworks (Klakegg & Haavaldsen, 2011; Klakegg, Williams, & Magnussen, 2009) • Authority to procure, implement, and execute governance frameworks and policies (Turner & Keegan, 1999)	Alignment of • Objectives for project, project sponsor, and project manager (Turner & Müller, 2004) • Organizational strategy and project objectives (Morris & Jamieson, 2005)

(Continued)

Table 6.1 (Continued)

	Process facilitators	Discursive abilities
Mechanisms	Idiosyncrasy of • Governance and organizational structures (Miller & Hobbs, 2005; Renz, 2007; Turner & Keegan, 1999, 2001) • Governance frameworks (Klakegg & Haavaldsen, 2011; Klakegg et al., 2009)	Communication mechanisms, such as • Steering Committee and other governance meetings (Crawford et al., 2008) • Workshops and gathering of people for ideating and planning (Lehtonen & Martinsuo, 2008)

Organizational enablers for governance of projects

include flexibility in corporate structures and ways of interactions, which allow for effectiveness in project selection and efficiency in project execution.

	Process facilitators	Discursive abilities
Factors	Presence of • Versatile governance structures (Blomquist & Müller, 2006; Turner & Keegan, 1999) • Choice of governance frameworks to adjust to program and portfolio needs (Aubry, Sicotte, Drouin, Vidot-Delerue, & Besner, 2012a; Klakegg & Haavaldsen, 2011; Klakegg et al., 2009) • Supportive governance institutions, such as PMOs and middle management (Aubry, Hobbs, Müller, & Blomquist, 2010)	Awareness of the • Organizational implications of doing business by projects (project versus operations way of working) (Aubry et al., 2012; Müller, 2009) • The roles of governance institutions, related policies, and objectives (Monique Aubry et al., 2012; Pemsel & Müller, 2012)
Mechanisms	Idiosyncrasy of the • Organization structures and governance frameworks to allow effective and efficient governance (Foss, 2012; Klakegg & Haavaldsen, 2011; Klakegg et al., 2009; Turner & Keegan, 2001) • Mandates of governance institutions, such as PMOs and Steering Groups, to address acute issues in programs and portfolios (Müller, 2009) (Aubry, Hobbs, & Müller, 2010; Aubry, Müller, & Glückler, 2011; Blomquist & Müller, 2006)	Communication mechanisms, such as • Structures for sharing and synchronizing information across projects, such as meetings and online platforms (Aubry et al., 2012; Müller et al, 2013) • Improved interactions and communication exchanges stemming from the flexible adjustment of policies and mandates and creation of new or temporary roles of governance institutions and individuals (Aubry et al., 2012; Lehtonen & Martinsuo, 2009)

Organizational enablers for governmentality

Organizational enablers for governmentality are the extent to which 'thinking in projects' pervades the organization and the extent to which individuals are mindful of the organization, self-responsible, and self-organizing to a degree that matches the goals of the corporation.

	Process facilitators	Discursive abilities
Factors	Presence of • Autonomy of projects (Bresnen, Goussevskaia, & Swan, 2004; Lindkvist, 2004) • A governance structure (Müller et al., 2013) • Provision of financial and human resources, and top management support (Lehtonen & Martinsuo, 2008)	Awareness of • The ideology of the organization and its values, alignment of corporate and project governance (Franck & Jungwirth, 2003; R Müller, Andersen, et al., 2013) • The importance of a culture of open discussions (Lehtonen & Martinsuo, 2008) • The temporality of the undertakings and its success measures (Bresnen et al., 2004)
Mechanisms	Idiosyncrasies of • A general 'under-specification' of structures (Lindkvist, 2004) • Individuals' flexibility in adapting formal and informal roles (Crawford et al., 2008) • Trust between individuals and governance structures (Müller et al., 2013)	Communication, such as • Synchronized reporting and communication structures across the projects and organization (Bresnen et al., 2004) • Creation and maintenance of network structures for information exchange (Lindkvist, 2004) • Knowledge exchange events (Müller et al., 2013)

The Variety in the Nature of Enablers

The nature of enablers changes with the level at which governance and governmentality is exercised. A helpful perspective for this is that of governance and governmentality as a hierarchy, with project governance as the lowest level, governance of projects as the next higher organizational level, and governmentality as the organizational culture and therefore the highest level. It shows that:

a At lower levels of governance, the more structural enablers dominate, such as policies, guidelines, and methodologies;

b At higher levels, the more people-related dimensions dominate, such as ideologies, sense-making of organizations, cultures, etc.;

78   *Ralf Müller*

c   Flexibility surfaces as a key characteristic of good governance, but the nature of the flexibility changes over the hierarchy—project governance requires flexibility in methodologies and processes to address the particularities of individual projects; governance of projects requires flexibility in organization structures and people's willingness to adapt to changing tasks, objectives, and timeframes; and governmentality requires flexibility from management in adapting to the governed, such as when a shift from strict control structures to a more liberal governmentality is needed.

Case study 3 provides an example of this with the transformation of Tasly Pharmaceuticals from a process-oriented to a project-oriented organization. This transformation was triggered by a new president of the organization, who put in place a PMO to develop and execute the transformation process. This PMO was established as a virtual organization, made up of a small team to build up the communication platform and databases for project managers to share information and a group of six line managers who established project management in the organization while simultaneously serving in their roles as, for example, vice-president or department manager.

For project governance, they developed the infrastructure like a governance framework, in the form of a project management methodology and related training and certification programs. They established policies, structures, and roles, and acted as the Steering Group for all projects. For governance of projects, they developed the portfolio management process and system, adapted organizational structures, developed project categorization systems, and adjusted the project management approaches to the needs of the different portfolios, such as drug development versus internal improvement projects.

Their approach to governmentality was to move the organization from authoritative to neoliberal governmentality by building a culture of mutual trust and respect between governance institutions and project managers. This was accomplished through, among other things, aligned incentives between line and matrix managers, recognition and career systems for both project and line managers, and development of individuals who were mindful of the wider organization and its capabilities, self-responsible, and self-organizing, in order to support the joint achievement of project and organizational objectives. This, in turn, led to new levels of motivation, supported by the necessary structural components, such as processes and information access, which fostered governance principles such as transparency, accountability, and responsibility, together with social aspects like fairness in career advancement and a general culture of being proud to work in projects.

The Role of Project-Related Organizational Enablers in the Wider Organizational Context

This section addresses the ways in which the above organizational enablers jointly interact within the wider organization. We first map the enablers

Tactical Organizational Enablers 79

identified above to the three pillars of institutional theory. This shows the role of the individual enablers in the wider organizational context. Based on this we theorize about how these roles collectively work in predominantly project-based organizations. More details about the underlying research can be found in Müller et al. (2015).

We used institutional theory (Henisz, Levitt, & Scott, 2012; Scott, 2004, 2012) as a theoretical lens for the categorization of enablers and their roles in organizations. Institutional theory proposes that organizations can be understood by categorizing organizational means into regulative, normative, and cultural-cognitive elements (Scott, 2004).

The *regulative* elements are often externally imposed on the organization and include formal regulations, laws, and property rights. These elements come to bear through relational contracts, public-private partnerships, complying with, for example, environmental laws, etc.

The *normative* elements of institutional theory include informal norms, values, and standards, as well as formal and informal roles. Examples of these are standards issued by professional associations, companies' internally developed project management methodologies, the formal project manager role, etc. Normative elements also include internal peer pressure to influence certain behaviors. Examples include formal mentoring, training, and informal interactions that help individuals to judge the appropriateness of their behavior in a variety of situations (Scott, 2014).

The *cultural-cognitive* elements are the "shared conceptions that constitute the nature of social reality and create the frames through which meaning is made" (Scott, 2014, p. 67) and the shared beliefs, symbols, identities, and logic of actions (Misangyi, Weaver, & Elms, 2008; Orr & Scott, 2008; Scott, 2012). Examples include people's construction of meaning (Scott, 2014), their identification with a certain occupation, a certain professional or personal network, or the entire organization (Grabher, 2004).

Collectively, these pillars serve as mechanisms for different aspects of organizations' stability or growth. Here, the regulatory elements are often perceived as providing the returns for the managers. The normative elements are recognized as providing the basis for shared commitments and identity construction of the individuals in an organization. The cultural-cognitive elements provide the sense-making of the organization and allow an organization's claims to be perceived as valid and self-evident within its particular context (Scott, 2014).

Mapping the enablers shown in Table 6.1 against the three pillars of institutional theory shows:

- Organizational enablers for project governance include regulative elements such as externally imposed governance frameworks like those enforced by clients or governments for the execution of their projects. Normative elements include the internally set governance infrastructure, often consisting of policies, roles and responsibility definitions, in-house

80 *Ralf Müller*

methodologies, and governance institutions, such as PMOs and steering groups. Cultural-cognitive elements include the alignment of objectives between project, portfolio, and organizational strategy, as well as communication events, especially the meetings with governance institutions.

- Organizational enablers for the governance of projects include regulative elements like choice of governance frameworks for different types of projects or portfolios and the possibility to establish a governance infrastructure that allows for the execution of governance within organizations and across organizational boundaries. Normative elements include the flexibility to adapt organizational structures to the particular needs of strategic projects, programs, or entire portfolios, as well as the flexible adaptation of the mandates of governance institutions to the organization's particular needs. Cultural-cognitive elements include the awareness of the implications of doing business by projects, the nature of temporary work, and the related infrastructure for information sharing and dissemination. Further, it includes the sense-making of the roles and support provided by governance institutions for the governance of projects.
- Organizational enablers for governmentality consist of regulative elements, such as top management support (both internal and external to the organization), as well as the general level of autonomy granted to projects. Normative elements include the level of self-responsibility and self-organizing expected from and exercised by individuals in the project or organization. The cultural-cognitive elements include the level of 'thinking in projects' in the organization and the individual's mindfulness of the organization as an open system for sense-making within the organization and beyond.

Table 6.2 summarizes the institutional theory-based categorization of enablers. It shows that regulative elements mainly provide a mechanism for project governance and governance of projects, as well as the autonomy for project managers to act on behalf of the project. Normative elements provide structures and processes for governance, and provide for self-responsible action in governmentality. Cultural-cognitive elements for governance provide for sense-making of the role of projects in the wider organization, and related governmentality elements allow for sense-making of the wider organization and its functioning.

Interpreting the nature of these enablers and their particular tasks in being regulative, normative, and cultural-cognitive suggests three roles that these organizational enablers play in the wider governance of the organization. These are providing flexibility, stability, and alignment.

Flexibility refers to the adaptation to changing requirements. However, the nature of flexibility differs with the level of governance. For project governance it is the flexibility in project management methodology. In Shenhar's (2001) words, we can say that "one-size [of methodology] does not fit all

Tactical Organizational Enablers 81

Table 6.2 Organizational Enablers by Institutional Theory Categories

	Project governance	*Governance of projects*	*Governmentality*
Regulative	Steering Groups Flat and flexible organization structures PMO*	Flexible organization structures Standardization Media and infrastructure	Autonomy of project managers
Normative	Project management methodologies Clearly defined roles*	Company-wide methodologies	Self-responsibility
Cultural-cognitive	Meeting schedules Top management support	Alignment of projects and business	Project-thinking Open-system thinking

Note: * large organizations only

[projects]" (p. 394). Governance structures must allow for adjusting project governance, including the methodology, to the projects' needs. Flexibility in governance of projects refers to structural flexibility, as when organizations adjust their structures to projects and portfolios to safeguard strategic and long-term projects from short-term revenue-generating projects by executing them in organizational structures distinct from their everyday projects. Flexibility also refers to the use of company-wide methodologies that allow different governance approaches for different groups of projects by taking care of the idiosyncrasies of particular portfolios or programs of projects. Flexibility in governmentality is addressed through cognitive flexibility, such as in people's ability to address organizational micro- and macro-level issues simultaneously, for example, when prioritizing tasks or resources while taking into account project-level, portfolio-level, and organization-wide implications of the decisions. Flexibility also refers to individuals' sense-making of their own and organization-wide capabilities before accepting responsibilities for themselves and others.

Stability and choice of elements at a lower level provide for flexibility at the next higher level. Using a variety of proven (stable) building blocks at the lower level allows for flexibility in choice (of proven and stable) building blocks at a higher level. The relationship between stability and flexibility is ambidextrous, similar to the exploration and exploitation of knowledge in organizations (O'Reilly & Tushman, 2004; Raisch & Birkinshaw, 2008), where the coexistence of both elements and their interaction allows for long-term efficiency of the organization. In the context of projects, the nature of stability differs. Stability in approaches to managing projects, such as through established methodologies with proven processes,

82   Ralf Müller

tools, techniques, roles, and responsibilities, allows for flexibility in methods used, and possible adaptation to a project will occur at a lower risk than by use of unstable, ad-hoc practices. Similarly, flexibility in the governance of projects builds on the stability of the framework of corporate-wide methods and standardization. For example, in risk reduction, when a narrow choice of standardized reporting practices is used, or a limited choice of methods used, it provides for low risk in flexibly aligning or selecting a suitable reporting practice and method after a reorganization or redesign of project portfolios. Flexibility in governmentality then builds on stability in people's understanding of the wider organization. Here, cognitive flexibility, as described above, is achieved through a stable understanding or model of organization. For example, to respond appropriately to upcoming business opportunities, cognitive flexibility may be achieved by taking a systems view of the organization, the way it works, its capabilities, resources, and their availability.

Alignment allows for the synchronization of governance structures and governmentality with the organization's internal and external characteristics, such as internal organizational structures, skill sets, and overall culture with externalities like markets and clients. For project governance, this is the alignment of the project governance structure with the nature of the project, such as more outcome-focused governance structures in innovation projects and more behavior-controlled governance in maintenance projects. The former requires freedom to act and 'out of the box' thinking to achieve innovative solutions, whereas the latter requires process compliance stemming from well-understood means-ends relationships between process and outcome. Governance of projects aligns the governance of groups of projects with the organizational strategy and its markets, as well as with corporate governance. This is exemplified in aligning the reporting and selection criteria in portfolio governance with the strategy of the organization, or the alignment of portfolio, program, or other organization-wide project activities to changes in markets or corporate governance structures through changing reporting metrics or contracting policies. Governmentality provides for the alignment of people's behavior with organizational structures and cultures, such as through neoliberal approaches to governmentality in flat and flexible organization structures, compared with more authoritarian governmentality in hierarchical and bureaucratic organizations. Table 6.3 summarizes the characteristics of the model derived from the study.

The above analysis suggests that stability in underlying dimensions is an antecedent for flexibility at the next higher level of governance. This stability changes over time and is not static. It changes when the understanding of the practices at the underlying lower level evolves, such as through development of better practices for planning or reporting in project governance.

The ambidexterity of stability and flexibility allows for various interpretations, such as it being a punctuated equilibrium (Gersick, 1991), which alternates between stable states, where flexibility can be applied due to

Table 6.3 Interaction of Organizational Enablers

	Stability	*Flexibility*	*Alignment*
Project governance	Stability in processes, techniques, and roles	Methodological flexibility	Aligning the governance structure of the project with the nature of the project
Governance of projects	Stability in methods and standardization	Structural flexibility	Aligning the governance of projects with the organization's strategy and its markets
Governmentality	Stability in understanding the organization and its capabilities	Cognitive flexibility	Aligning the governmentality approach with the structures and capabilities of the organization

stability in underlying practices, and change states, when flexibility should not be applied because the underlying elements are under reconfiguration. During the stable state, governance and governmentality can be adjusted to meet new or changing organizational contents, such as through changing organization structures, markets, or strategies. A different interpretation could be made as per Farjoun (2010), where stability and flexibility continuously reinforce each other, leading to a constant adjustment of governance practices. More research on the nature of this ambidexterity is indicated.

A number of studies in the context of projects support this theory, such as those emphasizing the ambidexterity in simultaneity of different modes of action, like following a plan (rationalization mode) versus adapting to deal with a situation (adaptation mode) (Aubry & Lievre, 2010). The need for ambidexterity in terms of knowledge exploration and exploitation at the project team level was shown by Liu and Leitner (2012) and at the PMO level by Müller et al. (2013). Complementarily, Sadowski, Sadowski-Rasters, and Duysters (2008) added a time dimension when they identified differences in ambidexterity across project life cycles, with emphasis on flexibility in the early phases, which turns into stability in the later phases of projects. In broadening the perspective to projects and their related programs, Pellegrinelli, Murray-Webster, and Turner (2015) showed that programs contribute to flexibility in an organizational transition, while projects contribute to stability through the reliable delivery of products. The latter

84 *Ralf Müller*

two studies refer to ambidexterity in the governance of projects and thus are especially supportive of the above theory.

In this chapter, we have discussed the nature of organizational enablers for each of the levels of project governance, governance of projects, and governmentality. In the next section we take an organization-wide view, which integrates the three layers and provides for more strategic organizational enablers in the realm of projects.

References

Ahadi, H. R. (2004). An Examination of the Role of Organizational Enablers in Business Process Reengineering and the Impact of Information Technology. *Information Resources Management Journal*, *17*(4), 1–19.

Aubry, M., Hobbs, B., & Müller, R. (2010). Images of PMOs: Results from a Multi-Phase Research Program. In B. Sandrino-Arndt, R. L. Thomas, & L. Becker (Eds.), *Handbuch Project Management Office* (1st ed., pp. 301–321). Düsseldorf, Germany: Symposion Publishing.

Aubry, M., Hobbs, B., Müller, R., & Blomquist, T. (2010). Identifying Forces Driving PMO Changes. *Project Management Journal*, *41*(4), 30–45.

Aubry, M., & Lievre, P. (2010). Ambidexterity as a Competence of Two Polar Expeditions. *Project Management Journal*, *41*(3), 32–44. doi:10.1002/pmj

Aubry, M., Müller, R., & Glückler, J. (2011). Exploring PMOs Through Community of Practice Theory. *Project Management Journal*, *42*(5), 42–56.

Aubry, M., Sicotte, H., Drouin, N., Vidot-Delerue, H., & Besner, C. (2012). Organisational Project Management as a Function Within the Organisation. *International Journal of Managing Projects in Business*, *5*(2), 180–194. doi:10.1108/17538371211214897

Blomquist, T., & Müller, R. (2006). Practices, Roles and Responsibilities of Middle Managers in Program and Portfolio Management. *Project Management Journal*, *37*(1), 52–66.

Bresnen, M., Goussevskaia, A., & Swan, J. (2004). Embedding New Management Knowledge in Project-Based Organizations. *Organization Studies*, *25*(9), 1535–1555.

Crawford, L., Cooke-Davies, T., Hobbs, B., Labuschagne, L., Remington, K., & Chen, P. (2008). Governance and Support in the Sponsoring of Projects and Programs. *Project Management Journal*, *39*(Supplement), S43–S55.

Dosi, G. (1982). Technological Paradigms and Technological Trajectories—a Suggested Interpretation of the Determinants and Directions of Technical Change. *Research Policy*, *11*(3), 147–162.

Farjoun, M. (2010). Beyond Dualism: Stability and Change as a Duality. *Academy of Management Review*, *35*(2), 202–225. doi:10.5465/AMR.2010.48463331

Foss, N. J. (2012). Selective Intervention and Internal Hybrids : Interpreting the Rise and Fall of the Oticon Spaghetti Organization. *Organization Science*, *14*(3), 331–349.

Franck, E., & Jungwirth, C. (2003). Reconciling Rent-Seekers and Donators—The Governance Structure of Open Source. *Journal of Management & Governance*, *7*(4), 401–421.

Gersick, C. J. G. (1991). Revolutionary Change Theories: A Multilevel Exploration of the Punctuated Equilibrium Paradigm. *Academy of Management Review*, *16*(1), 10–36.

Grabher, G. (2004). Temporary Architectures of Learning: Knowledge Governance in Project Ecologies. *Organization Studies*, *25*(9), 1491–1514. doi:10.1177/0170840604047996

Gulati, R., Sytch, M., & Tatarynowicz, A. (2012). The Rise and Fall of Small Worlds: Exploring the Dynamics of Social Structure. *Organization Science*, *23*(2), 449–471.

Henisz, W. J., Levitt, R. E., & Scott, W. R. (2012). Toward a Unified Theory of Project Governance: Economic, Sociological and Psychological Supports for Relational Contracting. *Engineering Project Organization*, *2*(1–2), 37–55.

Kjorlie Lee, D., & Ventres, S. (1981). The Nurse: The Enabler. *American Journal of Nursing*, *81*(3), 506–508.

Klakegg, O. J., & Haavaldsen, T. (2011). Governance of Major Public Investment Projects: In Pursuit of Relevance and Sustainability. *International Journal of Managing Projects in Business*, *4*(1), 157–167. doi:10.1108/17538371111096953

Klakegg, O. J., Williams, T., & Magnussen, O. M. (2009). *Governance Frameworks for Public Project Development and Estimation*. Newton Square, PA: Project Management Institute.

Lehtonen, P., & Martinsuo, M. (2008). Change Program Initiation: Defining and Managing the Program–Organization Boundary. *International Journal of Project Management*, *26*(1), 21–29.

Lehtonen, P., & Martinsuo, M. (2009). Integrating the Change Program with the Parent Organization. *International Journal of Project Management*, *27*(2), 154–165.

Lindkvist, L. (2004). Governing Project-Based Firms: Promoting Market-Like Processes within Hierarchies. *Journal of Management and Governance*, *8*(3–25), 3–25.

Liu, L., & Leitner, D. (2012). Simultaneous Pursuit of Innovation and Efficiency in Complex Engineering and Impacts of Ambidexterity in. *Project Management Journal*, *43*(6), 97–110. doi:10.1002/pmj

Maitlis, S., & Lawrence, T. B. (2007). Triggers and Enablers of Sensegiving in Organizations. *Academy of Management Journal*, *50*(1), 57–84.

Mesquita, L. F., & Brush, T. H. (2008). Untangling Safeguard and Production Coordination Effects in Long Term Buyer Supplier Relationships. *Academy of Management Journal*, *51*(4), 785–807.

Michailova, S., & Foss, N. (2009). Knowledge Governance: Themes and Questions. In N. Foss & S. Michailova (Eds.), *Knowledge Governance: Processes and Perspectives* (pp. 1–24). Oxford, UK: Oxford University Press.

Miller, R., & Hobbs, B. (2005). Governance Regimes for Large Projects. *Project Management Journal*, *36*(3), 42–51.

Misangyi, V. F., Weaver, G. R., & Elms, H. (2008). Ending Corruption: The Interplay Among Institutional Logics, Resources, and Institutional Entrepreneurs. *Academy of Management Review*, *33*(3), 750–770.

Morris, P., & Jamieson, A. (2005). Moving from Corporate Strategy to Project Strategy. *Project Management Journal*, *34*(4), 5–18.

Müller, R. (2009). *Project Governance*. Aldershot, UK: Gower Publishing.

Müller, R., Andersen, E. S., Kvalnes, Ø., Shao, J., Sankaran, S., Turner, J. R., Biesenthal, C., Walker, D.H.T, & Gudergan, S. (2013). The Interrelationship of Governance, Trust, and Ethics in Temporary Organizations. *Project Management Journal*, *44*(4), 26–44. doi:10.1002/pmj

Müller, R., Glückler, J., Aubry, M., & Shao, J. (2013). Project Management Knowledge Flows in Networks of Project Managers and Project Management Offices: A Case Study in the Pharmaceutical Industry. *Project Management Journal*, *44*(2), 4–19.

86 Ralf Müller

Müller, R., Pemsel, S., & Shao, J. (2014). Organizational Enablers for Governance and Governmentality of Projects: A Literature Review. *International Journal of Project Management*, 32(8), 1309–1320. doi:10.1016/j.ijproman.2014.03.007

Müller, R., Pemsel, S., & Shao, J. (2015). Organizational Enablers for Project Governance and Governmentality in Project-Based Organizations. *International Journal of Project Management*, 33(4), 839–851. doi:10.1016/j.ijproman.2014.07.008

O'Reilly, C. A., & Tushman, M. L. (2004). The Ambidextrous Organization. *Harvard Business Review*, 82(4), 74–81.

Orr, R., & Scott, W. R. (2008). Institutional Exceptions on Global Projects: A Process Model. *Journal of International Business*, 39(4), 562–588.

OxfordDictionaries. (2014). *The Concise Oxford English Dictionary* (12th ed.). Oxford, UK: Oxford University Press.

Pellegrinelli, S., Murray-Webster, R., & Turner, N. (2015). Facilitating Organizational Ambidexterity Through the Complementary Use of Projects and Programs. *International Journal of Project Management*, 33(1), 153–164. doi:10.1016/j.ijproman.2014.04.008

Pemsel, S., & Müller, R. (2012). The Governance of Knowledge in Project-Based Organizations. *International Journal of Project Management*, 30(8), 865–876.

PMI. (2013). *Organizational Project Management Maturity Model (OPM3) Knowledge Foundation*. Newtown Square, PA: Project Management Institute.

Prencipe, A., & Tell, F. (2001). Inter-Project Learning : Processes and Outcomes of Knowledge Codification in Project-Based Firms. *Research Policy*, 30, 1373–1394.

Raisch, S., & Birkinshaw, J. (2008). Organizational Ambidexterity: Antecedents, Outcomes, and Moderators. *Journal of Management*, 34(3), 375–409. doi:10.1177/0149206308316058

Renz, P. S. (2007). *Project Governance: Implementing Corporate Governance and Business Ethics in Nonprofit Organizations*. Heidelberg, Germany: Physica-Verlag.

Sadowski, B. M., Sadowski-Rasters, G., & Duysters, G. (2008). Transition of Governance in a Mature Open Software Source Community: Evidence from the Debian Case. *Information Economics and Policy*, 20(4), 323–332. doi:10.1016/j.infoecopol.2008.05.001

Scott, W. R. (2004). Institutional Theory: Contributing to a Theoretical Research Program. In K.G. Smith & M.A. Hitt (Eds.), *Great Minds in Management: The Process of Theory Development* (pp. 460–484). Oxford, UK: Oxford University Press.

Scott, W. R. (2012). The Institutional Environment of Global Project Organizations. *Engineering Project Organization Journal*, 2(1–2), 27–35.

Scott, W. R. (2014). *Institutions and Organizations: Ideas, Interests, and Identities*. Los Angeles, CA: SAGE Publications.

Seddon, B. P. B., Calvert, C., & Yang, S. (2011). A Multi-Project Model of Key Factors Affecting Organizational Benefits from Enterprise Systems. *MIS Quarterly*, 34(2), 1–11.

Shenhar, A. (2001). One Size does Not Fit All Projects: Exploring Classical Contingeny Domains. *Management Science*, 47(3), 394–414.

Turner, J. R., & Keegan, A. (1999). The Versatile Project-Based Organization: Governance and Operational Control. *European Management Journal*, 17(3), 296–309.

Turner, J. R., & Keegan, A. (2001). Mechanisms of Governance in the Project-Based Organization: Roles of the Broker and Steward. *European Management Journal*, *19*(3), 254–267. doi:10.1016/S0263–2373(01)00022–6

Turner, J. R., & Müller, R. (2004). Communication and Co-Operation on Projects Between the Project Owner as Principal and the Project Manager as Agent. *European Management Journal*, *22*(3), 327–336.

7 Strategic Organizational Enablers

Ralf Müller

The previous chapter looked at the organizational enablers at the operational levels of the individual project and of groups of projects. In this chapter, we take a more strategic perspective and address the organization-wide enablers for governance and governmentality in the realm of projects. We report on the research findings on the particular organizational enablers that crossover organizational and governance levels and boundaries. We identify the organization-wide enablers and look at their presence and expression in companies with different levels of success. This reveals the most successful practices. Based on these results, we theorize on the role of organizational enablers for project governance. The evolution of enablers over time, organizational growth, and organizational success is addressed next. The chapter finishes with a discussion of the enablers' contribution to the four governance principles.

Organization-Wide Enablers for Governance

To understand the organizational enablers at the strategic level and to develop a more generic theory of organizational enablers for governance in the realm of projects, we broadened the perspective to include all the enablers identified so far and all the levels of governance. In doing this, we combined the factors and mechanisms identified in Table 6.1 (Chapter 6) and tested their existence and expression in organizations through an international questionnaire study. We addressed the two questions of a) how do the factors and the mechanisms cluster together as distinct organizational enablers at the organizational level, and b) if organizational enablers work then they must have a measurable impact on the results of the project-based part of an organization, hence what is the impact of enablers on success?

From these two questions we derived the underlying model that organizational enabler factors impact or create organizational enabler mechanisms, which impact success at both the governance and organizational levels. This logic follows the predominant thinking that factors influence practices (i.e., mechanisms) in organizations, and these practices influence success. An example for this is a project sponsor with an agency perspective toward the project manager (a factor). This factor leads to certain behavior, such as skepticism and increased control structures (a mechanism). In practice, with this mechanism, additional costs in the form of agency costs arise, which have an impact on the financial results of the project (Müller & Turner, 2005; Turner & Müller, 2004). This leads to a so-called mediation model, where the impact of the organizational enabler factors on project success may be mediated by the enabler mechanisms. Hence, the impact of factors on success can range from nil to very strong, depending on the extent this impact is controlled by the mechanism.

To identify distinct factors and mechanisms, the questionnaire results were analyzed using factor analysis. This technique 'factors' together into new variables those enabler factors or mechanism items from the questionnaire that share similar content. At the same time, the new variables become statistically distinct from each other. Further details can be found in Müller, Shao, and Pemsel (2016).

This resulted in five distinct organizational enabler factors:

- *Embeddedness* in the sense of project managers' behavior (as representatives for their project) being influenced and constrained by their social relationships in combination with the structural embeddedness in the wider organization (Granovetter, 1985). In the context of projects as temporary organizations, this relates to the potential for project managers to deliberately draw (or not draw) on structures, practices, and resources from their project's parent organization or a network of organizations, influenced by the social relationships they have with the relevant actors in these organizations (Sydow, Lindkvist, & DeFillippi, 2004). The structural embeddedness of the project management role in the organization determines, for example, the degree to which project managers are allowed to negotiate and exchange information on behalf of the projects. Social embeddedness influences the degree to which project managers will make use of these structures or circumvent them if needed. In terms of an enabling factor, embeddedness is understood as the combination of the structural and social embeddedness of the project management role in the project's parent organization and the organization's interactions with business partners and markets, as well as with professional organizations. Hence, this represents the mental sphere of action for project managers, granted by a governance system for projects and their management. Measured as the project manager's permission to negotiate and exchange information on a scale from within projects, across projects, within organizations, and beyond organizational boundaries.
- *Leadership* is the extent to which governance was established by a strong leader and is maintained and further developed over time. Measured on a five-point scale from not at all to very much.

90 Ralf Müller

- *Governmentality* represents the mental predisposition of the governors toward those they govern. Typically measured on a scale from authoritative, through liberal, to neoliberal.
- *Project-Governance Flexibility* is the extent to which a project can adapt its structure, roles, meeting schedules, etc. to the emergent needs during project execution. Measured on a five-point scale from not at all to very much.
- *Governance-of-Projects Flexibility* is the extent to which programs and portfolios of projects can flexibly adapt to emerging needs, thus the extent the institutional functions, structures, and leadership styles, etc. are adjusted to the situational needs of groups of projects. Measured on a five-point scale from not at all to very much.

Using the same method, six enabling mechanisms were identified:

- *Governance orientation*, that is, the extent to which shareholder versus stakeholder orientation in the governance of the organization is used as a mechanism in governing projects toward organizational objectives. Measured on a five-point scale from purely shareholder oriented, through balanced, to purely stakeholder oriented.
- *Institutionalization* is a mechanism that allows practices in governance to become standardized, routinized, and institutionalized by, for example, the use of similar reporting methods across the projects in a portfolio of projects; use of the same institution to select projects into, and coordination of projects within a portfolio of projects; use of similar project management methodologies, institutions, and criteria for project selection and coordination; etc. Measured on a five-point scale from never to always.
- *Professionalism* is a mechanism that supports the professionalism of project managers by encouraging them to become certified, work with professional organizations, speak at conferences, etc. Measured on a five-point scale from strongly disagree to strongly agree.
- *Meeting structure* is an infrastructure mechanism that allows for governing communication through planned events, for example, meetings with project managers and management in the organization or external organizations for coordination or other issues. Measured on a five-point scale from never to always.
- *Review structure* is a mechanism for transparency, decision making, and information exchange of projects, programs, and portfolios. Measured on a six-point scale of never, when needed, annually, quarterly, monthly, weekly.
- *Incentives structure* is a mechanism to synchronize objectives of project managers and functional managers by determining the extent to which the income of both is impacted by project results. Measured on a five-point scale from strongly disagree to strongly agree.

Strategic Organizational Enablers   91

Assuming that organizational enablers impact (or 'cause'), to some extent, the success of projects in organizations, we used mediation analysis to regress two types of success measures against these enablers. These were:

a   Success of the project-based part of the organization. This includes measures on objective achievements in terms of time, cost, and quality in projects, achievement of plans and agreed upon outcomes, and satisfaction of employees and customers. Measured on a five-point scale from strongly disagree to strongly agree.
b   Success in the governance structure, measured as the perceived helpfulness of project governance for project managers, helpfulness in achieving organizational objectives, and its general acceptance by the project management community. Measured on a five-point scale from strongly disagree to strongly agree.

Organizational Enablers' Impact on Project Success

The mediation analysis showed that three of the five enablers correlate with success of the project-based part of an organization. These enablers are embeddedness, leadership, and governmentality. Jointly, these three enablers explain 22% of the success measure. This constitutes a moderate impact (Cohen, 1988) of enabler factors on project success. The two flexibility factors (flexibility in project governance and flexibility in governance of projects) did not surface as being significantly correlated with successful projects and governance structures. However, this should not rule them out as important factors. Their value may lie in a more indirect and more process-related role in the execution of governance.

The mediation analysis showed that none of the mechanisms impacted the link between factors and success to more than 20%, which, according to Hair, Hult, Ringle, and Sarstedt (2014), is a negligible effect. Hence, there is no mediation of the link between factors and success by the mechanisms stemming from the factors.

The results show the importance of organizational enabler factors for project success.

Organizational Enablers' Impact on Governance Success

A similar analysis as above was done on the impact of governance factors and their mechanisms on the success of the governance structure. The same three factors of embeddedness, leadership, and governmentality correlated with and explained 36% of the success measure. This constitutes a large effect (Cohen, 1988). However, the governmentality factor is mediated by the meetings mechanism. About 24% of the impact that governmentality has on governance success is absorbed by the way the meetings infrastructure is set up. This is a small but significant effect. It indicates

92   Ralf Müller

that the design of the communication infrastructure has an important bearing on the governmentality factor 'reaching through' to the project managers and making them accept the governance system. The broader the range of meetings that project managers are allowed to attend—ranging from project only to those within the wider organization and external to the organization—the more the impact of governmentality on governance success is controlled by the meeting structure. Here, the wider meeting structure provides for a more comprehensive set of perspectives, issues, etc., which slightly reduce the direct influence of governmentality on the success of governance.

In both analyses, leadership came out as the most important enabling factor for success, followed by embeddedness and then governmentality. Leadership weighted approximately twice as important as the other two factors. This is also shown in Chapter 15, in the pharmaceutical company, where a strong leader established project management and a PMO as a governance institution to continuously develop project management.

That means priority in enabling governance in the realm of projects lies with leadership, which is defined here as a person who establishes project management as a way of working along with the required infrastructure. Moreover, it includes the continuous development of project management as a task and a profession in the organization. To that end, leadership is the strongest enabling factor for project governance.

The second most important enabling factor for governance in projects is embeddedness. It is the level of self-governance granted to project managers, especially the scope of the sphere of activity granted by the organization, so that project managers can interact and negotiate beyond project and organizational borders. Wider scope and greater embeddedness correlate with more successful projects and governance structures.

The third most important enabling factor is governmentality, here defined as the mental predisposition of the governors toward those they govern. Higher levels of neoliberalism in governmentality are associated with greater success in both projects and governance structures, with the latter slightly controlled by the structure of meetings that project managers are allowed to attend.

Finally, we used correlation analysis to identify the link between factors and mechanisms; in other words: which mechanism supports which factor? The results show a hierarchy of mechanisms in terms of their support for enabling factors. Professionalism and meeting structure support all three main enabling factors of embeddedness, leadership, and governmentality and can therefore be seen as the most generic mechanisms for enabling governance. This is complemented by factor-specific mechanisms. Here, the embeddedness factor is supported by the review structure as an underlying mechanism, leadership is supported by institutionalization, and governmentality is supported by governance orientation and incentive structure as underlying mechanisms. Table 7.1 summarizes these relationships.

Strategic Organizational Enablers 93

Table 7.1 Organizational Enablers, Their Factors, and Mechanisms

	Process facilitators	*Discursive abilities*	
Factors	Embeddedness	Leadership	Governmentality
Specific mechanisms	Review structure	Institutionalization	Governance orientation Incentive structure
Generic mechanisms	Professionalism, Meeting structure		

The case study on Tasly Pharmaceuticals (Chapter 15) exemplifies the practicality of the above findings. Project management and its governance were introduced by a strong leader. When he took over as CEO, he built on his military background and experiences in managing projects, and introduced projects and their management as an alternative to the existing process orientation. Under his strong leadership, the whole company was turned into a project-based organization. He institutionalized projects as a way of doing business and project management as a role in the organization. He did this through a PMO, which had an extremely high level of embeddedness, as it was staffed with people from the existing line organization who were eager to change the organization in order to increase efficiency and organizational results. Interaction problems between line and project organization were minimized through this. This highly embedded PMO set up all the enabling mechanisms listed in Table 7.1, except for the governance orientation, which was provided by the company's strategy. The enabling mechanisms were gradually implemented, as shown in the chapter, starting with the institutionalization of work methods (i.e., developing and implementing a project management methodology), in parallel to setting review and meeting structures to enable information flows. This was followed by mechanisms to increase professionalism (such as IPMA certification) and, finally, the alignment of incentive structures of line and matrix managers. The case shows that success in implementing project governance does not come automatically by following the above enablers. It takes time and perseverance to solve the many problems and issues that emerge over time. However, as described in the case, the transition from process governance to project governance paid off for the company.

Toward a Theory of Organizational Enablers for Governance

From the above study results a preliminary theory can be derived.

Governance in the realm of projects is enabled through discursive abilities and process facilitators, with each of these consisting of factors that

94 *Ralf Müller*

trigger the enablers and mechanisms that provide the structure for factors to materialize in the organization. The strongest enabler for successful governance is the organization's discursive ability. This ability is driven by two enabling factors, which are leadership and governmentality. These factors are supported by the five mechanisms of professionalism, meeting structure, institutionalization for leadership, as well as governance orientation and incentives structure for governmentality. The other organizational enabler for successful governance is the process facilitator, which consists of embeddedness as the enabling factor and professionalism, meeting structure, and review structure as the supporting mechanisms. In the following section, we discuss each factor and its underlying mechanisms.

Discursive abilities provide for people's sense-making in the organization. In terms of the enabling factor leadership, it is twofold. First comes the leader's ability to construct and articulate persuasive accounts of the way of doing business by projects. This is done by using the cognitive combination of his or her expertise, legitimacy of the argument, and the opportunity at hand in order to establish both projects and project management in the organization. Second, once projects and their management are established in an organization, the leader steers the organization toward continuous improvement in the way projects are selected, set up, and executed; practices are institutionalized; and project management is done in the organization. The stronger this leadership, the better the results of the project-based part of the organization and the acceptance of the governance structure by the governed. This is the main factor behind a successful enabling of a governance structure in and for projects.

In terms of the enabling factor governmentality, it is the mentality and attitude governors have, and thus the tone they instill between parties, that has an enabling effect. Here, the more successful organizations apply more liberal and neoliberal approaches to governmentality. Hence, governors persuade through rationality in their argument, or by developing a culture that allows for project teams and managers to control themselves through subtle forces in the organization and society around them.

Five mechanisms underlie the discursive abilities enablers—these are professionalism and meeting structure as generic mechanisms, and institutionalization for leadership, as well as governance orientation and incentive structure for governmentality. Collectively, they allow both leadership and governmentality to prosper, determining the work-practices, which allows the factor to 'reach through' to the operational part of the organization.

Professionalism is a generic mechanism for all enabling factors. It fosters the development of project managers in their profession. Here, the leader's efforts to improve results surface as mechanisms such as professional certification for project managers, their engagement with professional organizations, speeches at conferences, etc. Through this, the work of project managers becomes more transparent and clearer in terms of their own and others' accountabilities and responsibilities, and the fairness of their doings, thus contributing to the corporate governance principles.

Meeting structures are another generic mechanism in support of all enablers. This mechanism provides the media infrastructure for project managers to communicate, negotiate, and decide on behalf of the project by attending a variety of meetings and acting beyond the boundaries of the individual project or organization. Through this, they convey the contents of the enabling factors to the rest of the organization and shape (and get shaped in the) sense-making of the organization. This allows for transparency in many aspects, including goals, performance, needs, etc., as well as for clarification of accountabilities and responsibilities in projects.

Institutionalization is a mechanism in support of the leadership factor and is implemented, among other ways, through clear role and process definitions for those working in and with projects, as well as standardized reporting requirements across projects. The former provides for clarity in accountabilities and responsibilities through a mutual understanding of 'who does what and how.' The latter provides for transparency of project plans, performance and ethical standards, etc., which support fairness in the treatment of projects and those working in them.

Governance orientation is a mechanism in support of governmentality. This mechanism provides for transparency of the organizational *raison d'être* by articulating the stakeholder or shareholder orientation of the organization, which provides for clarity in the aims and purposes of the organization, as well as guidance in people's decision making in projects, project management, and project governance.

Incentives are also a mechanism in support of governmentality. They provide for the alignment of the project-based and process-based (or functional) parts of the organization in terms of remuneration and benefits, and foster fairness and other ethical aspects of the business.

Process facilitators are the particular combinations of routines, practices, structures, and policies that allow for results to emerge. These are particular features that, when employed, are associated with higher chances of reaching organizational objectives in terms of project and governance results. The enabling factor underlying process facilitation is embeddedness, which are those structures and routines that allow project managers to self-govern their work, exemplified here by the extent to which an organization allows its project managers to go beyond project and organizational boundaries in communication and negotiation on behalf of their projects. Higher levels of embeddedness are associated with higher levels of success in projects and their governance structures. This factor is supported by the mechanisms of professionalism, meeting structure, and review structure.

Professionalism as a mechanism in support of embeddedness surfaces in the alignment of levels of embeddedness with the professionalism shown by the project managers, as more professional project managers are granted greater embeddedness in the form of authority and autonomy to act on behalf of the project than their more junior colleagues. To that end, it contributes to all four corporate governance principles. As described above, meeting structures as a mechanism in support of embeddedness provide the

96   Ralf Müller

media infrastructure for project managers to communicate, negotiate, and decide on behalf of the project.

Review structure is a mechanism that provides for socialization in support of the embeddedness of the project manager. The wider the meeting structure (i.e., the more the meetings are beyond project and organizational borders), the greater the embeddedness of the project manager. Hence, the enabling factor and mechanism need to be aligned in scope. Meeting structures that address wider contexts (from project only, through to organizational and external), contribute to more transparency and clearer accountabilities and responsibilities, through the involvement of more parties and the sense-making of the project in its context. This possibly results also in greater fairness and ethics in project selection and execution.

However, the above mentioned mechanisms are neutral in their role of turning enabling factors into specific behavior that is beneficial for governing the projects in an organization. Only in the case of acceptance of governance structures do the meeting structures play a minor role in controlling the impact that governmentality approaches have on governance success.

The strategic-level enablers of leadership, sovereignty, and governmentality allow governance and governmentality to be enabled at the strategic level. Here embeddedness at the strategic level corresponds with the tactical-level process facilitators listed for governance of projects and project governance in Table 6.1. These are mainly the authority to develop and select choices of governance frameworks and governance structures plus their supporting institutions, as well as roles and responsibilities at the governance of projects level. This is complemented at the project governance level with the authority to procure, implement, and execute these governance frameworks and establish the required governance. The discursive ability of leadership at the strategic level relates to discursive abilities at the operational level, such as institutionalization of governance by clarifying the organizational implications of doing business by projects, defining the roles of governance institutions, provision of information sharing structures, and flexible adjustments of policies and mandates, at the governance of projects level. This is complemented at the project governance level with the alignment of organizational and project objectives, as well as the use of governance institutions and their structures. Strategic-level governmentality relates to its tactical implementation by providing the general governance orientation, such as a stakeholder or shareholder orientation, and by using incentive systems and other means to make people willing to take responsibility, be mindful of the organization's capabilities, and 'think in projects.'

The above discussion has shown how leadership, governmentality, and embeddedness enable governance in the realm of projects. The implementation of these factors is done through enabling mechanisms, which, in turn, contribute to the four governance principles of transparency, accountability, responsibility, and fairness. These contributions emerge at the levels of individual projects, groups of projects, and at the top of the organization.

Through this, the levels are interlinked and each level contributes its particular part to corporate governance and its principles.

Evolvement of Enablers for Governance and Governmentality in Organizations

Organizational enablers cannot be assumed to be static over time or immune to impacts from within or outside the organization. We addressed this question through several case studies, including longitudinal studies, and validated the findings through global questionnaires. The details of these studies can be found in Müller, Shao, et al. (2016) and Müller, Zhai, & Wang (2016). In these studies, we identified three different forms of evolvement in organization enablers. We categorized them by their driving forces, which made us distinguish between context-driven, growth-driven, and maturity-driven evolvement in organizational enablers.

Context-Driven Evolvement of Enablers

Context-driven evolvement refers to those changes in enablers for governance and governmentality over time that can be traced back to the variations in external or internal circumstances. Müller et al. (2016) show that there is very little evidence that influences external to the organization, such as changes in terms of number of projects with customers, increasing or decreasing market share, or similar, lead to visible patterns in the changes of enablers of governance and governmentality. While most of the organizations we looked at did experience changes in their context, the reactions by the organizations and the related impact on organizational enablers was very diverse. For example, two large organizations of equal size and industry, which experienced the same increase in market share, reacted to this in opposite manners. One organization diversified its governance by increasing the embeddedness and autonomy of project managers, combined with establishing more neoliberal governmentality. The other organization consolidated its business and reduced embeddedness and autonomy, pushed decision-making authority to top management levels, and instilled an authoritative governmentality. No patterns were detectable in the link between external impacts on and changes in organizational enablers.

However, the data showed that most of the changes in enablers were triggered by the top managers and their decisions on changes that were needed for the organization to continue creating wealth for its shareholders and stakeholders, which ultimately impacted on the governance and governmentality of projects. Top management, typically the CEO, and his or her leadership appeared to be the main drivers for context-driven evolvement of governance and governmentality. As indicated in the above example of two similar firms, it was the decision by the CEO that made them develop in two different directions. This underscores the above study's findings of the importance of leadership and its role as the ultimate enabler for governance and governmentality. Leadership does establish, maintain, and change governance and governmentality over time.

This is supported by studies by Monique Aubry and her colleagues on the changing mandates of PMOs in organizations (Aubry et al., 2010; Aubry, Hobbs, Müller, & Blomquist, 2010, 2011). Similar to our findings, these studies concluded that the majority of changes in PMOs are triggered by the CEO of the organization, in many cases by a newly hired CEO. These changes addressed the scope of authority, mandate, the number and skills of employees, and in many cases the closedown of the PMO. About half the PMOs were closed down during the first two years of their existence, while almost all of those surviving the first two years continued to exist after five years; however, often with considerable changes, over time, in size, mandates, and skills (Aubry et al., 2011). Aubry and her colleagues concluded that governance institutions like PMOs are established to address existing or emergent issues, such as improvement of poor project portfolio results or implementing the use of project management methodologies in projects throughout the organization. Once these issues are resolved, the PMO is either closed down or charged with a new mandate, which often addresses the next important issue. Therefore, PMOs are not closed down because of poor performance, but because of successful accomplishment of their temporary mandate (Aubry, Müller, & Glückler, 2012).

Here, we see similarities with our study in terms of strong influences by top management and its chain of decisions over time. Examples include new CEOs, or those having to consolidate the business, reducing the embeddedness of projects and autonomy of project managers in the governance of projects, paired with an increasingly authoritative governmentality. Even though organizations adapt to their changing markets, the particular ways in which they react to these changes and the extent to which these reactions impact the enablers for governance and governmentality are top management, often CEO, decisions. To that end, it is the top management that ultimately causes changes in the organizational enablers for governance and governmentality in the realm of projects.

Growth-Driven Evolvement of Enablers

Growth-driven evolvement refers to the changes in governance and governmentality associated with the size, and therefore indirectly with the growth, of the organization. For analyzing this we distinguished between five categories of sizes of organizations, depending on the number of employees: (1) 1–250, (2) 251–1,000, (3) 1,001–10,000, (4) 10,001–30,000, (5) more than 30,000 employees. The measurements for the enabler dimensions are described above.

We assessed organizations on their expression of strategic organizational enablers (both factors and mechanisms). The results show that the smallest

Strategic Organizational Enablers

organizations (category 1) score highest in flexibility and embeddedness measures. Interestingly, the next higher-level category, with organizations between 251 and 1,000 employees, shows the lowest expression of organizational enablers among all the categories. With further increase in size (categories 3 to 5) the expression of organizational enablers increases again. Figure 7.1 shows the profile of category 1, 2, and 5 organizations, with the circle labeled 0 showing the average of all organizations. The right-hand side shows the enabling factors, while the bottom and left-hand side depicts the enabling mechanisms.

Thus, project-related governance is well established in small organizations, but falls below average in medium-sized organizations and approach average levels in the large organizations. Different organizational enablers appear to be emphasized in different organizational sizes or stages of organizational growth. The smallest organizations emphasize flexibility, shown by the high scores for related factors in both project governance and governance of projects, as well as flexible meeting structures. At the same time, they are relatively weak (i.e., below average) in leadership factors and institutionalization mechanisms.

Organizations in category 2 reduce significantly the expression of almost all of the enablers for governance. Moreover, the measures of almost all dimensions fall below average. When we addressed this effect in interviews

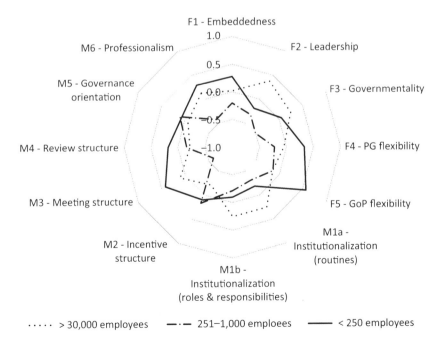

Figure 7.1 Enabler Profiles of Organizations of Different Sizes

100   Ralf Müller

with these organizations, we were told that projects, as a way to organize the flow of work, were too expensive for them. Additional costs, stemming from dedicated organizational and control structures, make projects a less attractive alternative in these organizations compared with process-oriented ways of working. However, these organizations engage in projects with their customers. So they look like project-oriented organizations from the outside. Nevertheless, once a project is contracted, it gets dismantled into specific tasks and the tasks are then fed into the organizational production processes. This approach supports the incremental development of parts of the project outcomes. The parts will then be integrated by a specialized integration team before the product is handed over to the customer.

Rodney Turner and his colleagues explained the reasons for this way of organizing work by the additional transaction costs that the project way of working incurs when compared with the process way of working. These are mainly costs stemming from dedicated governance structures (Turner & Keegan, 1999; Turner & Müller, 2003). In addition, we found in our studies that organizations of that size (251–1,000 employees) often have difficulties in balancing the diversity of skills needed in projects and the utilization of people possessing these skills. Rather than hiring resources with specialized skills that are at the risk of being not fully productive, they employ resources with skills that are frequently needed, thus making sure the hired resources are utilized and thereby productive. Once organizations grow beyond this particular size, the number of projects and associated skills (including specialized skills) increases, and it becomes efficient for the organizations to hire resources with more specialized skills.

Large organizations, like the ones shown with a dotted line in Figure 7.1, emphasize different enablers to the ones emphasized by small organizations. In particular, leadership and the two different forms of institutionalization are strongly expressed in large organizations, compared with smaller organizations. At the same time, the large organizations reduce significantly the flexibility at both project level and groups of projects level.

In summary, our studies show a strong impact by organization size on the governance and governmentality enablers. While the smallest organizations focus on flexibility-related enablers, the medium-sized organizations (251–1,000 employees) emphasize efficiency aspects and govern projects only to the extent needed for customer exchange, while organizing their internal work with a prioritization of processes and production efficiency. Organizations growing beyond this size increasingly organize their work as projects, supported by the institutionalization of roles, responsibilities, and work routines. The organizational enabler with the strongest increase corresponding to increasing organizational size is leadership, followed by governmentality. Thus, when organizations grow large they balance the governance and governmentality enablers, and thereby put equal emphasis on the science and the art of governance.

Maturity-Driven Evolvement of Enablers

Maturity-driven evolvement refers to the different expressions of enablers for governance and governmentality in organizations with different levels of success with their project-based parts. We assessed this by using the organizational success measures described above and calculated the profile of organizational enablers as the mean values of the measurement dimension. We did this for the four quartiles of average project success. Figure 7.2 shows the profiles of the expression of organizational enablers for organizations in the four quartiles of success (i.e., lowest level of success = quartile 1, dotted line, to highest level of success = quartile 4, solid line). The circle labeled 0 shows the mean of all the organizations.

Organizations with the lowest levels of success show extremely low expressions of embeddedness, leadership, governmentality, institutionalization of roles and responsibilities, as well as professionalism. The key enablers for successful projects are severely underdeveloped. Simultaneously, they show extremely high flexibility. Taken together, this is indicative of an ad-hoc approach to governing projects, where reactivity and flexibility prevail, lacking a set of project-related enablers to develop a stable and reliable governance structure.

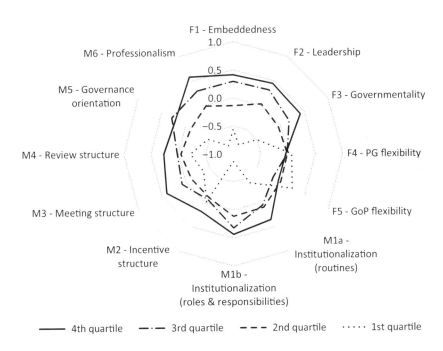

Figure 7.2 Enabler Profiles of Organizations at Four Levels of Success

102 *Ralf Müller*

The expression of the enablers increases with increasing success of the organization. Organizations in the second quartile are almost congruent in their profile with those having average levels of success (i.e., ring 0). Those growing beyond average levels of success (quartiles 3 and 4) also develop strongest in the three enabling factors of embeddedness, leadership, and governmentality, and support this by strong growth in enabling mechanisms for fostering professionalism and communication through strong meeting structures, as well as institutionalization of roles, responsibilities, and work routines.

The three factors of embeddedness, leadership, and governmentality feature again as the key enablers for successful governance. Flexibility appears to be strongly developed in organizations with less success and maturity in their project business, and is reduced in the more successful and mature organizations. Through its association with success for the organizations that apply them, the factors of embeddedness, leadership and governmentality—as shown in Figure 7.2—are strong indicators for successful practices, which may be generalized across organizations of different types and sizes.

The Contribution of Strategic Organizational Enablers to the Four Corporate Governance Principles

We cannot conclude this discussion on organizational enablers for governance in the realm of projects without taking a look at their contribution to organization-wide governance principles. The three key strategic organizational enablers—embeddedness, leadership, and governmentality—contribute simultaneously to several of the four governance principles.

Transparency is supported by embeddedness, and its enabling mechanisms of review and meeting structures, by setting up information exchange events for projects, programs, and portfolios. This provides for increased visibility and information exchange, and thereby transparency of projects. A further contributing factor is leadership and its underlying mechanism of institutionalization, as well as the mechanism for professionalism. This provides for transparency of the work methods, processes, roles and routines, which is needed to legitimize projects and the ways in which they are implemented, and with it the transparency and legitimacy of the wider organization.

The accountability and responsibility principles are supported through embeddedness in combination with its enabling mechanism review structure. This allows, for example, defining decision-making authorities for managers in the organization, which contributes to clearer accountabilities and responsibilities. Again, leadership surfaces as a contributor by assigning accountabilities and responsibilities for project managers and their governing institutions, such as PMOs.

The fairness principle is supported through the governmentality factor, among others, and its underlying mechanisms for clarifying governance orientation (stakeholder or shareholder) and aligned incentive structures. This provides for fairness and ethical management in the overall orientation of employees in their daily work and decision making, as well as their remuneration. Leadership should also contribute to a general culture of ethical conduct and fairness in the organization.

This chapter has developed a set of strategic organizational factors and their underlying mechanisms that enable governance in the realm of projects. We have discussed these enablers from various perspectives, including their roles, impact, relationship with success, and their evolution in line with company growth, maturity, and changes to the organization. We concluded the chapter by outlining some exemplary contributions of these enablers to the corporate governance principles.

References

Aubry, M., Hobbs, B., Müller, R., & Blomquist, T. (2010). Identifying Forces Driving PMO Changes. *Project Management Journal*, 41(4), 30–45.

Aubry, M., Hobbs, B., Müller, R., & Blomquist, T. (2011). *Identifying the Forces Driving Frequent Change in PMOs*. Newtown Square, PA: Project Management Institute.

Aubry, M., Müller, R., & Glückler, J. (2012). *Governance and Communities of PMOs*. Newtown Square, PA: Project Management Institute.

Aubry, M., Müller, R., Hobbs, B., & Blomquist, T. (2010). Project Management Offices in Transition. *International Journal of Project Management*, 28(8), 766–778. doi:10.1016/j.ijproman.2010.05.006

Cohen, J. (1988). *Statistical Power Analysis for the Behavioral Sciences*. Hillsdale: Lawrence Erlbaum Associates, Inc.

Granovetter, M. (1985). Economic Action and Social Structure: The Problem of Embeddedness. *American Journal of Sociology*, 91(3), 481–510.

Hair, J. F., Hult, G. T. M., Ringle, C. M., & Sarstedt, M. (2014). *A Primer on Partial Least Squares Structural Equation Modeling (PLS-SEM)*. Thousand Oaks, CA: SAGE Publications.

Müller, R., Shao, J., & Pemsel, S. (2016). *Organizational Enablers for Project Governance*. Newtown Square, PA: Project Management Institute.

Müller, R., & Turner, J. R. (2005). "The Impact of Principal-Agent Relationship and Contract Type on Communication between Project Owner and Manager. *International Journal of Project Management*, 23(5), 398–403.

Müller, R., Zhai, L., & Wang, A. (2016). A Framework for Governance in the Realm of Projects. In *Proceedings of EURAM 2016 (European Academy of Management) Conference*, June 1–4, 2016, Paris, France.

Sydow, J., Lindkvist, L., & DeFillippi, R. (2004). Project-Based Organizations, Embeddedness and Repositories of Knowledge: Editorial. *Organization Studies*, 25(9), 1475–1489. doi:10.1177/0170840604048162

Turner, J. R., & Keegan, A. (1999). The Versatile Project-Based Organization: Governance and Operational Control. *European Management Journal*, 17(3), 296–309.

Turner, J. R., & Müller, R. (2003). On the Nature of the Project as a Temporary Organization. *International Journal of Project Management*, 21(1), 1–7.

Turner, J. R., & Müller, R. (2004). Communication and Cooperation on Projects between the Project Owner as Principal and the Project Manager as Agent. *European Management Journal*, 21(3), 327–336.

Part III

Practices in the Private and Public Sector

This part presents the practices in organizational project governance and governmentality.

It starts in Chapter 8 by introducing tactical practices from the private sector for the level of project governance, governance of projects, and governmentality. Then the strategic organization-wide practices are presented and visualized in a multi-dimensional framework that captures organization-level practices of governance and governmentality.

The practices of the public sector are described in Chapter 9. The Norwegian governance scheme is used as an example for the successful application of a governance framework for large state-funded investment projects.

8 Private Sector Practices

Ralf Müller

This chapter addresses the practices of governance and governmentality in the private sector. Similar to the chapters on organizational enablers, we first address the tactical practices structured by project governance, governance of projects, and governmentality. Next, we address the strategic practices. Finally, we outline a multidimensional framework that allows the capture and visualization of strategic, organization-level practices of organizational project governance and governmentality. The chapter is based on, among others, studies published in Müller, Shao, and Pemsel (2016) and Müller, Zhai, Wang, and Shao (n.d.)

Tactical Practices

In line with Oxford Dictionaries (2014), we define 'tactical' practices as carefully planned actions aimed at an end beyond the immediate action. By this we refer to the operational-level actions and their institutions as a means set up to achieve governance objectives as an end.

In our 2014 study, we looked at the practices employed by organizations in the private sector across the world (Müller, Shao, & Pemsel, 2016). We first identified and proposed practices through a systematic literature review, and then tested, refined, and extended these in six case studies. We validated these results using a questionnaire with 208 responses from organizations worldwide and derived distinct patterns for practices in project governance, governance of projects, and governmentality.

Patterns for worldwide practices for tactical project governance include the use of project management methodologies, steering groups, and PMOs.

Project Management Methodologies

Ninety-nine percent of the respondents to our worldwide questionnaire, and all the companies we interviewed, indicated that their project management is governed by a project management methodology. For these companies, the use of a methodology ensures a proven approach to the management of their projects, and thus a risk reduction. Seventy-six percent of the respondents

108 *Ralf Müller*

"often to always" use the same methodology, which indicates a general stability and familiarity with the use of methodological ways to manage projects. According to the popular Prince2 project management methodology (Office of Government Commerce, 2005), a methodology supports project managers in their daily work by serving as a guideline for a controlled, well-managed, visible set of activities to achieve the desired results. It links to governance principles by providing transparency in the project's process and its status, for example, by requiring milestone or sprint reviews, as well as through identification of responsibilities, accountabilities, and authorities of individuals involved in a project. Moreover, it is designed to help reconcile the different perspectives of stakeholders in order to synchronize them into a cohesive and holistic perspective toward a project. A variety of methodologies exists, which can be categorized in different ways. For example, the Office of Government Commerce (2008) distinguishes between predictive, convergent, and emergent methodologies, where:

- *Predictive methodologies*, such as Prince2, refer to the most traditional methodologies, which emphasize upfront planning at the detailed level (where possible), followed by design freeze and subsequent careful implementation of the plan with closely controlled changes to the original plan; that is, a predominantly sequential approach to managing a project. These methodologies are especially important when a project's outcome must be complete by the time of its first productive use, like in products such as airplanes or services like those of travel agencies.
- *Convergent methodologies*, such as the Dynamic Systems Development Method (DSDM), refer to those where some planning is done upfront with a moderate level of detail, complemented by lean documentation and informal communication to allow for sequential and iterative approaches to project management, and which accommodate change.
- *Emergent methodologies*, like Lean or Agile/Scrum, are those where little planning is done at the detailed level in the beginning and iterative work methods support the continuous adjustment of project objectives to changing needs and the easy incorporation of change. These methodologies are of special interest for project outcomes that can be delivered incrementally, for example, where the most business-critical parts can already be used productively while less critical parts are still under development, as in many Information Systems projects.

Governance in respect to methodologies includes the decisions regarding the particular methodology for a project. The choice of methodology often determines the nature of the involvement of governance institutions, such as steering committees and the level of oversight they can exercise. Thus, the selection of a methodology should not be based solely on the criteria implied by the above categories, such as the volatility of the project's outcome in terms of product or service and the level of understanding of the product or service at the time the project is planned. The decision should also include criteria related to the possibility to exercise governance once the project is under way.

Steering Groups

The steering group is the most widely used governance institution. Ninety-seven percent of project managers indicated that they report to a steering group. Moreover, project managers reported that they spend most of their governance-related time with steering groups, followed by line managers and then PMOs. Customer and external governance institutions ranked four and five on that list. The composition of steering groups varies widely. In smaller companies this is often just the CEO, in medium-sized companies it is the CEO or someone delegated the responsibility by the CEO, such as the Head of Project Management. Larger organizations, or organizations in industries such as pharmaceuticals or aviation, may use several different steering groups, both internal and external to the organization. The principal roles and responsibilities of steering groups are described in Chapter 5. Project reviews by steering groups are mostly done on a monthly basis (indicated by 30% of the respondents to the worldwide questionnaire), followed by (bi)weekly reviews (28%) and when the need arises (23%).

PMOs

PMOs are popular in larger organizations with more than 1,000 employees. However, they vary considerably in their mandates, because they address the idiosyncratic issues of an organization. Chapter 5 describes the nature of PMOs as governance institutions. As such, they serve both individual projects and groups of projects, depending on their mandate. In terms of project governance, the quantitative study showed a slight preference for organizations to have PMOs ensuring compliance with the project management methodology in individual projects. About one-third of the PMOs have clearly defined and stable mandates, while about 50% have flexible mandates, which are adjusted to emerging issues or changing circumstances.

Patterns in practices for the tactical governance of projects include the use of business alignment and standardization.

Business Alignment

Business alignment refers to the association of projects with the organization's business, especially at the portfolio level. Developments in portfolio management software in recent years increased the transparency of projects' fit to business, and through this, the quality of portfolio-level decision

110 *Ralf Müller*

making. Hence, it contributed to the corporate governance principles. Many published studies (e.g., Müller, Martinsuo, & Blomquist, 2008) as well as the interviewees in our studies mentioned the need for this practice. Two-thirds of the respondents to our worldwide questionnaire said that portfolio decisions are institutionalized and often to always made by the same institution, compared with 24% of the organizations where this happens only sometimes. Governance of portfolios in terms of portfolio reviews is most often done monthly (28%), followed by quarterly reviews (20%). About 77% of the respondents said their portfolio decisions are made by sponsors and steering groups, followed by dedicated portfolio managers (31%) and PMOs (30%). The latter question allowed for multiple answers, as the portfolio decisions are typically made in groups composed of a variety of roles. It shows that portfolio steering groups dominate portfolio decision making, and thereby the alignment of an organization's projects with its business.

Standardization

Standardization of practices across projects is a major task in the governance of projects and constitutes the level of institutionalization of governance practices. Five major areas for standardization were identified in our studies:

- *Standardization of project selection.* This refers to the institutionalization of processes and roles for the initial decision to accept a project (as opposed to the sum of all portfolio decisions mentioned in the paragraph above). This includes the stability of project selection in terms of a) stability of the process of identifying, selecting, and prioritizing projects for the organization, and b) stability in the roles that are involved in project selection decisions, such as those listed above. Together, the two dimensions contribute to all four governance principles by providing greater transparency of the decision-making process and the status of the project selection, clearer accountabilities and responsibilities by use of defined roles for project selection, and fairness through transparency and predictable selection methods. Moreover, this builds the foundation for maturity in, for example, learning and continuous improvement of practices. Nearly 64% of the organizations in our sample indicated that they use the same process and roles "often to always" to select their projects.
- *Standardization of project reporting and review.* This addresses the similarity in project reporting requirements, such as in progress measures across projects (e.g., Earned Value results for every project), reporting periods, and level of detail required. This standardization allows for comparability of the performance of the projects in a portfolio or program. Examples include the popular red, yellow, and green reporting, which provides for a quick and easy portfolio-level overview of

projects and their status. A similar comparability is accomplished with the standardization of project reviews, where the use of established processes and review techniques aim for a comprehensive understanding of the project and its circumstances from a portfolio perspective in order to improve portfolio-level decisions. Both standardized reports and reviews contribute to the four governance principles by providing more transparency in the projects and their portfolio's status and circumstances, which provides for more fairness in portfolio decision making, as well as clearer accountabilities and responsibilities. Seventy-one percent of the organizations in our study use standardized review and reporting "often to always."

- *Standardization of project management methodologies.* This refers to the use of one or more predefined sets of methodologies in a program or portfolio. Advantages include the familiarity of project managers with their methodology, because they have to get familiar with only a limited number of different methodologies, as well as the efficiencies for procurement, training, and maintenance that stem from this limitation. Contributions to corporate governance principles are similar to the above. Fifty percent of the organizations in our study provided one methodology for their project managers, while 28% provided two, 14% provided three, and 6% provided seven or more methodologies.
- *Standardization of roles and responsibilities.* This refers to the clarity of the roles and responsibilities, as provided through policies or other governance means. In Chapter 6 we outlined that the clarity of roles and responsibilities is a characteristic of the more successful organizations and enables governance. In a similar vein, it is a common practice in organizations with more than 1,000 employees. Thus, it requires a critical mass of projects and resources before it can eventuate. This standardization obviously contributes to all four governance principles, as it provides more transparency of *what* is done and *by whom*, and contributes to accountability and responsibility by outlining exactly these two principles for each role. Finally, it contributes to fairness by communicating the expectations and requirements for each role and the persons aiming to fulfill them.

Patterns in practices for tactical governmentality include autonomy and self-responsibility of project managers, project thinking, and organizational open systems thinking.

Autonomy and Self-Responsibility of Project Managers

This refers to the level of freedom from external control, and thus the level of self-governance (OxfordDictionaries, 2014) granted to the project manager. We addressed it from the perspective of the project manager's autonomy to negotiate for and act on behalf of the project, ranging from within

112 *Ralf Müller*

the project's organization only, to higher hierarchical levels in the project's parent organization, up to external organizations and public events, such as conferences. The span of autonomy for project managers varies widely. The most autonomous project managers are found in the smallest and the largest organizations. The least autonomous are found in medium-sized organizations, especially those between 250 and 1,000 employees. The latter organizations often subordinate project management and its related tasks to the operational production processes of the wider organization, which often turns project management into a lobbying and coordinating internal role, while, at the same time, being the interface for external customers. The level of project manager empowerment featured as a dimension with significant differences between organizations that are more or less successful with their project business. The more successful organizations empower their project managers to a much larger extent than those with lower levels of success. However, it is reasonable to assume that organizations only grant higher levels of autonomy to those project managers who are self-responsible, and thus have the required standing to be answerable to the things under their control. The empirical studies showed a wide span of practices. As with autonomy, the practices range from organizations that invest little in the development of self-responsible project managers, such as the medium-sized organizations, where compliance with production processes dominates the governance practices, to practices of targeted development of project managers' self-responsible acting, as in the smallest and the largest organizations.

Project Thinking

This refers to the dominating ontology in the organization hosting a project, in terms of it being a project- or a process-based organization. In the former, the organization is mainly seen as a network of projects, which may share common resources and overarching coordination processes. The latter ontology understands an organization as a set of repetitive production processes, to which the project's tasks are mapped. Similar to autonomy, the smallest and largest organizations in our study were dominated by a project ontology. Examples include cases where references to work were made along the different projects the people worked on or the awareness of the temporariness of project organizations and their related goals and objectives, the consequences of matrix structures in terms of friction between line and project organization, etc. (for an example, see Chapter 15). In contrast, process-based organizations were described by their employees in functional departments, to which elements of their projects were assigned, and the processes that constitute the operations of the organization. Project and process ontology is another pattern that differs significantly between medium-sized organizations and others. Process ontology dominates the governance in the former organizations, which is contrary to the project ontology in the smallest and largest organizations. In-between stages were also met in medium-sized organizations, where management thinks and talks in projects, while employees perceive their work as following the operational processes.

Open Systems Thinking

This relates to project managers' and teams' view of the organization as an open system, with a variety of skills and opportunities, as well as both internal and external interfaces. Open systems thinking fosters the willingness to continuously combine and recombine existing skills, opportunities, and interfaces in new ways to match upcoming requirements. This reflects the cognitive aspects of good understanding of the project's parent organization. The quantitative study identified external orientation of project managers as a key practice, which needs to be enabled by the organization and implemented through the governance structure. Organizations practicing a culture of open systems thinking are significantly more successful in the governance of their projects.

No significant differences in governance practices were found between countries, industries, project size, and the level of project manager experience. This was despite a wide variety of governance approaches in all these strata. However, differences were found in company size and discussed above.

Strategic Practices

In line with the *Merriam Webster Dictionary* (2015), we define strategic practices as those that relate to the achievement of a plan over a long period of time. This section addresses the range of the strategic governance and governmentality approaches in organizations of different size, industry, and level of projectification. The section consolidates prior singular perspectives, such as governance structures for particular project types, e.g., NASA projects (Shenhar et al., 2005) or large capital investment projects (Miller & Hobbs, 2005), by providing a framework of the different approaches to governance and governmentality, as well as a way to visualize and profile them.

We do this by lifting the perspective from the nuts and bolts of operational governance and governmentality, as reported above, to the more generic and strategic governance concepts as they are addressed in the corporate governance literature. The span of subjects in corporate governance literature is very wide and only a fraction of these subjects applies to the project level. Therefore, we focus only on those concepts of governance and governmentality that are established at the corporate level and filter through to the governance of projects. For this, we follow Dean (2010) and focus on sovereignty, governance mechanisms, and governance institutions.

We also provide a tool to visualize the specific governance and governmentality profile of organizations, which allows us to compare approaches and to identify context-related differences.

114 *Ralf Müller*

Governmentality

Governmentality Approach

In accordance with the general management literature, we distinguish between *authoritarian, liberal,* and *neoliberal* approaches to governmentality (e.g., Dean, 2010). Authoritarian approaches to governmentality are indicative of reconcilability and totality of the various governance principles (Burchell, 1991), and are manifested in centralized decision making, giving clear direction, and significant power distance (Dean, 2010). The authoritarian approach "seek[s] to operate through obedient rather than free subjects, or, at a minimum, endeavor to neutralize any opposition to authority" (Dean, 2010, p. 155). Liberal approaches are indicative of a recognition of the heterogeneity and incompatibility of the different governance principles in a society or organization (Burchell, 1991). Here, decision making based on economic principles and a general market-mindeness help as guides through heterogeneity (Dean, 2010). Neoliberal approaches address the collective interests of people and the consent which leads them to voluntarily obey contextual frameworks. These cognitive frameworks shape, but do not necessarily determine, people's behaviors (Clegg et al., 2002; Clegg, 1994). Thus, neoliberal approaches are indicative of a system that does not directly steer individuals through their supervisors (e.g., state government), but through subtle forces imposed by the society they live in. This approach focuses mainly on the societal context and how to cultivate and optimize differences therein for the benefit of the governed system. It does not focus on the individual *per se* in order to normalize people's behaviors (Lemke, 2001).

In organizational project governmentality, the three approaches are:

- *Authoritarian governmentality,* which enforces process compliance and rigid governance structures, such as in major public investment projects (Klakegg & Haavaldsen, 2011; Miller & Hobbs, 2005).
- *Liberal governmentality,* which emphasizes outcome control within clearly defined but, when needed, flexible governance structures, such as in customer delivery projects (Dinsmore & Rocha, 2012).
- *Neoliberal approaches,* such as in community-governed open source development projects (Franck & Jungwirth, 2003). The goal here is to indirectly steer team members' behavior through their desire to contribute to existing values and ideologies, which foster self-control within rudimentary governance structures.

From a worldwide study, where we measured these three concepts quantitatively, we learned that these approaches are not mutually exclusive. The three concepts are in a complex relationship, where each of them contributes to different success measures in an organization. The following patterns of governmentality dimensions were found for the three approaches.

Private Sector Practices   115

Authoritarian and Liberal Approaches to Governmentality

These two approaches can be modeled on a continuum from liberal to authoritarian. Patterns for more liberal approaches include organizations that provide a certain level of freedom to their project managers, such as in making decisions on how to achieve their project objectives. What stands out in these organizations is their outcome control, as opposed to behavior control in more authoritarian regimes.

It becomes clear that in order to accomplish corporate values and carry out the ways in which projects should be managed, the organization moves toward more authoritarian approaches. In its mature form, authoritarian governmentality is shown through very clear directions, which are enforced by the governance institutions, supported by an emphasis on the communication and the achievement of organizational values. This is often supported by tactical PMOs, which provide for transparency in project management methods and goal accomplishments.

Authoritarian approaches contribute significantly more than other approaches to the accomplishment of the objectives in governance of projects, such as annual plan achievement, organization-wide customer satisfaction, and employee satisfaction measures.

In Figures 8.1 and 8.2, the liberal approaches are depicted as low levels of authoritarian governmentality.

Neoliberal Governmentality

Neoliberal governmentality is also modeled form low to high. An increase in neoliberalism is indicated when the project manager's freedom for decision making increases in parallel with the governance institution's efforts to communicate organizational values as criteria for decision making. In its highest measured form, neoliberal governmentality shows that organizations become flexible in adjusting their structures to project needs; governance institutions rarely steer the projects directly and assume that project managers make their own decisions and trust them to decide freely within their projects while they work in alignment with methodologies and policies.

The neoliberal approach to governmentality contributes significantly more than other approaches to project success measures in general and to customer satisfaction and employee satisfaction in particular.

Governmentality Precepts

In our studies on governmentality, we encountered strong differences in the terms of reference governors (such as steering committees) used when steering projects. They are independent from the governance approach. We

116 *Ralf Müller*

identified three different terms of reference, which we call "precepts." These are: organizational values, process compliance, and project wellbeing.

- An *organizational values precept* is indicated when governors mainly refer to the organizational values in their governmentality, and to a lesser extent to processes or results. Examples include steering committees that prioritize the accomplishment of core organizational values (such as exceptional performance, continuous learning, individual wellbeing, and individual engagement) over short-term profit gains.
- A *process precept* is indicated when governors, for example, refer mainly to the organizational processes for arriving at decisions or achieving project objectives. For standard situations, trust in the process is higher than in the individuals' own ways of doing their work. This is often found in high-risk industries, such as for airline pilots, firefighters, and the like.
- A *project precept* is indicated when the governors mainly refer to the project and its viability, the success of its deliverables, and the importance of the project outcome for the organization. Thus, the project is at the center of governmentality, which may demand flexibility in processes, values, or other of the above mentioned items.

Significant differences were found among the companies we investigated. A trend we identified is that smaller organizations tend to prefer a values precept in their attempt to acknowledge the individual employees and align them with organizational objectives. Medium-sized organizations tend to prefer a process precept, as they are often driven by short-term profit objectives. Organizing their business mainly by projects is felt to be too expensive for them. Large organizations tend to prefer a project precept, which emphasizes the need for the project's product or service to accomplish objectives in the market, as well as adhere to legal and other requirements during the life cycle of the project.

Sovereignty

Sovereignty is one of the most basic tenets of governance. It relates to the supreme power or authority in governance. Originally describing the rights to autonomy, mutual recognition, and control of the member states in the "Peace of Westphalia" in 1648 (Krasner, 2001), it is nowadays often defined in terms of internal control and external autonomy. In more practical terms, it refers to authority. Ayoob (2002, p. 82) defines it as "the right to rule over a delimited territory and the population residing within it," where the execution of this right has implications for the standards of behavior within and across societies. Since its invention, the concept has developed further. Examples include its extension to multilevel governance, such as in the European Union (EU). In that context, the focus of the discourse shifted from process

Private Sector Practices   117

to polity, which means, from discussing the EU and the European integration, the focus shifted to the EU's existence as a fact, where "the alleged *sui generis* character of the institution is kept in place" (Aalberts, 2004, p. 27).

In the context of project-related governance, the concept of sovereignty addresses the right to rule in and over individual projects as temporary organizations that bring about change (in the sense of Turner & Müller, 2003). Sovereignty applies here to several levels, such as in the right to autonomy of and ruling within both a single project and a program or portfolio of projects. This includes mutual recognition of projects within the organization and mutual control through resource sharing at governance levels, such as program and portfolio management. The concept of sovereignty is therefore broader in scope than autonomy, as it also addresses mutual recognition and external control.

In a series of studies we identified sovereignty of the project as a key concept that is important for the success of projects (Müller, Shao, & Pemsel, 2016; Müller, Zhai, Wang, & Shao, n.d.). Here, sovereignty was defined and measured in terms of the project manager role, such as being allowed to act outside the limitations set by the job description, negotiating on behalf of the project, assuming decision-making authority, acting entrepreneurially, and lending resources to other projects. Moreover, we measured the extent this was supported by an appropriate communication infrastructure.

Project manager role refers to the expected behavior by the governance system. A distinction is made between three major roles: *employee*, *manager*, or *entrepreneur*. The *employee* role limits the project manager's behavior to the fulfillment of tasks in a merely prescribed manner, combined with limited decision-making authority. The *manager* role refers to a slightly wider scope, which includes decisions on the resources and processes to be employed, with the governance system expecting merely a risk-averse behavior (Amihud & Lev, 1981), and application of professional and predictable decision-making heuristics (Busenitz & Barney, 1997). The *entrepreneur* role includes autonomous decisions on supplier contracts, negotiating resource priority with portfolio management, etc. It includes responsibility for the project in its entirety as a business and the right to decide on behalf of the project as long as it stays within the limitations set by the steering group or other governing bodies. This includes a wide scope of tolerated behaviors, such as those for risk taking and decision making (Begley & Boyd, 1987; McGrath, MacMillan, & Scheinberg, 1992). The results show that, on average, project managers are expected to act as managers and entrepreneurs, with the managerial role and its decision making on behalf of the project being expressed strongest, followed by the entrepreneurial role in terms of negotiation, entrepreneurial decision making, and lending resources. Least expressed is the employee role.

Infrastructure refers to the provision of supportive communication infrastructures by the governance system, which allows the execution of the granted levels of autonomy and authority. Examples include schedules for meetings, reviews, and events that are supportive of the project manager's

118 *Ralf Müller*

role and negotiation needs. Organizations that are successful with their projects have a significantly better developed infrastructure.

Through the above dimensions, we approximate sovereignty at the level of project manager as a combination of expected role and related authority in decision making, both within the confines of an established organizational communication infrastructure.

Governance Mechanisms

Trust and control are frequently referred to as the two mechanisms through which governance is exercised (Das & Teng, 1998; Dyer & Chu, 2003). Chapter 11 provides a detailed review of the two concepts.

Control, "the power to influence or direct people's behavior or the course of events" (*OxfordDictionaries*, 2014), represents the measurable, rational element in an evaluation (Eisenhardt, 1985), as in governing projects. It is often seen to supplement the subjective element of trust in governance. It is the primary governance mechanism in control-related definitions of governance, such as governance being a collection of control mechanisms (e.g., Larcker & Tayan, 2011), a system by which companies are directed and controlled (Cadbury, 1992), or a control function with the aim of balancing organizations' economic and social objectives as well as individual and communal objectives (Cadbury, 2002). Understanding governance predominantly as a control function is indicative of an underlying agency perspective (see Chapter 4). This leads to governance structures that aim to reduce the risk of hazards through formal control mechanisms (Williamson, 1991), for example, by enforcing process compliance, or "behavior control" (Ouchi, 1980), from its employees.

Trust is the "willingness of a party to be vulnerable to the actions of another party based on the expectation that the other will perform a particular action important to the trustor, irrespective of the ability to monitor or control that other party" (Schoorman, Mayer, & Davis, 2007, p. 712). It is a psychological state of a person, which impacts attitudinal, perceptual, behavioral, and performance outcomes (Dirks & Ferrin, 2001). It builds on a person's initial propensity for trust and prior experience, and is subsequently nurtured in collaboration among parties (Clases, Bachmann, & Wehner, 2003) and is based on relationship and prior experience.

Studies have shown that trust has the potential to reduce transaction costs in organizations, as it allows the reduction of control efforts (Das & Teng, 1998; Dyer & Chu, 2003). However, Nooteboom (1996) reminds us that increasing trust also increases the risk for opportunism, especially in temporary endeavors, such as projects, where the opportunistic behavior may remain unnoticed until the end of the endeavor. Hence, it will be risky to abandon control completely in the favor of trust.

The relationship between the two mechanisms of trust and control is still under debate (Hoetker & Mellewigt, 2009). However, the Organization for Economic Co-operation and Development (OECD), which defines governance as both a control function and a relationship between the managers and the shareholders of an organization (OECD Publishing, 2004), with the latter implying a level of trust, refers to the irreducibility of governance mechanisms to either trust or control alone. The two concepts are not mutually exclusive, but in a complex and non-linear relationship (Clases et al., 2003; Pinto, Slevin, & English, 2009). In terms of governance theories, trust as a governance mechanism indicates a stewardship perspective of the governing party (Davis, Schoorman, & Donaldson, 1997), assuming a pro-organizational and collectivistic attitude of actors, driven by a desire to accomplish mutually accepted goals.

Governance Institutions

This refers to the number of institutions (or organizational entities) in support of project-related governance. Examples include PMOs in their various roles of governing and managing projects in an organization, as described by Aubry and her colleagues (e.g., Aubry, Müller, & Glückler, 2012), or steering groups, program and portfolio management, or external governance bodies, such as national or industry standards, etc. The concept of institutions refers here to those entities that have a saying in the governance of projects in organizations. This measure (i.e., number of institutions) was chosen because it is indicative of the complexity in governance structures. Complexity increases with the number of institutions, as it requires the reconciliation of different governance approaches at the project level and coordination of their activities. Examples include the quality-related approaches from tactical PMOs, as opposed to the enterprise-wide approaches from strategic PMOs, or the industry-specific approaches from industry standards, etc. Every additional governance institution poses an additional agency problem to the project, arising from the need to agree and maintain performance in line with the terms of reference under which each of those institutions engage (Dixit, 2009). The pharmaceutical industry, for example, employs a variety of governance institutions both internal and external to the individual pharmaceutical organization. These institutions need to be synchronized for an overall governance of the projects in an organization. Another example is described by Aubry et al. (2012) in the context of a telecommunication provider that uses a network of several hundred PMOs to manage its projects. This network needs governance, for example, through PMO-specific mission statements to synchronize work across the network. In summary, we use the number of governance institutions as a proxy for complexity in governance. Empirical investigations showed us that project management is typically governed by a limited number of governance institutions.

120　*Ralf Müller*

Therefore, we use a scale of low (none or only one institution, e.g., a steering committee), medium (two or three), or high (more than three).

Projectification

A major contextual factor for organizational project governance is the extent to which projects are seen as a business principle, that is, as a way to conduct business and execute daily work in the organization. This is often referred to as projectification.

Projectification is a term originally coined by Christoph Midler in the 1990s and further developed by Lundin et al. (2015). The latter conceptualize projectification as a societal phenomenon of increased project thinking. They trace its development back to the 1960s, when modes of manufacturing started to become challenged through specialized business support firms, which offered their services to manufacturing firms on a project-by-project basis. This was followed by declining numbers of employees in manufacturing, which was balanced by increasing numbers of employees engaged in project-based business services or self-employment (Lundin et al., 2015).

Midler (1995) describes projectification as an organizational phenomenon, by describing the organizational transition process of the automobile manufacturer Renault from a bureaucratic, functional organization in the 1960s to a project-driven organization in the 1990s. He describes four phases of transition:

1　*Functional organization with informal project coordination in the 1960s.* This is the starting point, where the organizations focus on mass production with only a few projects, typically coordinated by top management, such as the CEO.
2　*Centralized project coordination from 1970 to 1988.* Under the pressure of changing and uncertain markets, organizations develop more responsive organization structures. Project coordinator and project committee roles are established, where the former collect data for faster decision making by the latter.
3　*Empowerment and autonomy of the project management structure in 1989.* The position of project management is established, with status and power equivalent to other management functions. Decision-making authority and autonomy of project managers is increased to ensure project success through more entrepreneurial behavior. Simultaneously, the communication structures were matched to those of the existing vertical structures.
4　*Transforming the permanent processes of the firm from 1989 onwards.* Project management and line management were transformed into complementary units, which balanced the permanent processes and departmental structures with those of projects. Related changes include new performance measures, career paths, status of projects, etc.

Chapter 15 of this book provides a case study of projectification in a pharmaceutical company. More details of the transformation and the associated implications can be found there.

The process described above and in Chapter 15 shows that projectification involves much more than changing organizational structures and management processes. It is a fundamental organizational transformation (Aubry et al., 2012), which starts with projects being a tool to implement organizational strategies and continues to projects becoming an element of the organizational strategies, including their programs and portfolios. Its continuation to the next stage, which addresses higher organizational levels, is known as "programmification" and is described by Maylor, Brady, Cooke-Davies, and Hodgson (2006).

These changes come at the cost of intra-organizational tensions, primarily created by the coexistence and codependence of inherently different structures and processes in line functions versus projects, and their competition for limited organizational resources and different planning horizons (Arvidsson, 2009).

This symbiosis of permanent (line or functional) organization and temporary (project) organization is set up to achieve the strategy of the organization. For this to work, the permanent organization needs to carefully design the context for the temporary organization to sustain. This includes project governance, institutions, and governmentality approaches, which must be enabled by the permanent organization in order to run projects efficiently and effectively (Müller, Pemsel, et al., 2014). Each level of projectification requires an idiosyncratic combination of project governance and its associated organizational enablers in a firm.

Based on the published work by Midler (1995) and Lundin et al. (2015), as well as personal discussion (Midler, 2015), we developed five dimensions to assess projectification at the organizational level:

- *Status of project management*: management's perception about the importance of project management for the achievement of organizational objectives.
- *Projects as a business principle*: including the types of relationships organizations have with their business partners or customers and whether these relations are based on joint projects, or merely handled as operations (like outsourced services).
- *Percentage of business done through projects*: the fraction of business (measured as revenue) stemming from projects.
- *Project mindset and culture*: the extent to which project thinking pervades the organization. For example, do employees, when they talk about their work, refer to the projects or the departments they work for?
- *Career system for project managers*: the existence and execution of career paths, training curricula, etc. for project managers in an organization.

Profiling Governance and Governmentality

Using the dimensions for governance and governmentality listed above, we developed and tested a visualization and profiling tool (see Figures 8.1 and 8.2) based on eight in-depth case studies in Europe and Asia, and then validated it through a worldwide questionnaire with 121 responses. Figure 8.1 shows the average project governance and governmentality profiles for organizations with low, medium, and high levels of project success. Success was measured as the compound of the achievement of time, cost, and quality objectives, as well as the achievement of the project's business objectives and customer satisfaction objectives. Governance profiles of projects in the lowest third of success are shown as a dotted line, the inner third of success as a dashed line, and the top third as a solid line.

Figure 8.1 shows that projects with low to medium levels of success tend to be governed along the measures on the left side of the profiling tool, which are ambiguous governmentality approaches with low levels of clarity on how the steering committee wants the project to be managed (neither communicated through directives nor through neoliberal "culture setting"). Approaches to governance vary considerably between low and high levels of sovereignty, paired with the tendency to prioritize control as a governance mechanism. Projectification is low to medium in these organizations.

The average profile of successful projects tends to be more related to the measures on the right side of the tool. Approaches to governmentality are, on average, both neoliberal and authoritative. At first sight, this seems to be contradictory. However, it is indicative of a need for flexibility in governance approaches, which varies by a project's particular circumstances. Just as the adjustment of leadership styles to the particular leadership situation marks a significant improvement in leadership success, it is reasonable to assume

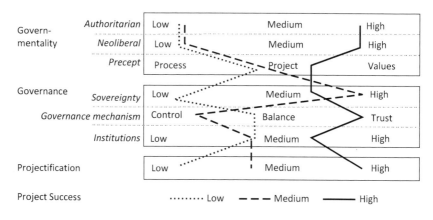

Figure 8.1 Governance Profiles of Organizations at Three Levels of Project Success

that the adjustment of governmentality approaches to governance situations will have a greater impact on governance success. Through the quantitative analyses we found that both approaches, neoliberal and authoritarian, are conceptually and statistically independent from each other (i.e., orthogonal factors), and both correlate strongly with project success. When testing all the governance and governmentality dimensions listed in Figures 8.1 and 8.2 against project success (with projectification as a control variable), a correlation of 53% (p=0.000) between these two approaches and project success was found. Thus, there was a moderate relation between governance/governmentality and project success (Hair, Babin, Money, & Samouel, 2003). In successful projects, the precept in governmentality is the project, which means the governance institutions mainly reference the wellbeing of the project and its product or service as a means to govern the project.

Governance in successful projects allows for medium levels of sovereignty, paired with high levels of trust as governance mechanisms. No difference was found in the average number of governance institutions (typically three: steering committee, owner/customer, and PMO). Successful projects appear to be found more in a context of highly projectified organizations.

Figure 8.2 shows the average profile of organizations with low, medium, and high levels of success in their project-based part of the organization. This reflects the governance of projects. Related success measures center on the achievement of annual plans, as well as customer and employee satisfaction levels. Similar to the project measures, this figure shows that organizations with low to medium levels of success apply more ambiguous approaches to governmentality, with low to medium levels of clarity (both in directives as well as context setting). Governance approaches vary widely and are in part contradictory, such as the combination of high levels of sovereignty and

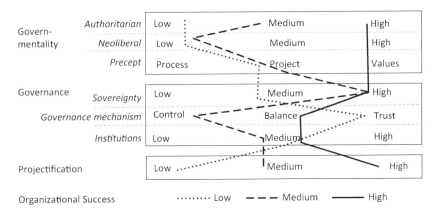

Figure 8.2 Governance Profiles of Organizations at Three Levels of Organizational Success

124 Ralf Müller

control as governance mechanisms. As before, these organizations show low to medium levels of projectification.

Organizations successful in their project-based part prefer approaches toward the right side of the profiling tool. That includes both neoliberal and authoritative governmentality, a focus on organizational values, and high clarity in the ways the project should be managed. Approaches to governance include high levels of sovereignty, paired with a balance between trust and control as governance mechanisms, and about three governance institutions. These organizations tend to be highly projectified.

The contribution of strategic practices to the four governance principles is manifold. Transparency is supported through clarity in governmentality approaches and the associated clarity with which governors make their expectations understood, as shown in Figures 8.1 and 8.2. Transparency is also supported through clarity on the type of precept selected by the governance system. Governance-related contributions to transparency are through sovereignty, which provides for transparency on the organizational positioning of projects, mechanisms that allow for transparency of the control system, and institutions for transparency in work methods (such as those provided by PMOs). In a similar vein, all strategic dimensions contribute to clearer accountability and responsibility. Examples include PMOs as institutions that often define the responsibilities of project managers and the steering committees as institutions accountable for project results. Fairness is indirectly supported through more transparency of practices, such as in governance and governmentality approaches, precepts, and mechanisms.

The Relationship Between Strategic and Tactical Practices

The division of this chapter into strategic and tactical practices for governance and governmentality brings up the question of their relationship. To answer this question, we look at the strategic practices and their related tactical expressions.

At the strategic level we identified the governance and governmentality dimensions and projectification as a context factor. To that end, we focus on governance and governmentality.

Governmentality at the strategic level was described as a combination of liberal, authoritative, and neoliberal approaches, combined with a precept of process, project, or organizational values. Governmentality practices at the tactical level were described as the level of self-responsibility and open systems thinking of individuals. To that end, the choice and strength of the strategic governmentality approach appears to influence the level of self-responsibility in project managers' actions at the tactical level. We described the governmentality approach as contingent on the idiosyncrasies of the projects and their context, such as more neoliberal approaches in community-based open source development projects versus more authoritarian approaches in large-scale infrastructure projects. The clarity of governor expectations, whether instilled through authoritarian or neoliberal approaches, or a combination of the two, sets the framework for managers of individual or groups of projects to assume a level of self-responsibility for the execution of their tasks, and thereby the extent of tactical level governmentality. The chosen governmentality approach allows project managers to develop (or constrain) their level of thinking of their organization and projects as open systems with various internal and external interfaces, skills, and opportunities that can be combined and developed to manage their day-to-day business.

A lever for the implementation of these governmentality approaches for the benefit of the project's and organizational results is the precept. Similar to the mechanisms (trust and control) in governance (described below), the precept is a point of reference for the particular way governmentality is implemented and executed in an organization. The choices of process, project, or organizational values are contingent on a number of factors. Examples include the relative importance of people, processes, and business results, the existence and quality of processes, the extent to which projects can be planned in advance, the skills levels of the people working in projects, the nature of the business and of the projects, the type of leadership in the organization, and so forth.

Governance at the strategic level was described as consisting of sovereignty, governance mechanisms, and institutions. The extent of sovereignty at the strategic level links with the tactical governance elements of autonomy to negotiate on behalf of the project as well as the underlying infrastructure to allow for this to happen. Higher levels of sovereignty of projects relate to more autonomy of project managers. Similarly, greater numbers of institutions support the institutionalization of governance: this is shown in the many studies that describe PMOs as the institutions to develop and implement project management methodologies, best practices, and reporting and reviewing standards. These developments are then used by other governance institutions, such as steering committees, to conduct reviews, or portfolio managers, to align projects with the business. The governance mechanisms of trust and control support the execution of the two governance dimensions of sovereignty and institutions. Both sovereignty and the work of and with institutions can be governed through trust, control, or a combination of both. Thus, the choice of strategic level governance mechanisms governs the particular tactical level practices in execution of autonomy and the work of governance institutions.

Table 8.1 summarizes the relationships between strategic and tactical practices and the mechanisms that link them.

This chapter outlined the strategic and tactical practices of governance and governmentality in the private sector. The next chapter addresses the practices in the public sector.

126 *Ralf Müller*

Table 8.1 Relationship between Strategic and Tactical Practices

	Governance		*Governmentality*
Strategic level	Sovereignty	Institutions	Authoritarian, liberal, neoliberal
Mechanism	Trust/control	Trust/control	Process, project, values
Tactical level	Autonomy	Methodology, PMOs, Steering Groups, Standardization	Self-responsibility, Open systems thinking

References

Aalberts, T. E. (2004). The Future of Sovereignty in Multilevel Governance Europe—A Constructivist Reading. *Journal of Common Market Studies, 42*(1), 23–46. doi:10.1111/j.0021–9886.2004.00475.x

Amihud, Y., & Lev, B. (1981). Risk Reduction as a Managerial Motive for Conglomerate Mergers. *The Bell Journal of Economics, 12*(2), 602–617.

Arvidsson, N. (2009). Exploring Tensions in Projectified Matrix Organisations. *Scandinavian Journal of Management, 25*(1), 97–107.

Aubry, M., Müller, R., & Glückler, J. (2012). *Governance and Communities of PMOs*. Newtown Square, PA: Project Management Institute.

Ayoob, M. (2002). Himanitarian Intervention and State Sovereignty. *The International Journal of Human Rights, 6*(1), 81–102.

Begley, T. M., & Boyd, D. P. (1987). Psychological Characteristics Associated with Performance in Entrepreneurial Firms and Smaller Businesses. *Journal of Business Venturing, 2*(1), 79–93. doi:10.1016/0883-9026(87)90020-6

Burchell, G. (1991). Peculiar interests: civil society and governing "the system of natural liberty." In G. Burchell, C. Gordon, & P. Miller (Eds.), *The Foucault Effect* (pp. 119–150). Chicago: The University of Chicago Press.

Busenitz, L. W., & Barney, J. B. (1997). Biases and Heuristics in Strategic Decision Making: Diffcrences Between Entrepreneurs and Managers in Large Organizations. *Journal of Business Venturing, 12*(1), 9–30. doi:10.5465/AMBPP.1994.10341736

Cadbury, A. (1992). *The Financial Aspects of Corporate Governance*. London, UK: Gee (a division of Professional Publishing Ltd.).

Cadbury, A. (2002). *Corporate Governance and Chairmanship: A Personal View*. New York, NY: Oxford University Press.

Clases, C., Bachmann, R., & Wehner, T. (2003). Studying Trust in Virtual Organizations. *International Studies of Management & Organization, 33*(3), 7–27.

Clegg, S. R., Pitsis, T. S., Rura-Polley, T., & Marosszeky, M. (2002). Governmentality Matters: Designing an Alliance Culture of Inter-organizational Collaboration for Managing Projects. *Organization Studies, 23*(3), 317–337.

Das, T. K., & Teng, B. S. (1998). Between Trust and Control: Developing Confidence in Partner Cooperation in Alliances. *Academy of Management Review, 23*(3), 491–512.

Davis, J. H., Schoorman, F. D., & Donaldson, L. (1997). Toward a Stewardship Theory of Management. *Academy of Management Review, 22*(1), 20–47.

Dean, M. (2010). *Governmentality: Power and Rule in Modern Society* (2nd ed.). London, UK: SAGE Publications.

Dinsmore, P. C., & Rocha, L. (2012). *Enterprise Project Governance*. New York: AMACOM.

Dirks, K. T., & Ferrin, D. L. (2001). The Role of Trust in Organizational Settings. *Organization Science, 12*, 450–467.

Dixit, A. (2009). Governance Institutions and Economic Activity. *The American Economic Review, 99*(1), 5–24.

Dyer, J. H., & Chu, W. (2003). The Role of Trustworthiness in Reducing Transaction Costs and Improving Performance: Empirical Evidence from the United States, Japan, and Korea. *Organization Science, 14*(1), 57–68. doi:10.1287/orsc.14.1.57.12806

Eisenhardt, K. (1985). Control: Organizational and Economic Approaches. *Management Science, 31*(2), 134–149.

Franck, E., & Jungwirth, C. (2003). Reconciling Rent-Seekers and Donators—The Governance Structure of Open Source. *Journal of Management & Governance, 7*(4), 401–421.

Hair, J. F., Babin, B., Money, A., & Samouel, P. (2003). *Essentials of Business Research Methods*. Hoboken, NJ: John Wiley & Sons Inc.

Hoetker, G., & Mellewigt, T. (2009). Choice and Performance of Governance Mechanisms: Matching Alliance Governance to Asset Type. *Strategic Management Journal, 30*(10), 1025–1044. doi:10.1002/smj

Klakegg, O. J., & Haavaldsen, T. (2011). Governance of major public investment projects: in pursuit of relevance and sustainability. *International Journal of Managing Projects in Business, 4*(1), 157–167. doi:10.1108/17538371111096953

Krasner, S. D. (2001). Rethinking the sovereign state model. *Review of International Studies, 27*(5), 17–42. doi:10.1017/S0260210501008014

Larcker, D., & Tayan, B. (2011). *Corporate Governance Matters*. Upper Saddle River, NJ: Pearson Education Inc.

Lemke, T. (2001). The birth of bio-politics: Michel Foucault's lecture at Collège de France on neo-liberal governmentality. *Economy and Society, 30*(2), 190–207.

Lundin, R. A., Arvidsson, N., Brady, T., Ekstedt, E., C, M., & Sydow, J. (2015). *Managing and Working in Project Society*. Cambridge, UK: Cambridge University Press.

Maylor, H., Brady, T., Cooke-Davies, T., & Hodgson, D. (2006). *From projectification to programmification*. International Journal of Project Management, 24(8), 663–674.

McGrath, R. G., MacMillan, I. C., & Scheinberg, S. (1992). Elitists, risk-takers, and rugged individualists? An exploratory analysis of cultural differences between entrepreneurs and non-entrepreneurs. *Journal of Business Venturing, 7*(2), 115–135. doi:10.1016/0883-9026(92)90008-F

MerriamWebsterDictionary. (2015). Strategic. *Merriam Webster Dictionary*. Retrieved December 17, 2015, from http://beta.merriam-webster.com/dictionary/strategic

Midler, C. (1995). "Projectification" of the firm: The Renault Case. *Scandinavian Journal of Management, 11*(4), 363–375.

Midler, C. (2015). *Dimensions of projectification*. Personal communication, 20 February 2015.

Miller, R., & Hobbs, B. (2005). Governance Regimes for Large Projects. *Project Management Journal, 36*(3), 42–51.

128 *Ralf Müller*

Müller, R., Martinsuo, M., & Blomquist, T. (2008). Project Portfolio Control and Portfolio Management in Different Contexts. *Project Management Journal*, *39*(3), 28–42.

Müller, R., Pemsel, S., & Shao, J. (2014). Organizational enablers for governance and governmentality of projects: A literature review. *International Journal of Project Management*, *32*(8), 1309–1320. doi:10.1016/j.ijproman.2014.03.007

Müller, R., Shao, J., & Pemsel, S. (2016). *Organizational Enablers for Project Governance*. Newton Square, PA: Project Management Institute.

Müller, R., Zhai, L., Wang, A., & Shao, J. (2016). A Framework for Governance of Projects: Governmentality, Governance Structure and Projectification. *International Journal of Project Management*. *34*(6), 957–969. http://dx.doi.org/10.1016/j.ijproman.2016.05.002

Nooteboom, B. (1996). Trust, Opportunism and Governance: A Process and Control Model. *Organization Studies*, *17*(6), 985–1010.

Office of Government Commerce. (2005). *Managing Successful Projects with PRINCE 2*. London, UK: The Stationery Office.

Office of Government Commerce. (2008). OGC Governance. *OGC Governance*. Retrieved from http://www.ogc.gov.uk

Ouchi, W. G. (1980). Markets, Bureaucracies and Clans. *Administrative Science Quarterly*, *25*, 129–141.

OxfordDictionaries. (2014). *The Concise Oxford English Dictionary* (12th ed.). Oxford, UK: Oxford University Press.

Pinto, J. K., Slevin, D. P., & English, B. (2009). Trust in Projects: An Empirical Assessment of Owner/Contractor Relationships. *International Journal of Project Management*, *27*(6), 638–648.

Schoorman, F. D., Mayer, R. C., & Davis, J. H. (2007). An Integrative Model of Organizational Trust : Past, Present, and Future T. *Academy of Management Review*, *32*(2), 344–354.

Shenhar, A., Dvir, D., Milosevic, D., Mulenburg, J., Patanakul, P., Reilly, R., . . . Thamhain, H. (2005). Toward a NASA-Specific Project Management Framework. *Engineering Management Journal*, *17*(4), 8–16.

Turner, J. R., & Müller, R. (2003). On the Nature of the Project as a Temporary Organization. *International Journal of Project Management*, *21*(1), 1–7.

Williamson, O. E. (1991). Comparative Economic Organization: The Analysis of Discrete Structural Alternatives. *Administrative Science Quarterly*, *36*, 269–296.

9 Governance in Public Projects
The Norwegian Case

Ole Jonny Klakegg and Gro Holst Volden

This book mainly focuses on governance through the lenses of private sector organizations and projects. In this chapter, we try to supplement and contrast this perspective with a description of governance in public sector projects and the differences these represent. One main point highlighted is the use of governance frameworks implemented to secure successful investment projects. Throughout this chapter, Norway will be used as the main example. The reason for this is not only that both authors are Norwegian with wide experience doing research on Norwegian public projects, but also because Norway is a pioneer in the area of governance of public projects, having introduced a governance scheme applied to all the largest state-funded investment projects across sectors, with external quality assurance of the planning documents as the essential element.

The overall objective is to develop front-end management and project governance as an academic subject. Project governance as seen from the financing party's perspective has long been neglected in project management. In recent years, it has been widely recognized that there is a need for a more holistic and interdisciplinary orientation with a specific focus on the front-end stages of a project. This chapter aims at contributing to this by reporting the practices and results achieved in Norwegian public projects.

Public Sector—Governance for the Common Good

An Overview of Recent Developments

In this book, most of the chapters focus on the private sector, but this chapter aims at filling in the gap with regards to the public sector, to indicate differences and similarities between private and public sectors in terms of governance relating to projects.

One obvious characteristic that defines the difference between public and private is ownership: the public sector consists of organizations owned by the federal, state, regional, or municipal authorities. Private interests own private sector organizations. Another characteristic is that they are normally under different jurisdictions. A third characteristic lies in what they do: the major issue in the public sector has always been providing basic services needed to develop and maintain society. Public goods, defined by economists as non-excludable and non-rivalrous, are a special case—such goods will not be provided in a free market since it is impossible to make a profit from them. Therefore, they must be provided (not necessarily produced) by the government. But the public sector also provides and produces purely private goods, such as health and education, based on the principle that everyone should have access to them regardless of their income. Someone needs to look after and continue to develop these goods. This is why we have public organizations. The public sector is organized through central, regional, or local government bodies and their agencies, whereas the private sector is organized through many forms of corporations and small businesses or private firms.

A fourth characteristic has to do with incentives: private firms have owners who, precisely because they have invested their own money, have incentives to introduce the necessary regulations and processes that ensure profit maximizing decisions. Since most firms operate in a competitive environment, they have to be efficient and innovative to stay in the market and make profits. Goal achievement is easy to verify, and leaders who do not deliver will have to go. Public enterprises, on the other hand, are financed through taxes (or mandatory fees collected by a monopolist), and cannot go bankrupt. Goal achievement is more difficult to verify and reward, and there is no natural incentive to ensure efficient use of resources in the same way as in the private sector.

We focus on the difference between the private and the public sector. There is, however, a large and growing group of organizations that form 'grey zones' between the public, private, and third sector (Not-for-profit sector, voluntary sector). For example, there are organizations with public ownership that are operated under private sector legislation, 'to be equally efficient,' as some politicians hold. There are private companies operating services on behalf of (and paid by) the government that are normally considered public, 'because the public sector does not have the capacity needed.' There are private sector organizations taking over responsibility that traditionally has been in the public domain, 'so public entities can focus on their most important tasks.' The increasing amount of services bought from private actors in a market is called outsourcing, and we call the tendency to transfer organizations from the public sector to the private sector privatization. We also see new forms of collaboration between public and private organizations emerge—both on a permanent basis (partnering) and in joint ventures (in single projects) across the public–private divide. The point is: the division between the private, public, and third sector is getting more complex and more difficult to define.

Focusing on the public sector, researchers in economics and political science have described the development over the past decades as implementing management models from the private sector in public sector organizations.

Governance in Public Projects   131

The trend started in the US under President Ronald Reagan and in the UK under Prime Minister Margaret Thatcher. Scholars have branded this development 'new public management' (NPM) and it had great influence in Western countries, including Scandinavia (Busch, 2005).

The driving force behind the development that started in the 1980s was a growing awareness that the public sector is growing in scope and cost, and there is a need for making the most out of the available, limited public funding. Traditionally, the tendency was that the public sector took responsibility for the whole value chain, from buying (decision making), owning the resources, financing, and executing the production of services. Now, a wave of changes moved toward buying execution of services in the private sector using market forces as driving forces to increase efficiency. Management theories and methods widely used in the private sector became more common in the public sector, for example, in the use of: goal-oriented tasks and performance measurement, contracts and other regulative means like external control, and relational management and new forms of authority.

Branded post-NPM, a "second-generation reform" or even "rebuilding the State" has since occurred (Christensen, 2009, p. 43). The driving force seems to be a search for more coherence in the public sector, after NPM created a highly disaggregated and fragmented public sector. However, the sum of changes did have a large impact on public and private sectors and the effects are important for the topic of this book: governance related to projects. The biggest change is maybe the change in the use of authority and means to regulate behavior.

Another important and parallel development seen is that project work has had an increasing importance across sectors and industries, including the public sector, as the mode of operation. An increasing portion of the total amount of work is organized as projects, and everyone is involved in projects (Jensen, 2012). According to Andersen (2008), somewhere between a quarter and a third of all value-creation in society is done in projects. Turner et al. (2010, p. 1) state it is close to one-third or US $16 trillion. Projects as a concept have even influenced pedagogy, language, and rhetoric in general, and in specific areas like cultural policy (Velure, 2014). This development in society and the public sector is in itself an interesting issue to study, but not the issue we focus on in this book. We will now look more at some specific differences between public and private sectors that matter when we discuss governance further.

Characteristics of the Private and Public Sector and Their Projects

The following description has many limitations. It is not intended to represent the whole scope of differences and similarities between private and public organizations and their projects. We have chosen some characteristics that we see as relevant to the discussion in this book, and our descriptions

132   *Ole Jonny Klakegg and Gro Holst Volden*

are probably colored by the research we have done from a privileged corner of the world.

As indicated above, the public sector is not looking for profit, but looking out for the common good for society, delivering basic services that everyone is entitled to have access to. This indicates that:

- Organizations in the public and private sector normally have very different goals and measures of success. The public sector obviously has a broad set of goals and corresponding success criteria. The private sector normally has a relatively narrow array of success criteria, and the usual expression of this is financial result, maximizing profits.
- One reason for this is that the public sector has a wide array of external stakeholders. Everyone is a stakeholder in some sense: as a taxpayer, as a consumer of public services, or as a user of public commodities. In comparison, the private sector has (or at least takes notice of) a narrow set of stakeholders.
- The degree of involvement from these external stakeholders is also very different. In the private sector the stakeholders are either 'in' or 'out.' In the public sector, all citizens are stakeholders, even when they actively choose not to be involved. They are often represented by others, indirectly through the media or interest groups, or even through the public agencies placed there to take care of their needs.
- How to organize for taking care of common goods is also an area with a few differences and similarities. Although not necessarily very different in structure, the public sector is associated with a more bureaucratic working modus operandi, whereas the private sector is sometimes described as more able to make quick decisions, with a shorter distance to the decision makers. The difference is probably less important the bigger and more complex the organizations become.
- Mindset is probably a better explanation for differences than formal structures. Having responsibility for a wide array of stakeholders and the sustainability of common goods obviously makes decision making much more complex in a public organization than in a typical private sector organization. Since it is close to impossible to express simple success criteria in the public sector, the decision making is bound to be more time-consuming. It often requires more studies and discussions before a decision can be made. Due to the common interest, and thus a lot of pressure from interest groups and the media, every decision is under more scrutiny in the public sector compared with the private sector. This means every detail matters more, and the chance that someone will criticize is bigger. These factors seem to build up to a mindset that is more directed toward safety (doing the right thing, avoiding criticism) than speed (efficiency).
- Dependence on each other is another aspect that we need to mention here. The public sector cannot, and should not even try, to do everything

Governance in Public Projects 133

in society, for it is completely dependent on a well-functioning private sector as a supplier of vital services. The reverse is also true: the private sector is completely dependent on a well-functioning public sector to be able to develop—not only as customer of their services, but also as a facilitator for commercial business, provider of vital infrastructures, and manager of the common goods that the private sector cannot take care of.

- Decision making is another aspect that differs between the public and private sector. Not only are major decisions more complex and critical in the public sector, but the decision-making process is also very different (or can be—there are many variations here on both sides). Typically, in a Western country there is an element of democracy in decision making. This democracy represents involvement of stakeholders and is a quality assurance (QA) element of great importance. It does have its cost in terms of the time and effort it takes to reach a conclusion. Private sector organizations may, or may not, accept more power to make decisions concentrated in one or a few individuals. We need to consider that there are also cultural elements in decision making and that even within the same organization, whether public or private, there are different ways of reaching a conclusion. There are also differences in who is mandated to make those decisions, how powerful they are, and how easily decisions are changed once they are made.
- Financing is an issue that often comes up in discussions about differences between public and private sectors and major public projects. The public sector is at best robust, with its financing based on taxes. The tax money is far from 'free' financing, but it is a solid platform for investments in good times. This means well administered countries are also creditworthy and able to finance more and cheaper than most other investors. The ability to finance by taxes is more limited on a local level, at least in Norway. In relation to major public projects, we have seen a growing use of local taxes on travelers to finance transport infrastructure in Norway. Private sector investors, on the other hand, may turn to banks and other financial institutions whenever they need more money. If the risk is acceptable, they will have financing at a price set by a financial market. This is obviously different from the public sector. When necessary, the public sector has found room for mixed models. In the 1980s and 1990s, we saw the growth of public-private financing in the UK to help the public sector finance investments in large-scale infrastructure, and the same principle has been tried in Norway, although with a different rationale.
- Projects in the public sector are generally bigger in terms of money and the number of stakeholders than in the private sector. The complexity dimension varies across sectors and may be difficult to use as a distinction between public and private. Criticality or urgency is another dimension that represents a major challenge to governance, but there

134　*Ole Jonny Klakegg and Gro Holst Volden*

is little support to claims that this is basically different in private and public sectors.

- However, there is one similarity we need to remember when discussing the division between public and private sectors: it is basically about human beings with their strengths and weaknesses on both sides of the divide. It has a lot to do with the competence, attitudes, and skills to solve any task at hand, wherever it may be. Individuals and their relations (groups and networks) are the main resource in any value-creating operation.

As indicated above, there are numerous challenges in the difference between public and private sectors that may trigger interesting discussions. For the purpose of this chapter, we need to limit our scope to discuss investment projects, and even focus only on large public investment projects. We will look at the case of major projects financed by the state or municipality. The research we refer to in the remaining part of the chapter is all about how governance is set up in the public sector to make sure good decisions are made and carried out in the form of major public investment projects. The Sugarloaf Alliance Case Study in Chapter 13 illustrates well many aspects of public sector investment projects.

Samset (2003) shows that in order to be a true success, public projects need to perform well strategically, tactically and operationally. The strategic and tactical dimension points toward the need for the solution to be relevant for key stakeholders, not have unacceptable side effects, and to be effective and sustainable. The operational dimension concerns efficiency in the process of creating that result. Further, Samset argues that success in projects needs to be considered at three different levels or perspectives: project, users, and society. The project organization is naturally preoccupied with operational issues and efficiency in transforming resources into results. The users are most dependent on the effect achieved upon taking the result into operation. Society acts as investor and owner, and specifically in the public sector as steward of common goods, and is thus concerned with the relevance and sustainability of the investment.

To secure successful public investment projects, the investing organization needs to ensure some crucial factors: true cost-benefit analysis, transparency, accountability, incentives for efficiency, taking risk into account, preventing rent-seeking from stakeholders, etc. Flyvbjerg, Bruzelius, and Rothengatter (2003) point out that many problems in projects are similar across the public and private sectors, and that enforcing stronger accountability is necessary. They point out the contrast between the private sector, where competition can ensure accountability, and the public sector, which depends on transparency as a means of strengthening accountability.

Governance can be divided into two main types: structure-based governance and relationship-based governance (Klakegg & Meistad, 2014). Structure-based governance typically incorporates five elements: stage gate

Governance in Public Projects   135

approval process, stakeholder representation, formal roles and responsibilities, quality assurance, contracts, and sign-offs (Narayanan & DeFillippi, 2012). Relationship-based governance typically includes non-hierarchical elements, like: leadership, motivation and incentives, resource allocation, trust and ethics, alliances and involvement of stakeholders, informal relations, and communication (Klakegg & Meistad, 2014). Some authors have discussed the relative strength of governance instruments to try to find the right balance between incentives (carrot), regulation (stick), and information (Bemelmans-Videc et al., 1998; Yoshimori, 2005).

The rest of this chapter will focus on governance schemes and their content (regulation, incentives, information). The main focus will be on the Norwegian case, but we will also comment on other countries to illustrate differences. The descriptions will unveil that no organization implements purely structural or purely relational governance. Elements of both are mixed in the pursuit of maximizing value for limited public funds.

Norway and the Governance Framework for Major Public Projects

Norway is a pioneer in the area of structure-based governance of public projects, having introduced a governance scheme applied to all the largest state-funded investment projects across sectors, with external QA of the planning documents as the essential element. No system can be understood as independent from its context. Therefore, we briefly present the country and the context that it represents before we introduce the governance framework itself.

The Context and Background

Norway comprises the western part of Scandinavia, and has a population of about 5 million. The country has an extensive coastline, which is rugged and broken by huge fjords and thousands of small islands. Traditionally, sea-based activities such as fishing, shipping, and shipbuilding have been economically important, and they still are. In the 1960s, petroleum and natural gas reserves were discovered and have since boosted the country's economic fortune.

Norway is a small, open economy, highly dependent on international trade. The country maintains a combination of market economy and the so-called Nordic welfare-model, with high tax levels, high levels of public ownership, and high standards of social welfare. The society's egalitarian values are strong, and Norway is on top of the Human Development Index (UNDP, 2015). Public expenditure accounts for over 40% of the GDP. Generally, this works well with a moderate level of bureaucracy, low levels of corruption, and a relatively good ranking on the Global Competitiveness Index (no. 11 in 2014; see Schwab, 2015). But there are concerns regarding

136 *Ole Jonny Klakegg and Gro Holst Volden*

decreasing productivity levels, not least in the building and construction sector, with low competition, low innovation, too much regulation, and relatively low private ownership (NOU, 2015, p. 1).

Some initiatives have been taken recently to "modernize the public sector," i.e. promoting efficiency, flexibility, and a more user-oriented approach. State ownership has also been addressed, including the need to separate the ownership role from the regulatory functions. However, the great advantage which Norway enjoys as a result of its oil wealth has masked the need for broad reforms, and the incentives to make efficient gains are not strong. Rattsø and Sørensen (2008) describe how the oil wealth has created challenges with demanding citizens and soft budget constraints in public institutions.

There is a clearly articulated goal, agreed upon by all political parties, that people in rural areas should have access to the same public goods and standard of living as people in urban areas. This implies that the state is heavily subsidizing local infrastructure projects. Local co-financing is normally not required—the exception is road projects, where there may be a certain level of user fees. Norway has about 430 municipalities, many of them very small and, in contrast to the state, financially weak. Despite this, the decision processes in public projects are often sectoral and locally based, with strong involvement from local stakeholders.

Volden and Samset (2015) introduced the term "perverse incentives" to describe the imbalance between influence and financial liabilities that would typically result in attempts from local parties to overestimate the benefits and underestimate the costs of 'their' projects. These effects are described by Flyvbjerg and his colleagues as deception (see, for example, Flyvbjerg, Garbuio, and Lavallo, 2009). The problem is complicated further by the fact that Members of Parliament, too, are often heavily involved in, and supportive of, their respective constituencies. Decisions regarding even small- and medium-sized public projects are made at the parliamentary level and are highly "politicized." Whist and Christensen (2011) show how the early phase of state-funded investment projects in Norway is often characterized by "local rationality" and complex coalitions, while the more rational and analytical processes play a minor role. Welde et al. (2013) demonstrate the total lack of correlation between the cost-benefit ratio and project selection, based on more than 200 Norwegian road projects. The OECD (2003) also supports the notion that the informal, consensus-based approach to regulatory processes is not well adapted to evidence-based decision making.

Another problem was the extent of cost overruns in major public projects. The problem received particular attention in 1986, when the new headquarters of the National Bank was being planned. Independent experts raised doubts about the official estimate presented to the Parliament and claimed that it should be five times higher. After the project was completed, it turned out that the external experts were right; the final cost was more than five times the initial estimate.

Governance in Public Projects   137

In short, there has long been a need to introduce stronger incentives for efficiency and cost control, and for increased rationality and transparency in public decision-making processes. The governance scheme for major public projects could, at least indirectly, provide a solution to several of these challenges.

The Governance Framework

The following description is based on Samset and Volden (2013). It should be noted that the scheme is primarily about governance of projects, and not about project governance or governmentality, as per the terminology used elsewhere in this book. Samset and Volden (2013), however, use the term "project governance" as a collective concept including both governance of projects and project governance.

In 1997, the Norwegian government initiated a systematic review of the systems for planning, implementation, and monitoring of large public investment projects. The results were discouraging. Only three of 11 projects were completed within budget; cost overruns for the other eight were as high as 84%. The study concluded that the projects were presented to Parliament at a premature level of investigation with inadequate analyses or analyses based on false assumptions. The study also found a number of factors related to procedures, qualifications, responsibilities, etc.

In 2000, the Ministry of Finance introduced a governance framework applying to major public projects. The main feature was the requirement that major investment projects' cost estimates and management base must undergo external QA before the project was submitted to Parliament for approval and funding (currently known as QA2). A tender was conducted and framework agreements signed with five groups of consultants, all with extensive expertise in project management and project cost estimation, to perform the assessments.

When the framework agreements were renewed in 2005, the scheme was extended to include QA of the choice of conceptual solution prior to the Cabinet's decision on whether to proceed to the pre-project phase (referred to as QA1). The term "concept" refers to the conceptual solution that is chosen to meet a specific societal need. For example, the need to connect an island to the mainland can be solved in different ways; for instance, by constructing a bridge, a subsea road tunnel, or continued ferry transport (the zero option)—in this case, three conceptual alternatives. Rather than start with a chosen project, the idea is to clarify the underlying problem that needs to be resolved, describe the conditions and requirements that will have to be fulfilled, and then identify solutions and assess their feasibility against these conditions and requirements. The ultimate aim is that the chosen concept is the one that is considered the best use of public funds. By introducing QA1, the government recognized that the choice of concept is the most important decision for the State as the project owner. It is at this early stage that benefits and costs are compared to determine a project's viability and societal relevance. The competence requirements for quality assurers were correspondingly extended to include economics and social sciences.

There was now a system with two consecutive control points, QA1 and QA2, preceding two different types of decisions and thus having entirely different contents and perspectives. QA1 is meant to secure tactical and strategic success, and is designed to assess the outcome and long-term benefits, relevance, and viability of the project. QA2 is meant to ensure the operational success, and is aimed to ensure that cost frames (project budgets) are realistic and project outputs are produced on time and in a cost-effective manner. This is illustrated in Figure 9.1. The figure also demonstrates that the input to the QA reviews is essentially produced by the respective government agencies which, in turn, will be responsible for following up on the resulting recommendations. The quality assurers will review the documentation, check for consistency and whether the assumptions are realistic, undertake their own independent analyses, and finally give their recommendations. The decisions are taken at the political level without any obligation to follow the recommendations by the quality assurers.

Subsequent framework agreements signed in 2011 and 2015 have largely been a continuation of this system.

Cost estimates calculated as part of the QA2 scheme are based on stochastic estimation (probability-based numbers). By means of stochastic estimation, using mathematical analytical methods or simulation tools, the result is a cumulative probability distribution of investment cost as in Figure 9.2.

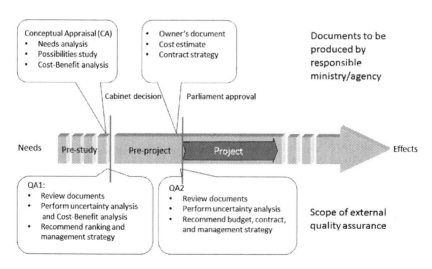

Figure 9.1 Content of the Norwegian Governance Framework for Major Public Projects

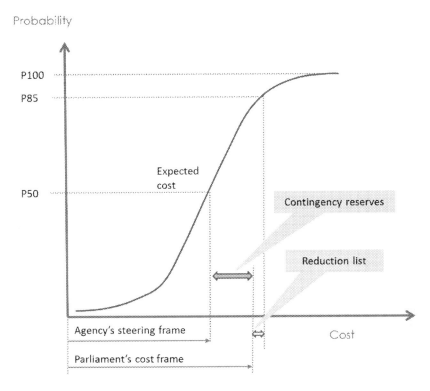

Figure 9.2 Stochastic Cost Estimation: Definition of Key Terms

PX means that there is an X % probability that the final investment cost will be at or below this level. Two key figures are P85 and P50 (the median) for the investment cost, which are estimated by external quality assurers.

The cost frame approved by the Parliament should take into account the anticipated uncertainties related to the implementation. The proposed cost frame is normally P85 minus deductions for possible simplifications and reductions (reduction list) that can be handled during the project if the cost frame is in danger of being exceeded. The budget available to the agency is lower in order to avoid incentives to use contingency reserves and normally corresponds to the median, i.e., P50 on the cumulative probability distribution for the investment cost. (The agency should have a budget for the project manager that is even lower).

The control aspect is essential in the QA2 review, to ascertain that the basis for the cost frame proposed to the Parliament is sufficient. But it also has a forward-looking perspective to ascertain that key challenges in the implementation of the project are identified. It is important that the owner's document defines the needs, objectives, and scope of the project, as well as the key requirements, timeframe, budgets, and uncertainty.

140 *Ole Jonny Klakegg and Gro Holst Volden*

What the Framework is—And What it is Not

In order for projects to reach their goals, many conditions must be met, such as:

i   the basis for decisions is adequate and realistic,
ii the decision-making process is transparent and as rational as possible, and
iii project management and control is satisfactory.

The Norwegian governance framework focuses primarily on condition (i) above. As regards (ii), it affects decision processes only indirectly. The decisions are taken at the political level without any obligation to follow the recommendations by the quality assurers. However, with the requirement that decision documents should adopt a broader societal perspective and be reviewed by an independent third party, the implication in the long run could be that it will be more difficult to get state funding for projects that are economically non-viable or ineffective.

Regarding (iii), neither QA1 nor QA2 affect project management directly. Governance regimes pertaining to major investment projects may be more or less detailed. Previous studies indicate that a good approach for the authorities is to establish general requirements for structures, processes, results, etc., but not interfere in project implementation as such (Klakegg et al., 2009; Samset et al., 2006). The current QA system has established general requirements for the type of documentation that must exist, but does not require that agencies use specific tools, formats, etc. and will not interfere during implementation once the project has been initiated. This is in line with the new public management reform discussed earlier. The idea is that this provides the best preconditions for efficiency.

In principle, the Norwegian governance framework is rather simple, in the sense that it has only two interventions, no detailed requirements, and applies only to the biggest state-funded projects, about 20 each year.

It implicitly assumes that the individual agencies have appropriate procedures for project implementation, including good leadership, tools and techniques, competence and capacity, culture and ethics, and project management practices more generally. However, indirectly, the intention is of course to also promote and improve these elements. The idea is that such an independent review has a disciplining effect and that agencies will take action to improve their practices.

As part of the scheme, there is also an emphasis on exchange of information and experience among civil servants and consultants involved in the scheme. The Ministry of Finance holds a yearly quality assurance forum where different aspects of the scheme are discussed, including the need for guidance concerning the elements in the analyses. The general rule is that the public agencies, such as the Norwegian Public Roads Administration

Governance in Public Projects 141

in the case of road projects, create and follow their own guidelines, but in some areas they might collaborate on the development of joint guidelines and uniform practice. In addition, a trailing research program, the Concept program (presented below), follows the scheme and the projects included in it continuously, helping to identify and disseminate best practices and to develop better tools and methods.

Brief Comparison with Other Countries

Several other countries have established similar formal, cross-sectorial project models for public investment projects in recent years. Samset et al. (2016) describe and compare five models in addition to the Norwegian. See also Klakegg et al. (2015) for a comparison of the schemes in Norway, the Netherlands, and the UK.

Around the turn of the millennium, Norway and the UK were the first to establish stage-gate models requiring QA before certain decision points. The British system is more ambitious, with 4–7 gates, not just in the front-end but also during implementation and after project completion. On the other hand, each assurance in the UK is simpler and less time-consuming, as the quality assurers do not perform their own independent analyses. Also, it is more flexible in the sense that the scope of the assurance and approval process may vary from project to project. Both schemes have developed over time, with increasing focus on the very early stage and the strategic perspective. Other countries, such as Canada (Quebec), Denmark, Sweden, and the Netherlands have since introduced similar schemes, largely inspired by the Norwegian and British models. The original justifications for introducing the schemes differ to some extent (e.g., value-for-money, cost control, faster project implementation).

One of the characteristics of the Norwegian model is the use of private consultants, instead of public employees, to perform the QA. Denmark and the UK also use private consultants, and Quebec did so until recently when a separate public organization was established to deal with QA instead.

Moreover, Norway seems to be alone in using probability-based cost and steering frames. The UK and Denmark use adjustment factors (a proportional factor is added to the base estimate of both time and risk) depending on project type and risk tolerance. Other countries, like Sweden, are more focused on the total cost-benefit analysis than on getting the cost estimate right.

The conditions for financing are also different in each country. Several countries seem to be aware of the problem here labeled perverse incentives. Therefore, in addition to the QA they require co-financing from those who receive the benefits of the projects. For example, the Netherlands requires co-financing from the initiating party as the main principle. The Scandinavian countries generally do not require co-financing.

142 *Ole Jonny Klakegg and Gro Holst Volden*

Practices in Norwegian Public Projects

This section addresses specific issues concerned with governance within the context of projects. Acknowledging that the project is a part of a bigger whole, we need to put it into context: the Norwegian governance framework for major public projects is dominant in the public sector and thus relevant for this section too. This section as a whole will give a summary of the results of the framework and its influence on Norwegian projects, as well as some indications as to why it is so powerful.

Project Governance in Autonomous Public Agencies

The Norwegian project governance scheme is not primarily about project governance. This was clear from when it was first introduced in 2000. It was about strengthening the decision making and control of investments at a higher level (Klakegg, Williams, and Magnussen, 2009, p. 94). The underlying intention was, of course, to improve the performance of individual projects. The focus, however, was on a higher level in the organization—associated with governance of projects (see next section). The idea was that if the owner became more professional in defining projects, setting up a good framework for planning and executing projects, and becoming a more demanding customer, the agencies, project managers, and private sector suppliers would follow and become more professional too (Klakegg, 2010). This has been proven to be a correct assumption. Obviously, all improvements in the period after 2000 did not come because of the introduction of the QA scheme, but there is little doubt that it helped. By introducing demanding requirements at the top of the pyramid, the effect trickled down through the project organization and set higher standards; results improved accordingly (Klakegg et al., 2009; Klakegg et al., 2015; Samset & Volden, 2013).

The Ministry of Finance assumed that the agencies would not accept being told from above how to do their projects. This is consistent with the way the Norwegian Government is organized and the egalitarian Norwegian culture. Therefore, they designed a framework that had few interventions, so that everything in between these controls was up to the agency to decide. During the interventions, on the other hand, the projects are subject to critical scrutiny (Klakegg et al., 2009). This leaves the agencies fully responsible for their own projects and the way they organize and manage their projects, but at the same time gives the ministries assurance that their projects are taken care of well.

In terms of governance, this leaves a lot of flexibility to the agencies. They can find the best ways to plan and execute their projects according to the situation and the needs in their specific area of responsibility. It means, for example, that infrastructure projects are planned and executed differently in the road sector than in the railway sector, and differently again in the sea transport sector and aviation. This approach has its strengths as

Governance in Public Projects   143

well as weaknesses. Among the positive elements is the ability to define best practices for each mode of transport—designed to best fit the technical and organizational challenges in each agency. It also leaves the agency in charge of all aspects of planning and management so that no agency is forced into practices they do not want or see fit for their specific area of responsibility.

On the other hand, the control effort at the two critical decision gates is very demanding, and the different practices in different agencies increase the variety of methods and procedures, which adds to the complexity. The agencies and the project organizations have to put in a lot of effort to accommodate the controls during QA. The QA reports are also powerful and normally seen (by the Ministry of Finance and the decision makers) as an important source of information about the benefits of the investment (in QA1) and the investment cost, risks, and execution strategy (in QA2).

This fine balance between flexibility that leaves the agencies wide room to maneuver in terms of their operational choices and the rigidity of the two QA interventions is challenging but gives good returns. In the Norwegian work culture, this marks the responsibility for each party and allows them the freedom to decide for themselves. Behind this balance of power lies a fundamental balance between trust on the one hand and distrust on the other. If the controls in one of the two major decision gates expose any critical issues that are not adequately dealt with, the QA will not recommend that the project pass into the next phase without meeting the specific requirements proposed by the responsible sectoral ministry (e.g. transport and communication, defense, health and care services) and Ministry of Finance.

The influence of governance on projects works directly through the decisions made and the requirements included in the Norwegian model. To be able to meet the requirements, the projects have to perform certain activities and use practices that are considered proper for the job. These practices are partly adapted from international best practices and partly developed in Norway by the ministries, agencies, consultants, and researchers together—in the Concept research program or one of the other arenas designed for learning and improvement following the QA scheme.

Alignment of strategy and project objectives is a key issue in project governance. The Norwegian scheme addresses this by intentionally giving more of the decision-making power to the central government and high-level political arenas, where it belongs (Klakegg et al., 2009, p. 93). By making crucial decisions on the purpose of the investment, the strategic intent, and the objectives and execution strategies at a high level, along with critical scrutiny that focuses on consistency throughout the planning of the project, the scheme strengthens the alignment between government strategies and project planning and execution. There is still great tension between, for example, local authorities and central authorities over planning preconditions and scope decisions. However, the scheme leaves the final say with the central authorities. This clearly limits the possibility of projects parting from the intended strategy.

Stakeholder Management

There is still tension between stakeholders over how agencies plan and execute projects. As described above there are different practices. There is a widespread tradition for involvement of stakeholders in Norwegian public projects. Directly affected parties are normally taken into consideration, and often they are involved in discussions and even negotiations over premises and solutions. Sometimes, it is they who propose the project in the first place. The planning legislation requires that stakeholders, e.g., neighbors and other affected parties, should have their say in all projects building physical infrastructure. This is independent of the governance scheme and falls either into the period before QA1, as part of developing the conceptual alternatives for choice of concept, or between QA1 and QA2 before the final decision to approve the project, as part of the local approval of the plans.

Major public projects like rail and road projects affect a lot of people. Therefore, rail and road authorities often hold open public meetings and workshops for developing goals and planning. This way, people who want to be involved can have updated information on the projects under development, and this is also a good opportunity for the project to learn about people's expectations and views on suggested solutions. These gatherings have become more common in recent years, and also more professional in format. This practice is not a part of the governance framework, but is compatible with it and has increased transparency in these large, complex projects.

Large building projects and other infrastructure projects take up similar practices. Some beneficial practices are described in the Sugarloaf Alliance Case Study (Chapter 13). This kind of stakeholder involvement has proven a good source of knowledge for the project planners and managers, and positive for stakeholders' understanding of the projects. This is expected to reduce the potential for conflict. On the other hand, it may also increase expectations and thus increase conflict later if expectations are not met. Norwegian media frequently report on such situations in public projects. This is one area where further research could be beneficial; we should know more about the effects of stakeholder involvement on specific projects.

Related to alignment of strategies and projects on the one hand and the freedom for projects to maneuver on the other, we should look at the use of steering committees, project boards, and reference groups in projects. These are organizational entities, or decision-making arenas, specifically connected to one project and hence elements of project governance. The governance framework introduced by the Ministry of Finance contains no rules regarding the organization of projects.

Governance of Projects: Striving for Better Public Decision Making on Major Projects

This section presents the research and documented results of introducing the governance framework in the public sector in Norway.

Governance in Public Projects 145

The Concept Research Program

In parallel with a governance scheme being introduced for major public projects in Norway, a research program was established to accumulate information about the projects over time, develop improved methods of analysis, and study the effects of QA and other measures taken during the front-end phase. The Concept research program is based at the Norwegian University of Science and Technology and funded by the Ministry of Finance, but cooperates broadly with other research and study centers in Norway and abroad in their respective fields. The overall objective of the program is to develop front-end management and project governance as an academic subject.

The Concept research program performs trailing research on major public investment projects in Norway. The first projects that were included in the Norwegian governance framework have been completed and are now in their operational phase. This allows for a preliminary review of how the system works. The presentation below is based on Kvalheim et al. (2015), Samset and Volden (2013), and Welde (2015).

The Projects Subject to the Model

After 15 years of operation (2015), there have been about 220 QA reviews under the framework. About 160 projects have been subjected to QA2, of which 80 are now completed and in their operational phase. The QA1 scheme has been in operation only since 2005, and about 70 projects have so far been through a Conceptual Appraisal (CA) followed by an external QA1 review. None of these projects have been finalized thus far, but 11 projects have reached the QA2 stage.

With few exceptions, the projects subjected to the model represent major public investments with an expected investment cost above the threshold value of approximately EUR 80 million. About half of the projects are within the transport sector (mainly road and rail), and the other half is mostly defense and construction projects and information/communication technology (ICT) projects in different parts of government.

Improved Cost Control on the Portfolio Level

So far the 'hard facts' about the effects of the scheme have been restricted to the effects of QA2. Welde (2015) presents the most recent update of the cost figures for 67 completed projects where the final cost has been established and reported. There are some challenges with the data, not least related to the agencies' reporting, but any discrepancies between the reported and the actual final cost are presumably small and constitute at most no more than a few percent of the total cost (see Welde, 2015).

The data show that 53 of the 67 projects, i.e., 79%, were completed within or below the cost frame. The total net savings for the projects taken as a whole were almost EUR 600 million, or about 7% of the total investment.

The cost frame largely corresponds to the quality assurers' recommendations, i.e., the P85 estimate minus a reduction list. Ideally, therefore, at portfolio level, one would expect that approximately 85% of the projects are delivered within the cost frame, but 79% are rather close. There are no striking differences between sectors, but the defense sector notably has had no projects with cost overruns (100% within the cost frame). Another interesting finding is that there is a slight tendency for cost overruns in the middle period, i.e., projects approved in the period 2004–2008. This may be due to strong cost increases in the construction industry that occurred in this period and that might not have been adequately addressed in the uncertainty analyses. Alternatively, the subsequent Global Financial Crisis of 2007–2008 may have had unforeseen consequences, for example pushing the prices down, helping subsequent projects.

The agencies' project budgets largely correspond to the quality assurers' recommendations, i.e., around P50. With a sufficiently large portfolio we should therefore expect the average for the whole portfolio to be close to P50. The results are approximately as expected. The differences are almost symmetrically distributed around zero, indicating that cost control at the portfolio level is good. The distribution is slightly skewed to the right, however, with 48% of the projects below and 52% above the budget. There is an average positive deviation of 2.8%.

A closer look at the projects shows that not only are the financial results satisfactory, but overall there is a high rate of operational success. Few projects experience delays or shortcomings related to quality and functionality. The projects also seem to be essentially well organized and executed. Most of the risk factors that did materialize were identified in the QA2 reports. However, there are also examples of projects where expensive adjustments and upgrading were necessary in the first few years of operation. This finding shows the importance of focusing on the life cycle cost, and not exclusively on the investment cost. A study of the use of reduction lists in railway projects found that they have limited use as an active tool for controlling costs, since the saved amounts are relatively small and not sufficient to avoid large overruns. The study concluded that to function as intended, the possible reductions must have the support of the relevant stakeholders and be technically and contractually possible to implement in a late phase of the projects (Olsson, 2015).

Caution should be used when comparing these results with the cost overruns from the 1990s. At that time cost frames were not based on stochastic cost estimation and thus not directly comparable with either P50 or P85. However, looking retrospectively, there are clear indications that the situation has improved. What we do know with reasonable certainty is that at the portfolio level, major Norwegian projects today cost what they say in advance that they will cost. This suggests that the QA2 scheme and the methodology used for cost estimation have produced reliable cost estimates.

A More Systematic Approach to Projects in the Earliest Phases

Ten years after the first QA1 report was produced, it is still too early to evaluate the effects of this part of the State Project Model. However, there is little doubt that the quality of the Conceptual Appraisal (CA) reports (see Figure 9.1) has improved steadily over time and that there is a convergence toward a common best practice. The same trend can be observed with the QA1 reports—quality assurers have gained years of experience and shown a positive learning curve. Some reviews in the literature have already examined the performance of the CA/QA1 process in the transport sector and the agencies' experience with the scheme; see, for example, Bjertnæs (2012), Rasmussen et al. (2010), and Statens vegvesen (2012).

These studies suggest that the CA/QA1 process is time and resource consuming, but, overall, the scheme is perceived as useful by the involved agencies. In particular, the scheme provides a more systematic approach to the early identification of project ideas than the previous system. Rather than going straight to selecting road sections and determining a technical solution, planners are forced to take a broader perspective and to discuss societal aspects, which allows ideas to mature and stimulates creativity in the agencies. The QA1 scheme allows the government to have a more direct influence in the early stages of the process in comparison with local stakeholders, who have traditionally had a significant influence, especially in road projects.

However, there is still room for improvement. One in-depth study of 17 projects (Samset et al., 2013) specifically examines how the opportunity space is defined and used in CA reports. A recurring problem is that the conceptual solution has already been selected before the CA process, either because of path dependency in the agencies or political constraints and limitations. Another study (Statens vegvesen, 2012) suggests that quality assurers seem to give disproportionate attention to economic considerations and that they should balance economic viability with the achievement of various political objectives. Finally, some ministries and agencies have drawn attention to the futility of undergoing the full CA/QA1 process in cases where, in their opinion, there are simply no alternatives apart from one feasible conceptual solution.

An important prerequisite for QA1 has been that the quality assurers' recommendations are only advisory and the final decision is a political one. The results so far confirm that this is still the case. In studying the CA and QA1 recommendations and the resulting decisions for the first 70 QA1 projects, trailing researchers have found that quality assurers agree with the agency/sectoral ministry on the ranking of concepts in one third of the cases. In these cases, the Cabinet normally follows that recommendation.

However, in the remaining two thirds of the cases, the quality assurer and the sectoral ministry diverge on the ranking of concepts. The QA1 reports more often recommend the zero alternative or a more economically feasible

148 *Ole Jonny Klakegg and Gro Holst Volden*

concept. In such cases, the Cabinet follows the recommendation by the agency/sectoral ministry more often than the QA1 recommendation, but in other cases, project proposals are withdrawn and sent back to the sectoral ministry for new CA or the Cabinet chooses a completely different concept (Grindvoll, 2015). The fact that political decision makers do not follow the quality assurers' recommendations is not surprising. Public investment decisions in Norway are often complex and highly politicized. The QA1 scheme can ensure only that decision makers are well informed about both alternatives and their economic implications. Over time, however, it may become more difficult to select conceptual solutions that are obviously ineffective and are clearly inferior to other alternatives.

One noticeable impact of the CA/QA1 scheme is that the ministries' opportunity space has been broadened during the appraisal process owing to the advice from quality assurers, as they play a role as not only controllers but also advisers. In several cases, the opportunity analysis in the CA was rejected by the external reviewers, resulting in a second round in the appraisal process, with new conceptual alternatives. In addition, there is reason to believe—although it is difficult to prove—that many of the most poorly conceived investment proposals are now screened out before they even reach the CA/QA1 stage. Such proposals can be rejected early because of the improved processes and procedures in the involved ministries and agencies, which likely constitute the most important beneficial effect of the QA1 scheme.

The governance framework in its current form appears to be suitable for the purpose for which it was designed. However, governance regimes should not be static. They need to be flexible so that they can be altered if they do not work as intended or if changes in operating conditions and characteristics of the projects should necessitate change.

One can also observe significant spinoffs from the framework in terms of increased awareness in government, altered practices, research and new knowledge, skills development and training on front-end management, and governance of major projects. In addition, similar schemes are being introduced also for smaller projects and in other sectors. Several of the biggest municipalities in Norway have introduced similar schemes for their biggest projects. It is the same for investment projects run by health authorities and high voltage electricity transmission and distribution projects, which are not included in the model since they are not owned by the state directly, but by state-owned enterprises. There is also diffusion to other countries as discussed above.

Cultural Aspects of the Norwegian Public Sector

If there is one thing that sticks out in the descriptions above, it is the importance of people as individuals and in groups. As indicated in the characterization of the public sector in the beginning of this chapter, people and

Governance in Public Projects   149

culture may be of specific importance in the public sector. This is useful for explaining some aspects of why the Norwegian model actually works.

Changes do influence the Norwegian government, as described in the introduction to this chapter, but the Norwegian society, government, and culture have remained stable during the past couple of decades. Strong democratic tradition, good economy, egalitarian culture, and a population with a high level of education are among the factors that explain this. The Norwegian work culture and overall regulation and organization of work life, including a strong position of workers' rights, are also a part of the explanation. These stability factors build a strong platform for organizing tasks as projects.

Integration is a key issue in making structural and relational governance work in any context, and not least in major public projects. Alignment between organizational structures and cultures in order to avoid a mismatch between formal structures and people's behavior has been a guiding principle in the development and implementation of the model.

Looking back at the reported problems before the introduction of the Norwegian governance scheme in 2000 (Berg et al., 1999; Klakegg et al., 2010), some of the problems were structural in nature: Every department of government had its own decision-making structures and budgeting routines. There was little to connect them across the sole responsibility of each Minister. The scheme introduced a common structure by which governance could be addressed, further developed, and made valid across the whole area of application. It has even proven influential beyond the area of application through a 'trickle down' effect that makes it influential also at a regional and municipal level (Welde et al., 2015). An even wider range of public organizations introduces similar structures and requirements, and the private sector fulfills these requirements as suppliers to public customers.

Given the poor performance of the Norwegian public projects in the 1990s, one would imagine the introduction of improvement measures like the QA scheme would be non-controversial. This was not the case. On the contrary, it challenged the traditional independence of each minister and agency, and even the culture of egalitarian independence that is deeply rooted in Norwegian work life. There was opposition (Berg et al., 1999), but over just a few years, the good results of the QA scheme convinced first the professionals, then the leaders in government agencies that this was an improvement. An interesting observation is that top management in both the ruling parties and the opposition parties had a strong focus on the major public projects in this early period, which may have helped the projects to achieve better results. The first projects under the new scheme had good top management support, access to the best individuals (project managers and experts), and generous investment budgets. After a few years, the conditions for projects normalized, but by then the results had convinced most parties, and as shown above the good results have continued.

Norwegian work culture can be characterized as egalitarian and independent, meaning people in formal positions are given a fair amount of room to

150 *Ole Jonny Klakegg and Gro Holst Volden*

maneuver within their area of responsibility. They do not like to be told how to do their job. Similarly the framework is not a detailed recipe for how agencies should do project management or solve other aspects of planning and execution of projects. This was also a conscious choice. Copying best practices from other countries or the private sector is held to be ineffective in this context and was never considered an option. However, learning from the private sector and other industries (oil and gas industries in the Norwegian case) is held to be important.

The development of the governance framework is done with respect to the specific conditions in Norwegian public projects and work life. Agencies and project managers need to have the opportunity to choose or develop their own practices. They can select whatever best practices they find suitable as long as they meet the performance requirements in the two QA gates of the Norwegian governance framework. Experience over the past decade shows that the projects and agencies are increasingly choosing to implement international best practices and share experiences of their own free will. One of the arenas for doing this is the Concept research program, and another is ProjectNorway (a research-based collaboration of members that consists of project-based organizations from the private and public sectors).

This combination of free choice and the modern willingness to take part in networks and communities of practice is important in terms of building a strong platform for governance. These networks are resourceful because organizations and individuals come together and learn from each other by sharing knowledge and experience. The effect is improved performance in each organization and in individual projects, but it also has a strong effect in terms of leveling out differences and strengthening good practices across organizations. We need to mention a couple of cultural factors in this context: Norway is a small country. Together with egalitarianism, this opens up for close relations and sharing across organizations. The level of trust in work relations (inside an organization and across organizational borders) is generally high. The resulting Norwegian work culture is traditionally very open, in some aspects even bordering on being naïve (lately there have been indications that this may be changing).

Finally, one cultural element, which also has a legal aspect, is that the Norwegian attitude is that the system bears more responsibility than the individual. The Scandinavian model is slightly different from, for example, the Anglo-American tradition. Instead of blaming the individual when things go wrong, we blame the system. For example, the Norwegian State is responsible for the actions of its employees. The State can be sued, but not the individual. On the other hand, the State can seek restitution from its employee, but this rarely happens unless there is a case of proven fraud (Klakegg et al., 2010, p. 93). This adds to the openness in the work culture, since there is less opportunity for losing a job over a case of miscommunication. The public sector is also obliged to keep all its communications open as per the Freedom of information legislation, which is generally strongly upheld in Norway. Article 100 of the Constitution gives access to public documents. The basic principle of the law is that everyone has the right to access State and municipal documents and to be present at sittings of courts and elected assemblies.

The advantage of this cultural setting is that knowledge and experience flow across organizations, and this helps strengthen governance and management in both the public and private sector. The disadvantage is that it also makes it possible for people to move relatively easily between the different sectors and organizations, thus creating a lack of continuity in the public sector. The extent of this challenge, however, is beyond the scope of this chapter.

The Norwegian workforce is well educated and disciplined. This has enabled a Norwegian work life that allows mindful and self-organizing individuals and teams. It is not supportive of hierarchical power and formal structures. Instead, it makes any attempt to use structural means without careful consideration of the relational and human aspects difficult. The powerful position that the governance initiative for Norwegian State projects has is only possible because the Ministry of Finance was aware of this from the beginning and made good choices. The result has been a governance initiative that has kept its fundamental structure unchanged since 2005 but with a constantly developing and improving content and maturing practice.

Conclusion

The purpose of this chapter is to address the differences between the public and private sectors and the consequences of these differences in terms of project governance and governance of projects. It does this by presenting a perspective of the public sector that shows how it is different from the private sector, which is the focus of the rest of the book. The specific case presented here is the Norwegian governance framework for major public projects. The last part of the chapter complements the description of the governance framework with the documentation of its results in terms of influence on project governance and governance of projects.

The Concept research program and other published material by researchers and professionals involved in the development of the framework document the effect of the initiative. In light of the concepts promoted by this book, this research addresses both project governance and governance of projects, and also indirectly governmentality. Structural governance has been given more attention than other aspects in this research. Structural governance is easier to address due to its formal character and visible elements, as shown in the Norwegian case. However, relational governance may be just as important in implementing effective governance and needs further study.

A high degree of formalization characterizes the public sector compared with the private sector. The flexibility to make quick decisions and take

152   Ole Jonny Klakegg and Gro Holst Volden

action is lower. This hampers decision making at the strategic and political levels, but it is also one of the reasons why projects are so popular: projects actually help this situation. By giving projects access to resources and room to maneuver, they can be made efficient, like in the private sector. The descriptions of the Norwegian culture, government, and the governance approaches to projects show a predominantly non-authoritarian approach to governmentality. We find that authoritarian approaches would be counterproductive in the given culture and environment. To that end, the neoliberal governmentality approach chosen for the Norwegian work life and public sector is a vital part of the success of projects and project management.

The success story told here leaves out some improvement initiatives taken by the industry itself, and the improved technological and educational effort made by organizations in both public and private sectors during the same period. It is also worth noticing that this initiative has proven its qualities in this specific Norwegian context, and that any attempt to copy its success needs to consider carefully how to address the specific conditions in other situations. Just copying the whole or parts of this initiative and implementing them under other circumstances will probably not prove a success, neither in the short-term nor the long-term. The Norwegian governance framework does not solve every problem or answer every question related to public projects. However, the Norwegian case illustrates the strengths of the governance concepts promoted by this book.

As previously mentioned, 'good governance' includes four principles that constitute sustainable and ethical project governance, namely, transparency, accountability, responsibility, and fairness (Millstein, Albert, Cadbury, Feddersen, & Tateisi, 1998). The Norwegian governance framework introduced here has a significant influence on all these dimensions of public projects.

In terms of transparency, the governance framework itself requires an almost total openness and transparency, not only about who makes the decisions, but also on what basis and how. Every project above the activation threshold is critically scrutinized by external experts with no previous connection to the project. By publishing every assessment made in QA1 and QA2, there is no doubt that all the involved parties will act professionally and perform to their best. All mistakes or omitted aspects will be critically reviewed and known among governors, customers, and pairs—a very strong motivation to do the right thing. In line with this principle of transparency, the infrastructure agencies have developed practices that involve stakeholders far more than before, adding to the transparency and opening up to the affected neighbors and the general public.

In terms of fairness, the governance framework contributes by ensuring that all relevant aspects of the project are considered in comprehensive concept assessments with reference to the positive and negative effects for all relevant parties in society. Specifically, themes like external effects of these public investments, disadvantages for neighbors and the local

Governance in Public Projects   153

community, accessibility for the disabled, and other aspects of fairness are explicitly challenged. Unfair effects will be assessed and weighted against the ultimate objective: whether the disadvantages are ethically acceptable given the positive and intended effects on the greater society. Certainly, there are aspects of these considerations that are not purely objective, for the political aspect of decision making allows room for value-based considerations when it comes to the final decision. All involved (professional) parties are highly aware of this aspect that limits the power of rational analysis.

Responsibility is a key aspect of the governance framework. In the Norwegian case it is anchored at the highest political level at the Prime Minister's office, and represents a clear line of responsibility down through levels of organization to the agency responsible for executing the project. By means of the 'trickle down' effect, this responsibility is made effective also at the lower levels of the organization. However, there is no active element in the governance framework that ensures this responsibility is promoted all the way down through contracts to those physically performing the activities on the ground. These details are left to the agencies and their project managers to handle professionally. This is one area where there is room for improvement, and lately, social responsibility has become a focus in Norwegian work life. This development is not a result of the implementation of the governance framework but more a result of cases of unacceptable business ethics cases being exposed in the media and by professional organizations.

All in all, the strengthened transparency, fairness, and responsibility add up to an increased level of accountability in public sector organizations and their projects. Not only do projects deliver within budget, but also more often in time and according to planned standards. Whether there will also be more relevant and sustainable projects is unknown until a significant number of projects are finished after being subject to the QA1 procedure. However, the indications so far are positive, and almost all involved parties acknowledge that the implementation of the governance framework has had positive effects, mostly in line with its intentions.

References

Andersen, E. S. (2008). Prosjektifiseringen av samfunnet [Projectification in Society]. Kunnskapsfrokost, November 6, 2008, BI Norwegian Business School.

Bemelmans-Videc, M., Rist, R., & Vedung, E., (Eds.) (1998). *Carrots, Sticks, and Sermons: Policy Instruments and Their Evaluation.* New Brunswick, NJ: Transaction Publishers.

Berg, P., Andersen, K., Østby, L.-E., Lilleby, S., Styrvold, S., Holand, K., Korsnes, U., Rønning, K., & Johansen, F. (1999). *Styring av statlige investeringer. Sluttrapport fra styringsgruppen.* [Control of State Investments. Final Report from the Steering Group] Oslo, Norway: Norwegian Ministry of Finance.

Bjertnæs, A. M. (2012). Konseptvalgutredninger—intensjon og forbedringer, Masteroppgave i organisasjon og ledelse, NTNU.

154 Ole Jonny Klakegg and Gro Holst Volden

Busch, T. (2005). Grensen mellom privat og offentlig sektor i endring [The Interface Between Private and Public Sector Is Changing]. In Busch, T.; Johnsen, E.; Klausen, K. K. and Vanebo, J. O. (Eds.), *Modernisering av offentlig sector: Utfordringer, metoder og dilemmaer* [Modernization of Public Sector: Challenges, Methods and Dilemmas] (2nd ed., pp. 70–81). Oslo, Norway: Universitetsforlaget.

Christensen, T. (2009). The Norwegian Front-End Governance Regime of Major Public Projects—a Theoretically Based Analysis. Concept report no 23. Concept Research Program, NTNU, Trondheim, Norway. Retrieved November 21, 2015, from http://www.ntnu.no/concept/

Flyvbjerg, B., Bruzelius, N., & Rothengatter, W. (2003). *Megaprojects and Risk: An Anatomy of Ambition.* Cambridge, UK: Cambridge University Press.

Flyvbjerg, B., Garbuio, M., & Lovallo, D. (2009). Delusion and Deception in Large Infrastructure Projects: Two Models for Explaining and Preventing Executive Disaster. *California Management Review, 5*(2) (Winter 2009), pp. 170–193.

Grindvoll, I., & Lise, T. (2015). Hva har skjedd med KS1-prosjektene? Status Per Mars 2015, Concept Working Paper. Concept research program, NTNU, Trondheim, Norway.

Jensen, A. F. (2012). *The Project Society.* Aarhus, Denmark: Unipress.

Klakegg, O. J. (2010). *Governance of Major Public Investment Projects: In Pursuit of Relevance and Sustainability.* Doctoral thesis at NTNU, Retrieved October 15, 2015 from http://ntnu.divaportal.org/smash/record.jsf?pid=diva2:294404

Klakegg, O. J., & Meistad, T. (2014). Individual Relations—The Core Line in Project Based Organizations. Panel 5: *In the Middle of a Crowded Intersection: The Governance of Public and Non-Profit Organizations Facing the Challenge of Balancing Performance, Democracy and Accountability.* Paper in Proceedings. XVIII IRSPM Conference 2014, April 9–11, 2014, Ottawa, Canada.

Klakegg, O. J., Williams, T., & Magnussen, O. M. (2009). *Governance Frameworks for Public Project Development and Estimation.* Newtown Square, PA: Project Management Institute.

Klakegg, O. J., Williams, T., & Schiferaw, A. T. (2015). Taming the 'Trolls': Major Public Projects in the Making. *International Journal of Project Management, 34*(2016), 282–296.

Klakegg, O. J., Williams, T., Walker, D. H. T., Andersen, B., & Magnussen, O. M. (2010). *Early Warning Signs in Complex Projects.* Newton Square, PA: Project Management Institute.

Kvalheim, E., Christensen, T., Samset, K., & Volden, G. H. (2015). Har regjeringen fått et bedre beslutningsgrunnlag? Om effekten av å innføre konseptvalgutredning (KVU) og ekstern kvalitetssikring (KS1 og KS2) for store, statlige investeringsprosjekter. [Has Government Received Better Decision Making Basis? On the Effect of Introducing Concept Choice Assessment and Quality Assurance for Major State Financed Projects.] Concept Working Paper.

Millstein, I. M., Albert, M., Cadbury, A., Feddersen, D., & Tateisi, N. (1998). *Improving Competitiveness and Access to Capital in Global Markets.* Paris, France: OECD Publications.

Narayanan, V. K., & DeFillippi, R. (2012). The Influence of Strategic Context on Project Management Systems: A Senior Management Perspective. In T. M. Williams, & K. Samset (Eds.), *Project Governance: Getting Investments Right* (pp. 3–45). Basingstoke, UK: Palgrave Macmillan.

Governance in Public Projects 155

NOU. (2015). Produktivitet—grunnlag for vekst og velferd—Produktivitetskommisjonens første rapport.

OECD. (2003). The OECD Review of Regulatory Reform. Norway. Preparing for the future now.

Olsson, N. (2015). Implementation of Pre-Defined Potential Scope Reductions in Projects. *Procedia Computer Science*, 64, 387–394.

Rasmussen, I., Heldal, N., Homleid, T., Ibenholt, K., Skjelvik, J. M., & Vennemo, H. (2010). På vei til kvalitet? Evaluering av KS1 i transportsektoren, Vista Analyse rapport 2010/10.

Rattsø, J., & Sørensen, R. (2008). Pengerikelighetens utfordringer i offentlig sektor, Magma 4/2008

Samset, K. (2003). *Project Evaluation, Making Projects Succeed*. Trondheim, Norway: Tapir Akademisk Forlag.

Samset, K., Berg, P., & Klakegg, O. J. (2006). Front-End Governance of Major Public Projects, paper presented at the EURAM 2006 Conference.

Samset, K., & Volden, G. H. (2013). Investing for Impact: Lessons with the Norwegian State Model and the First Investment Projects that have been Subjected to External Quality Assurance. Concept Report no. 36. Concept Research Program, NTNU, Trondheim, Norway. Retrieved November 21, 2015, from http://www.ntnu.no/concept/

Samset, K., Volden, G. H., Olsson, N., & Kvalheim, E. V. (2016). *Governance Regimes for Major Public Projects. A Comparative Study of Principles and Practices in Six Countries*, Concept Report no 47 (forthcoming). Concept Research Program, NTNU, Trondheim, Norway.

Schwab, K. (ed.) (2015). The Global Competitiveness Report 2014–2015. Insight Report. World Economic Forum.

Statens vegvesen. (2012). Evaluering av KVU/KS1. Færre og bedre KVU-er.

Turner, J. R., Hueman, M., Anbari, F., & Bredillet, C. (2010). *Perspectives on Projects*. Abingdon, UK: Routledge.

UNDP. (2015). Human Development Report 2015: Work for Human Development. United Nations Development Programme. New York, NY. Retrieved from http://hdr.undp.org

Velure, H. (2014). *"Et prosjekt er et prosjekt er et prosjekt": En analyse av prosjektbegrepets utvikling og betydning i det norske språket, med hovedvekt på kulturpolitisk retorikk og scenekunstdiskurs.* ["A Project is a Project is a Project": An Analysis of the Concept of a Project—Its Development and Influence on the Norwegian Language, Focusing Culture Policy Rhetoric and the Dramatic Arts Discourse]. PhD thesis. University of Bergen.

Volden, G. H., & Samset, K. (2015). Perverse Incentives in the Front-End: Public Funding and Counterproductive Projects. Conference paper presented at the IRNOP conference, London.

Yoshimori, M. (2005). Does Corporate Governance Matter? Why the Corporate Performance of Toyota and Canon is Superior to GM and Xerox. *Corporate Governance: An International Review*, 13(3), 447–457.

Welde, M. (2015). Oppdaterte sluttkostnader—prosjekter som har vært underlagt KS2 per September 2015. Concept Working Paper.

Welde, M., Aksdal, J., & Grindvoll, I. L. (2015). Kommunale investeringsprosjekter. Prosjektmodeller og krav til beslutningsunderlag. [Municipal Investment Projects. Project Models and Requirements for Decision-Making] Concept report no 45.

Concept research program NTNU, Trondheim, Norway. Retrieved November 21, 2015, from http://www.ntnu.no/concept/

Welde, M., Eliasson, J., Odeck, J., & Börjesson, M. (2013). Planprosesser, beregningsverktøy og bruk av nytte-kostnadsanalyser i vegsektor. En sammenligning av praksis i Norge og Sverige. [Planning Processes, Calculation Tools and Use of Benefit/Cost Analysis in the Road Sector. Comparative Study of Praxis in Norway and Sweden] Concept Report no. 33.

Whist, E., & Christensen, T. (2011). Politisk styring, lokal rasjonalitet og komplekse koalisjoner, Concept Report no 26. Concept Research Program, NTNU, Trondheim, Norway.

Part IV

Consequences for and of Governance

This part presents the relationships between governance approaches and their characteristic project results, governance mechanisms, and ethical issues.

The relationship between project success and governance is addressed in Chapter 10. This chapter also looks at the relationship between project management methodologies and project success and provides guidance in using governance as an enabler for project success.

The impact of governance mechanisms, such as trust and control, on project management is presented in Chapter 11. It shows the different aspects of project management that are impacted by trust and control, as well as the different levels of expression of trust and control in different governance paradigms.

The association of project governance structures with particular mixes of ethical issues is presented in Chapter 12. Here the typical types of ethical issues by governance paradigms are presented, together with the measures organizations take to avoid or mitigate the occurrence of ethical issues.

Chapter 12 discusses the conditions for theorizing a causality where governance impacts the phenomena presented in the chapters of this part of the book. Using the occurrence of particular ethical issues in projects as an example, this chapter theorizes the conditions and timely development of a causality in organizational project governance determining the management phenomena in projects.

10 Governance and Project Success

Robert Joslin

This chapter addresses the direct and indirect relationships of governance and project success. We look at the relationships of four governance paradigms with five success dimensions. Then we address the impact of the same governance paradigms on the relationship between a project methodology and success. We report on the research findings that explain which governance paradigms are more conducive to directly and indirectly influencing success and which success dimensions are influenced more than others by the governance paradigms, and why.

The chapter finishes with a discussion on how governance acts as an enabler to achieve success if aligned to the environmental factors.

Project Success

To understand the relationship between governance and project success, we first need to define the concept of project success. Project success should be considered in terms of first the outcome of a project (i.e., the success of the product or service that the project created), which is typically referred to in the research literature as 'project success,' and second in the way the project is run, referred to as 'project management success' (which is measured on the last day of the project in terms of achieving success criteria, such as time, cost, and quality objectives). It is possible for a project manager to succeed in one but fail in the other; for example, achieve project management success but fail in terms of the project outcome, or achieve project success but fail in the actual project management. For ease of understanding, from this point on 'project success' is taken to mean both project management success and success in the project outcome.

Project success is a multidimensional construct that includes both the short-term project management success (efficiency) and the longer-term achievement of desired results from the project, that is, effectiveness and impact (Judgev, Thomas, & Delisle, 2001; Shenhar, Levy, & Dvir, 1997).

Project success and how it can be measured is described in terms of success criteria outlined in the next section.

160 *Robert Joslin*

Success Criteria

To achieve agreement among stakeholders on whether a project was successful, measurable success criteria should be defined in terms of what constitutes project success. Morris and Hough (1987) define success criteria as the measures used to judge the success or failure of a project; these are dependent variables that measure success.

Defining objective and measurable success criteria for any project, even with comprehensive definitions for project success criteria, is not an easy task because some project criteria are subjective by nature; for example, product usability, acceptance of new processes, and reputational impact. Methods and techniques exist to help quantify subjective measures and reduce subjectivity, but, invariably, an element of subjectively always remains. When subjective criteria are combined with objective criteria to collectively determine whether a project is considered a success, projects with diverse groups of stakeholders are unlikely to reach a unanimous agreement among them, especially if the subjective criteria can be viewed from the interest and position of each stakeholder. Müller and Jugdev (2012) succinctly describe the subjectivity aspect on project success as "predominately in the eye of the beholder," (p. 768) meaning one stakeholder may consider a project successful, whereas another stakeholder might consider it a failure.

In the quest to reduce the level of subjectivity in defining success, project success criteria have evolved from time, scope, and cost criteria (known as the triple constraint concept, or iron triangle) to dozens of success criteria that model the multidimensional aspects of success (Khan et al., 2013). To aid in the correct selection of success criteria, measurement models for success exist for different types of projects, including the different aspects of success, such as the ones developed by Pinto and Slevin (1988), Shenhar, Tishler, Dvir, Lipovetsky, and Lechler (2002), Hoegl and Gemünden (2001), and Turner and Müller (2006).

The ability to measure success assumes the ability to achieve success, which leads us to the next section of understanding the factors that impact success.

Success Factors

Project success criteria determine if a project has met its objectives, but to ensure a high probability of success, success factors must be identified and implemented in a timely manner throughout the project life cycle.

Project success factors are the elements of a project which, when influenced, *increase the likelihood of success; these are the independent variables that make success more likely* (Morris & Hough, 1987; Payne & Turner, 1999).

From the more than seventy project success factors that have been identified from 40 years of project management research (Khan et al., 2013), for

Governance and Project Success 161

any given project every success factor may vary in the way it individually and collectively impacts project success over the project and product life cycle phases from project completion to production, and finally to preparation for product/service decommissioning/replacement.

The selection process for determining relevant (positively correlated) success factors is not without risk. Implementing success factors that have absolutely no impact on project success waste management time and resources (Atkinson, 1999). The selection or timing of the implementation for non-relevant success factors are called type 2 errors. There are also type 1 errors, which are success factors correlated to success but incorrectly or suboptimally implemented.

Attention should be given not only to the selection of individual success factors but also to the combination or grouping of related success factors that are contingent on the project life cycle (Belassi & Tukel, 1996). This requires a good understanding of the complex interaction of success factors throughout the project life cycle, which is aided through the development of success frameworks.

A success framework can be defined as a *basic structure, underlying system, or context that supports the project life cycle to meet the project's success criteria.*

Success frameworks typically consist of concepts, definitions, and existing theory for a particular study and can relate to either success criteria or success factors. In both cases, success frameworks can vary from being conceptual with a list of success factors or success dimensions, where the latter is associated with success criteria, or more practitioner-oriented, where figures illustrate lists or groups of success factors that may have process flows or links relating to project life cycles. The use of success frameworks should help to reduce type 1 and type 2 errors, but must be selected according to the context of the project.

Success Dimensions (Factors)

The definition of project success is dependent on context and perspective, which is why some success criteria are appropriate for one type of project but not another. Success dimensions (factors) are constructs that reflect commonality between the underlying success criteria variables. The relative importance of success dimensions varies across sectors, industries, roles, geography, and time. Examples of success dimensions include meeting design goals, impact on customer, and benefits to the organization (Shenhar et al., 1997), and Appendix A, taken from Khan et al. (2013), shows the breakdown of five success dimensions with their respective success criteria variables.

This section has explained that project success can be defined in terms of success in the outcome and success in the way the project is run from a project management perspective. The problem of subjectivity was discussed

162   *Robert Joslin*

in terms of how project success is perceived and techniques that can be used to reduce this subjectivity by defining measurable success criteria was described. Success factors were then described, as well as the importance of ensuring the right success factors are in place in a timely manner to increase the chances of success. Finally, success dimensions were described, including the list of success criteria per dimension used in the study described in this chapter.

Methodology

The focus in project management has shifted from individual tools and methods to methodologies that encompass multiple methods and tools. The first formal project methodologies that were established by government agencies to primarily control budget, plans, and quality, but as the understanding of project success increased, methodologies have also evolved to reflect this multidimensional view of success. For example, the Project Management Institute (PMI)'s latest Body of Knowledge V5 has an additional knowledge area and the International Project Management Association (IPMA) has released version 4 of their project management competency baseline, reflecting the competencies required to achieve today's broadened understanding of project success.

Several decades of methodology development would imply a common understanding of the term 'methodology.' However, the opposite is true; for example, PMI (2013a) describes a methodology as "a system of practices, techniques, and procedures, and rules," whereas the Office of Government Commerce (OGC, 2002) describes its Prince2 not as a methodology, but as a method, which contains processes and not techniques. Ericsson's PROPS is not called a methodology but a model, which describes all of the project management activities and documentation (Ericsson, 2013). PMI has changed the name of some of the elements of a methodology from knowledge areas to domains. In other cases, former knowledge areas have been renamed supporting processes. Although there is an apparent inconsistency of describing what a methodology is, the types of methodologies used have been described in Chapter 8.

Irrespective of the type of project methodology, all methodologies comprise a heterogeneous collection of practices that vary from organization to organization. To structure the contents of methodologies, Joslin and Müller (2015a) coined the term 'methodology elements,' which implies a structure within any given methodology irrespective of the origin of the heterogeneous collection of practices. Methodology elements may contain subelements, where the lowest-level element is defined as *a unit of knowledge* (Joslin & Müller, 2015a).

Literature on project methodologies mainly focuses on methodologies as a whole or on elements of methodologies. Research looking at a methodology as a whole focuses on those methodologies that are standardized,

Governance and Project Success   163

tailored, or a combination of both, and their correlation with project success. Research on a methodology element, such as project time management or finance management or any subelement (e.g., critical chain, earned value management, or a financial project selection method) looks at how an element influences success. Irrespective of whether the literature is focused on the whole or an element of a methodology, they are all applied within project environments.

Relationship Between Governance and Project Success

Introduction

Governance influences people indirectly through the governed's supervisor and directly through subtle forces in the organization (and society) in which they live and work. Corporate governance, from which project governance is derived, "should provide proper incentives for the board and management to pursue objectives that are in the interests of the company and its shareholders" (OECD, 2004, p. 11). Project governance should (if properly implemented) influence and motivate the way individuals view project management. This, in turn, is reflected in the structures through which projects are set up, run, and reported.

This section looks specifically at different types of governance and their direct and indirect relationship with project success.

Governance's Indirect Impact on Project Success

The literature on project governance shows a diversity of governance approaches covering topics such as the optimization of the management of projects; interrelationship of governance, trust, and ethics in temporary organizations; risk, uncertainty, and governance in megaprojects; governance in particular sectors such as information technology; and the normalization of deviance. Quantitative studies on project governance and success were mainly done in the IT industry, where Wang and Chen (2006) used structural equation modeling to show that an equilibrium of explicit contracts, implicit contracts, reputation, and trust as governance mechanisms mediates the relationship between project hazards and project success. Research on governance has shown how governance has an indirect impact on project success where it acts as a type of moderator variable, which modifies the nature or strength of the relationship between the independent and dependent variable, or as a mediator variable, which is postulated to be a predictor of one or more dependent variables and simultaneously predicted by one or more independent variables. This section's aim is to understand governance's impact on the relationship between project methodology and project success.

According to Joslin and Müller (2015b), the application of a comprehensive methodology, where the term comprehensiveness is taken to mean including or dealing with all or nearly all the methodology elements or aspects of something, can influence project success up to 22.3%. A comprehensive project methodology can be considered one of the key project success factors, so if one or more contextual factors impact a methodology's effectiveness, then this impact should be understood. From now on, we focus on one of the contextual factors—governance.

To understand the influence of governance on project success, it is important not only to consider a top-down view, i.e., shareholder versus employee in an organization, but also the influences of the bottom-up perspective, i.e., employee versus shareholder. To achieve this the governance models from Müller (2009) are used as shown in Figure 10.1 (see also Chapter 4). The top-down approach is represented by the shareholder–stakeholder continuum, while the bottom-up approach uses a behavioral approach, i.e., 'follow the process' versus an outcome approach, i.e., 'get it done.' The governance models draw on the theories of transaction cost economics, agency theory, and institutional theory, using legitimacy to emphasize conformance.

Three independent variables are used to represent a methodology: an incomplete methodology that has been supplemented by missing methodology elements (including tools, techniques, processes, knowledge areas, and capability profiles); a comprehensive methodology that required no supplementing; and an applied methodology including all the relevant methodology elements. All three independent variables were correlated to success. Then governance was tested in the form of two moderators, one

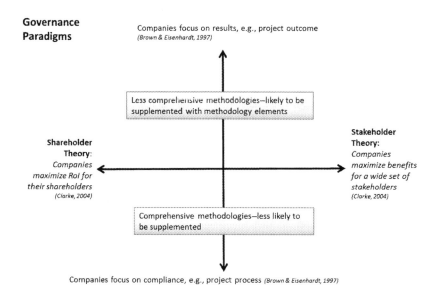

Figure 10.1 Governance Paradigms and Their Influence on the Comprehensiveness of a Methodology

representing the shareholder–stakeholder (top-down) continuum and the second representing the bottom-up (behavior versus outcome) continuum.

The first test determined if the moderator variable (shareholder versus stakeholder) influenced the effectiveness of a methodology to achieve success. The findings showed that this independent variable acted as a quasi-moderator, meaning it has indeterminate impact on the relationship between methodology and project success. So a shareholder versus stakeholder oriented governance may influence the relationship between the methodology and success or directly influence project success. The second test was carried out using the second moderator variable (behavior versus outcome), where the findings showed that it has no influence on the relationship between methodology and success. This indicates that increasing or decreasing environmental procedures and controls has no impact on the relationship between the methodology used and project success.

So governance has an indeterminate impact on the relationship between applying a comprehensive methodology and project success, but what is the influence of governance on the selection and evolution of a methodology before it is applied to a project?

In their mixed-methods study, Joslin and Müller (2016) showed that organizations that are more shareholder and outcome oriented are more likely to adopt an existing methodology rather than take the time to develop their own in-house methodology. This is especially so if the organizational culture is one of standardization more than customization. The risk in using standardized methodologies is that they do not cover the needs of specific projects; therefore, they require tailoring or supplementing to achieve the desired project outcome. Organizations that are more outcome oriented, i.e., 'get it done,' are more likely to expect project managers to supplement the standardized methodologies based on their own experience and knowledge of methodologies. The findings showed that project managers who need to supplement project methodologies are less effective than if they are given a comprehensive methodology to apply. This is because the thought and effort required to make a methodology comprehensive, consistent, and aligned to the environment will be far greater than if a project manager just has to decide on what methodology elements should be used to plug the gaps. A comprehensive methodology that comprises tools, techniques, processes, knowledge areas, and capability profiles has, over time, been integrated into the project environment, including the boundaries of the organization. A project manager who has to add a tool or technique in situ may plug an obvious methodology gap, but the level of effectiveness will be less than an institutionalized tool or technique. Organizations that are more control/process oriented are more likely to tailor their methodologies before they are used, thus reducing the need for project managers to supplement a methodology in situ. Control oriented organizations' methodologies are more comprehensive, and may or may not have originated from an international standard.

166 Robert Joslin

Additional insights were gained from the qualitative study on how interviewees referred to a methodology as being standardized where they only considered it with respect to the present time and not the history of the implemented methodology. Questions associated with the history of the implemented methodology showed that 65% of methodologies were derived from an international standard, and, of these, 75% (derived from international standards) were customized to varying degrees. The degree of customization ranged from organizational-level customization to that of the project team's skills. Two other levels of customization exist between the two extremes, which include customization to the business unit/line of business and customization to the project type.

Thirty-five percent of the organizations interviewed had more than one methodology that was customizable up to project type. In organizations that run projects that cover both software and hardware infrastructure, two or more methodologies may be employed, such as an Agile[1] approach for software development, e.g., SCRUM,[2] or extreme programming,[3] which links to more traditional non-agile methodologies for infrastructure design, development, and deployment, where the latter typically uses a waterfall life cycle.[4] In this situation, the challenge for the project manager is: first, to ensure the smooth integration of methodologies, with their different approaches and philosophies; and second, to prepare the organization for the cultural prerequisites required for it to succeed. The topic of successful integration and application of two or more methodologies is outside the scope of this chapter.

Understanding the history of a methodology is a good indication of the future of a methodology and whether a particular governance paradigm promotes its evolution or not. If a methodology does not evolve, it requires the project manager to overcome its deficiencies or shortcomings by supplementing it with methodology elements or subelements to meet any given project's requirements.

If there is a governance paradigm change, for example, from a stakeholder orientation to a shareholder orientation and from process orientation to getting it done output orientation, there is a risk that the incumbent methodology will be changed in some way, as observed in the Joslin and Müller (2016) study. For example, a highly evolved methodology that was aligned to the needs of the different business divisions in an engineering company was replaced with a standardized methodology with catastrophic results—project success rates dropped from 90% to 55%. Rapid changes to the governance paradigm of an organization are likely to indirectly impact project success through the change to the incumbent methodology.

Governance's Direct Impact on Project Success

Project governance is based on and aligned with corporate governance, but focuses on the governance of individual projects. The PMI defines project

Governance and Project Success 167

governance as "an oversight function that is aligned with the organization's governance model and that encompasses the project lifecycle [and provides] a consistent method of controlling the project and ensuring its success by defining and documenting and communicating reliable, repeatable project practices" (PMI, 2013b, p. 34).

In the previous section the governance moderator variable (shareholder versus stakeholder) was shown to act as a quasi-moderator on the relationship between a comprehensive methodology and project success. A quasi-moderator suggests there may be a direct relationship of governance on success, which this section investigates using the findings from Joslin and Müller (2016).

The operationalized governance paradigms were used from Müller and Lecoeuvre (2014), with the success dimensions[5] from Khan et al. (2013), shown below:

- Project efficiency
- Organizational benefits
- Project impact
- Future potential
- Stakeholder satisfaction

Using the operationalized governance paradigms from Müller and Lecoeuvre (2014), a multivariate regression analysis was carried out, with project success as the dependent variable and shareholder–stakeholder and behavior–outcome as independent variables. The findings showed that the shareholder–stakeholder independent variable was correlated with all five project success dimensions, but only on the stakeholder side of the variable, as can be seen in Figure 10.2.

Referring to Figure 10.2, the success dimension "future potential," which relates to enabling, motivating, and improving an organization's capability to undertake future project work, is the most strongly correlated with the governance orientation. This is supported by the notion that stakeholder orientation is underpinned by balancing the requirements of several stakeholder groups simultaneously, instead of shareholders only (such the shareholders of a project delivery organization), which is the basis for long-lasting business relationships. This finding is supported by Donaldson's and Preston's (1995, p. 67) thesis that "corporations practicing stakeholder management will, other things being equal, be relatively successful in conventional performance terms (profitability, stability, growth, etc.)." The lowest correlated success dimension is stakeholder satisfaction, where one explanation for this is that not all of the stakeholders will personally benefit from the projects, nor will all of the stakeholders approve of the way projects are run, which is in part impacted by the governance approach that is adopted. Looking from an agency lens, the findings could imply that principal–agent issues exist that are impacted by the governance of the project when these

168 *Robert Joslin*

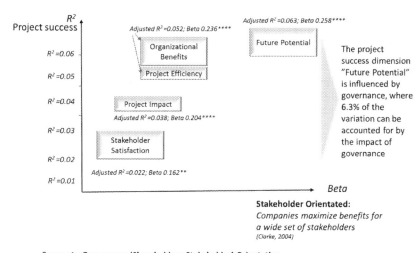

Figure 10.2 Impact of Governance on Project Success

agents do not personally benefit during the life of the project or through the project outcome. This is especially true when the project goals provide increased transparency or processes and controls that reduce the opportunity for personal gains. A stakeholder oriented governance is correlated to project success, but only 6.3% variation in project success can be accounted for by project governance. Perhaps, as with governance's indirect impact on success, governance has already positively influenced the environment within which the project is run, therefore providing the foundation for success. For example, governance impacting the selection and evolution of a comprehensive methodology, governance influencing the selection of a competent project manager, or governance impacting trust and ethics, which are three of seventy identified success factors.

Surprisingly, the second independent variable (behavior–outcome) is not correlated with project success. This is indicative of a situational contingency of control structures in that organizations where governance is more behavior-control oriented do not necessarily achieve higher rates of project success than organizations that are outcome oriented. This finding challenges the governance aspects of frameworks, such as the Carnegie Mellon University's Capability Maturity Model Integration (CMMI) or the governance process/outcome orientation behind the PMI Organizational Project Management Maturity Model (OPM3®) (PMI, 2013b), where the premise is that stronger process control leads to better organizational results. Along this line, Yazici (2009) showed that maturity models have only helped to improve project success on a replicable basis in certain organizational cultures. Using the competing values framework (Cameron & Quinn, 2006), Yazici demonstrated that clan culture, which represents the importance of stakeholder participation, cohesion, shared values, and commitment, is the model most linked to project success. This underpins stewardship theory, which proposes that the behavior of individuals in organizations is aligned and supportive to organizational and collectivistic goals instead of individualistic and self-serving goals. Project managers (agents) are tasked with complex projects and need to get things done; therefore, flexibility and trust is required from their principal (Turner & Müller, 2004).

It is important to understand the governance orientation of the organization governing projects and the potential enabling effect of a stakeholder orientation in project governance for project success. Yazici (2009) found that culture impacts project success; organizations that are more stakeholder participative, cohesive, and have shared values and commitment are most likely to achieve project success. Stakeholder oriented organizations that have shared values suggest stewardship relationships are in place. However, this can only occur when the necessary situational factors and structures are present, including individuals with the appropriate psychological profiles (Toivonen & Toivonen, 2014). When there is a change of culture in the organization due to external pressures, for example, a push for short-term benefits where management trust turns into excessive control, it will lead to agency tendencies (Clases, Bachmann, & Wehner, 2003).

Closing Summary

This chapter discussed the direct and indirect relationships of governance on project success. Using Müller's governance paradigms to understand the different types of governance, we were able to show that each paradigm influences an aspect of how a methodology is selected and evolves and its comprehensiveness in terms of fitness for use without the need to supplement missing methodology elements. Once the comprehensive methodology is applied to a project, governance plays an intermediate role in the effectiveness of the methodology, but governance does influence the project environment in terms of directly increasing the probability of success if the project environment is stakeholder oriented.

Notes

1   Agile is a time-fixed, iterative approach to software delivery that builds software incrementally from the start of the project, instead of delivering it all at once on or near project completion.
2   SCRUM is an iterative and incremental agile software development methodology for managing application and product development.
3   Extreme programming is an agile software development methodology intended to improve software quality and responsiveness to changing customer requirements.

170 Robert Joslin

4 The waterfall model is a sequential design process used in software development processes, in which progress is seen as flowing steadily downwards (like a waterfall) through the phases of conception, initiation, analysis, design, construction, testing, production/implementation, and maintenance.
5 The underlying success criteria are shown in Table 10.1.

References

Atkinson, R. (1999). Project Management: Cost, Time and Quality, Two Best Guesses and a Phenomenon, It's Time to Accept Other Success Criteria. *International Journal of Project Management*, *17*(6), 337–342.

Belassi, W., & Tukel, O. I. (1996). A New Framework for Determining Critical Success/Failure Factors in Projects. *International Journal of Project Management*, *14*(3), 141–151.

Cameron, K. S., & Quinn, R. E. (2006). *Diagnosing and Changing Organizational Culture. Bk: Addison-Wesley Publishing Company* (2nd ed.). San Francisco, CA: Jossy-Bass. Retrieved from http://scholar.google.com/scholar?hl=en&btnG=Search&q=intitle:Diagnosing+and+Changing+Organizational+Culture#8

Clases, C., Bachmann, R., & Wehner, T. (2003). Studying Trust in Virtual Organizations. *International Studies of Management and Organization*, *33*(3), 7–27.

Donaldson, T., & Preston, L. E. (1995). The Stakeholder Theory of the Corporation: Concepts, Evidence, and Implications. *The Academy of Management Review*, *20*(1), 65–91.

Ericsson. (2013). *PROPS Manual for Project Managers*. Stockholm, Sweden: Ericsson.

Hoegl, M., & Gemünden, H. G. (2001). Teamwork Quality and the Success of Innovative Projects: A Theoretical Concept and Empirical Evidence. *Organization Science*, *12*(4), 435–449.

Joslin, R., & Müller, R. (2015a). New Insights into Project Management Research: A Natural Sciences Comparative. *Project Management Journal*, *46*(2), 73–89. doi:10.1002/pmj.21472

Joslin, R., & Müller, R. (2015b). Relationships between a Project Management Methodology and Project Success in Different Project Governance Contexts. *International Journal of Project Management*, *33*(6), 1377–1392. doi:10.1016/j.ijproman.2015.03.005

Joslin, R., & Müller, R. (2016). The Impact of Project Methodologies on Project Success in Different Project Environments. *International Journal Managing Projects in Business*, *9*(2), 364–388.

Joslin, R., & Müller, R. (2016). The Relationship Between Project Governance and Project Success. *International Journal of Project Management*, *34*(4), 613–626.

Judgev, K., Thomas, J., & Delisle, C. L. (2001). Rethinking Project Management: Old Truths and New Insights. *International Project Management Journal*, *7*(1), 36–43.

Khan, K., Turner, J. R., & Maqsood, T. (2013). Factors that Influence the Success of Public Sector Projects in Pakistan. In *Proceedings of IRNOP 2013 Conference*, June 17–19, 2013. Oslo, Norway: BI Norwegian Business School.

Morris, P. W., & Hough, G. (1987). *The Anatomy of Major Projects: A Study of the Reality of Project Management*. New York, NY: John Wiley & Sons.

Müller, R. (2009). *Project Governance*. Farnham, Surrey, UK: Gower Publishing.

Müller, & Jugdev, K. (2012). Critical Success Factors in Projects: Pinto, Slevin, and Prescott – the Elucidation of Project Success. *International Journal of Managing Projects in Business*, 5(4), 757–775. doi:10.1108/17538371211269040

Müller, R., & Lecoeuvre, L. (2014). Operationalizing Governance Categories of Projects. *International Journal of Project Management*, 32(8), 1346–1357.

OECD. (2004). *OECD Principles of Corporate Governance 2004*. Paris, France: OECD Publishing.

OGC. (2002). *Managing Successful Projects with PRINCE2* (2nd ed.). London, UK: The Stationery office.

Payne, J., & Turner, J. R. (1999). Company-Wide Project Management: The Planning and Control of Programmes of Projects of Different Type. *International Journal of Project Management*, 17(1), 55–59.

Pinto, J. K., & Slevin, D. P. (1988). Critical Success Factors Across the Project Life Cycle. *Project Management Journal*, 19(1), 67–75.

PMI. (2013a). *A Guide to the Project Management Body of Knowledge*. (5th ed.). Newtown Square, PA, USA: Project Management Institute, Inc.

PMI. (2013b). *Organizational Project Management Maturity Model* (OPM3®) (3rd ed.). Newtown Square, PA, USA: Project Management Institute.

Shenhar, A., Levy, O., & Dvir, D. (1997). Mapping the Dimensions of Project Success. *Project Management Journal*, 28(2), 5–13.

Shenhar, A., Tishler, A., Dvir, D., Lipovetsky, S., & Lechler, T. (2002). Refining the Search for Project Success Factors: A Multivariate, Typological Approach. *R&D Management*, 32(2), 111–126.

Toivonen, A., & Toivonen, P. U. (2014). The Transformative Effect of Top Management Governance Choices on Project Team Identity and Relationship with the Organization—An Agency and Stewardship Approach. *International Journal of Project Management*, 32(8), 1358–1370.

Turner, J. R., & Müller, R. (2004). Communication and Co-Operation on Projects Between the Project Owner as Principal and the Project Manager as Agent. *European Management Journal*, 22(3), 327–336.

Turner, J. R., & Müller, R. (2006). *Choosing Appropriate Project Managers: Matching Their Leadership Style to the Type of Project*. Newtown Square, PA: Project Management Institute.

Wang, E. T. G., & Chen, J. H. F. (2006). The Influence of Governance Equilibrium on ERP Project Success. *Decision Support Systems*, 41(4), 708–727. doi:10.1016/j.dss.2004.10.005

Yazici, H. (2009). The Role of Project Management Maturity and Organizational Culture in Perceived Performance. *Project Management Journal*, 40(3), 14–33.

Appendix A

Below is an example of the diversity of success dimensions taken from Khan et al. (2013).

Table 10.1 Success Dimensions from Khan et al. (2013)

D1	*Project Efficiency*	D3	*Project Impact*
	Finished on time		Project's impact on beneficiaries are visible
	Finished within budget		Project achieved its purpose
	Minimum number of agreed scope changes		End-user satisfaction
	Activities carried out as scheduled		Project has a good reputation
	Met planned quality standard	D4	*Future Potential*
	Complied with environmental regulations		Enabling of other project work in future
	Met safety standards		Motivation for future projects
	Cost effectiveness of work		Improvement in organizational capability
D2	*Organizational benefits*		Resources mobilized and used as planned
	Learned from project		
	Adhered to defined procedures	D5	*Stakeholder satisfaction*
	End product/service used as planned		Sponsor satisfaction
	The project satisfied the need of the users		Steering group satisfaction
	New understanding/knowledge gained		Met client's requirements
			Met organizational objectives

11 Governance Mechanisms in Projects

Ralf Müller

This chapter describes how trust and control work as governance mechanisms in projects. We first describe trust and the interaction of person trust and system trust in governance. Then we describe the role of control and its role in projects. Finally we describe the different mixes of trust and control found in the four governance paradigms. The chapter shows that popular governance mechanisms of trust and control regulate different aspects of governance and therefore are not mutually substitutable in the governance of projects as temporary organizations.

The text below refers mainly to two studies, of which one researched the role of trust in project governance (Müller et al., 2013; Müller, Turner, Andersen, Shao, & Kvalnes, 2014), and the other looked into the role of control as a governance mechanism and its particularities in the context of ethical issues in projects (Müller, Turner, Andersen, Shao, & Kvalnes, 2015).

Trust and control are frequently referred to as the major mechanisms for executing governance in organizations. Their theoretical underpinnings in terms of governance can be found in agency and stewardship theories. While agency theory implies control as its predominant governance mechanism, stewardship theory implies trust (Schoorman, Mayer, & Davis, 2007).

Trust as Governance Mechanism

Trust is a broad and popular concept that has been studied extensively in the past. For example, economists tried to identify situations under which it is rational to trust (Banerjee, Bowie, & Pavone, 2006), while sociologists argue that trust stems from sociologically embedded norms that govern relationships (Banerjee et al., 2006), and psychologists describe trust as a psychological state which influences attitudinal, perceptual, behavioral, and performance outcomes (Dirks & Ferrin, 2001).

Management studies supported the notion that trust as a governance mechanism reduces transaction costs and improves performance in organizations (Das & Teng, 1998; Dyer & Chu, 2003; Gulati & Nickerson, 2008).

174 *Ralf Müller*

Transaction costs are thereby reduced because of lower control efforts and more informal and less hierarchical relationships, which together provide for better collaboration (Gulati & Nickerson, 2008). Other effects are that increased trust improves information processing capabilities in organizations, because higher information flows and development of trust reinforce each other (Carson, Madhok, Varman, & John, 2003).

In this chapter, we use the popular conceptualization and definition of trust by Mayer, Davis, and Schoorman (1995, p. 712), which is the "willingness of a party to be vulnerable to the actions of another party based on the expectation that the other will perform a particular action important to the trustor, irrespective of the ability to monitor or control that other party." Here trust is seen as a function of trustworthiness, which, according to Mayer, Davis, and Schoorman (1995), is a combination of:

- *Ability:* the skills, competencies, and characteristics that allow a person to influence within a specific area
- *Benevolence*: the extent to which the person being trusted wants to do good to the person who trusts him or her
- *Integrity:* the trustee's (person being trusted) adherence to a set of principles as judged by the trustor (person trusting)

Hence, we focus more on reliability and dependence on other actors than affection and emotional bonds in trust. Thus, we refer to cognitive-based trust (McAllister, 1995), where trust is reduced to the dyad of trustor and trustee.

Clases, Bachmann, and Wehner (2003) show that trust starts from a person's initial propensity for trust, which differs in individuals, and develops with experience over time, and is fostered through proactive collaboration among parties. Similarly, Luhman (2000) tells us that trust is contingent on experiences and the local milieu, and that it requires activity that establishes trust, but also warns that lack of trust leads people to withdrawal from joint activities.

The broadness of the concept has led to several classifications of trust, where people trust and system trust are among the most popular classifications. People trust is characterized by the extent the governance system trusts the people, and thereby, the extent the governance system trusts people's ability, benevolence, and integrity to fulfill their role in the organization. Ways to improve system trust include professional certification or experience of individuals (Grey & Garsten, 2001).

System trust—people's trust in the system—is people's belief that the creators of the management and governance system had the ability, benevolence, and integrity to design and implement a suitable system for the organization. Luhmann (2000) refers to this as "confidence," where lack of confidence leads to feelings of alienation and retreat into other "life worlds."

Research in the realm of projects showed that in trustful settings too much control can erode trust, because it signals to employees that they are not trusted and their governance system expects them to behave opportunistically (Kadefors, 2004). This was further investigated by Turner and Müller (2004), who found that low-trust structures impact project results negatively. Enterprise resource planning projects in Taiwan were found to be in need of a balance of the four governance dimensions, of which trust is one, together with explicit contracts, implicit contracts, and reputation (Wang & Chen, 2006). Trust as an antecedent for project success was described by Pinto, Slevin, and English (2009), but with different meanings of trust based on the contractor or owner role in projects. For both roles, trust varies in its impact on satisfaction with relationships in projects and positive project outcomes. On the other hand, too much trust is also risky, because it increases the possibility for opportunistic behavior or fraud (Nooteboom, 1996) as well as longer-term harm to organizations, caused by inadequate monitoring of too highly trusted, especially self-managed, individuals or teams (Langfred, 2004).

In a study on the trust between project managers and their governance structures, we asked project managers to what extent their governance system authorizes (i.e., trusts) them to decide on and implement measures on ethical issues in projects. Seventy percent of the project managers said their governance system trusts them to make the decisions and handle the implementation of measures on ethical issues. Conversely, we asked them to what extent they trust their governance system, and 80% answered they trust their governance system to help them address ethical issues in projects. This indicates a reciprocal relationship between system and people trust. If the system trusts the people to do their job well, then the people trust the system is supportive of their work (Müller et al., 2014). However, the continuation of a trustful mutual relationship is contingent on the project managers' long-term acceptance of the governance structure. This depends on the usefulness of the governance structure for the issues that project managers face. When accepted, the governance structure may continue to be the framework for ethical decision making in the future. When not accepted, the governance structure may be circumvented by the project manager in the future. The following prerequisites for successful governance structures were derived from this study:

1   *Freedom to act*: A governance structure has to provide sufficient flexibility for project managers to handle challenges. Too tight control may reduce the project manager's decision making to 'following the process,' which leads to a spiral of mistrust in the governance structure.
2   *Appropriateness of the governance structure for the issue at hand*: A governance structure must be relevant for project managers' issues and circumstances, and sufficiently wide and flexible to address many

176 *Ralf Müller*

unforeseen circumstances. Moreover, it must provide guidance for handling events that are outside the scope of the governance system.

Through this, the governance system leaves a sufficient amount of room to maneuver for the project manager, which builds trust and motivates the project manager to continue using it in the future. In cases of inappropriate guidance by the governance structure, or when its suggestion is in conflict with the law or the moral standards of the project manager, it may lead to mistrust and circumvention of the governance structure in the future.

The above positions trust as an important contextual factor for project managers' acceptance of governance structures.

Control as Governance Mechanism

Control is known as the measurable, rational element in a performance evaluation (Eisenhardt, 1985) and is often positioned as the objective supplement to the subjective trust mechanism in governance. Ouchi and colleagues (e.g., Ouchi, 1980; Ouchi & Johnson, 1978; Ouchi & Maguire, 1975) as well as Brown and Eisenhardt (1997) structure approaches in controlling employees in organizations along three dimensions:

- *Outcome control*, which controls at the level of meeting pre-established expectations. This type of control may pervade an entire organization using similar, often simple control measures, which provides for legitimate evidence of performance.
- *Behavior control*, which is frequently used when the nature and the means-ends relationship of a task is well known. As a control measure, it diminishes upwards through the hierarchy, as it is best suited for managers who understand well the task of those being led; thus it is good for controlling well understood adjacent levels of a particular level in a corporate hierarchy, or for less hierarchical settings, such as in smaller firms.
- *Clan control*, which is a socially exercised type of control. It builds on people's desire for belonging to certain groups, such as those in the same profession or professional organization. This makes them adopt the particular professional work practices and behaviors of their desired group.

Chapter 4 introduced the concept of governance paradigms. Outcome and behavior control make up the control dimension of the paradigms. Clan control is exercised in each of the four governance paradigms through the work practices demanded by the governance institution and the related professional standards or methodologies, such as those of Prince2 in a flexible economist paradigm or those of Agile/SCRUM in an agile pragmatist paradigm.

Governance Mechanisms in Projects 177

Control as a governance mechanism varies at micro and macro levels. While the macro level determines the above approach of outcome or behavior control, the micro level approaches define the nature and timing of control at the project level, such as the contents and frequency of milestone or review meetings in projects.

Few studies have investigated the role of control as a governance mechanism in projects. One study looked at the role of control as a governance mechanism in handling ethical issues and found that only control, and not the trust mechanism, relates to the occurrence of ethical issues in projects. Higher levels of control were found in projects with higher levels of ethical issues (for a discussion on causality, see Chapter 12). The same study showed that project-level control mechanisms supplement corporate-level control mechanisms, with the former providing more granular guidance on what is appropriate or inappropriate in projects (Müller et al., 2015).

Hence, control as a governance mechanism at the project level addresses very different aspects of project governance than the trust mechanism. This indicates that the project-level control mechanism in governance is more the extension or supplement of corporate governance's control mechanism, albeit at the project level.

Trust and Control in Different Governance Paradigms

The use of trust and control varies by governance paradigm (see Chapter 4 for an explanation of governance paradigms). The worldwide studies referred to at the start of this chapter showed that in:

- *Versatile artist paradigm settings (outcome control with shareholder orientation)*, governance builds on trust between project managers, sponsors, team members, and stakeholders, while control is minimized. At the same time, governance institutions expect that issues will be handled by the project manager or escalated immediately when they arise. For this, organizations provide training, escalation procedures, processes, and tools, such as 24-hour hotlines, etc.
- *Flexible economist paradigm settings (outcome control with stakeholder orientation)*, trust among project managers, team, and stakeholders is low. Medium levels of control are applied, often from a distance, where governance institutions expect monthly status reporting and scheduled review meetings.
- *Agile pragmatist paradigm settings (behavior control with a stakeholder orientation)*, both high levels of trust among stakeholders and high levels of control in project governance prevail. Governance in these settings builds on strict process compliance, such as in Agile/ SCRUM-driven projects, and often allows for direct surveillance due to geographic proximity of the actors. This allows for the immediate escalation of issues as well as building of trust among the stakeholders.

178 *Ralf Müller*

- *Conformist paradigm settings (behavior control with shareholder orientation)*, low levels of trust and high levels of control prevail. The latter is enforced by the governance institutions through emphasis on strict process compliance, paired with a multitude of formal control mechanisms, which jointly form an organization-wide 'closed control system.'

Trust was found to be low in all shareholder oriented paradigms and high in all stakeholder oriented paradigms. When project managers ask for help in handling issues, only those in the versatile artist paradigm turn to their steering committees for help, which indicates that they feel closer to their project governance institution than to their functional home organization. Project managers in the three other paradigms turn on average to their managers in their functional organization, indicating a stronger bond with their home organization than their project.

This chapter has outlined the role of trust and control as governance mechanisms. The perspective of governance mechanisms as a consequence of a governance approach was taken. We showed that trust and control impact projects differently and are therefore not complementary or substitutes of one another. Moreover, we showed that different levels and combinations of trust and control as governance mechanisms prevail in different governance paradigms.

References

Banerjee, S., Bowie, N. E., & Pavone, C. (2006). An Ethical Analysis of the Trust Relationship. In R. Bachmann & A. Zaheer (Eds.), *Handbook of Trust Research* (pp. 303–317). Cheltenham, UK: Edward Elgar Publishing Limited.

Brown, S., & Eisenhardt, K. M. (1997). The Art of Continuous Change: Linking Complexity Theory and Time-Paced Evolution in Relentlessly Shifting Organizations. *Administrative Science Quarterly, 42*(1), 1–34.

Carson, S. J., Madhok, A., Varman, R., & John, G. (2003). Information Processing Moderators of the Effectiveness of Trust-based Governance in Interfirm R&D Collaboration. *Organization Science, 14*(1), 45–56.

Clases, C., Bachmann, R., & Wehner, T. (2003). Studying Trust in Virtual Organizations. *International Studies of Management & Organization, 33*(3), 7–27.

Das, T. K., & Teng, B. S. (1998). Between Trust and Control: Developing Confidence in Partner Cooperation in Alliances. *Academy of Management Review, 23*(3), 491–512.

Dirks, K. T., & Ferrin, D. L. (2001). The Role of Trust in Organizational Settings. *Organization Science, 12*, 450–467.

Dyer, J. H., & Chu, W. (2003). The Role of Trustworthiness in Reducing Transaction Costs and Improving Performance: Empirical Evidence from the United States, Japan, and Korea. *Organization Science, 14*(1), 57–68. doi:10.1287/orsc.14.1.57.12806

Eisenhardt, K. (1985). Control: Organizational and Economic Approaches. *Management Science, 31*(2), 134–149.

Grey, C., & Garsten, C. (2001). Trust, Control and Post-Bureaucracy. *Organization Studies, 22*(2), 229–250.

Gulati, R., & Nickerson, J. A. (2008). Interorganizational Trust, Governance Choice, and Exchange Performance. *Organization Science, 19*(5), 688–708.

Kadefors, A. (2004). Trust in Project Relationships—Inside the Black Box. *International Journal of Project Management, 22*(3), 175–182. doi:10.1016/S0263-7863 (03)00031-0

Langfred, C. W. (2004). Too Much of a Good Thing? Negative Effects of High Trust and Individual Autonomy in Self-Managing Teams. *Academy of Management Journal, 47*(3), 385–399. doi:10.2307/20159588

Luhmann, N. (2000). Familiarity, Confidence, Trust: Problems and Alternatives. In D. Gambetta (Ed.), *Trust: Making and Breaking Cooperative Relations* (electronic, pp. 94–107). Oxford, UK: University of Oxford. Retrieved from www.sociology.ox.ac.uk/papers/luhmann94-107.pdf

Mayer, R. C., Davis, J. H., & Schoorman, F. D. (1995). An Integrative Model of Organizational Trust. *Academy of Management Review, 20*(3), 709–734.

McAllister, D. J. (1995). Affect- and Cognition-Based Trust as Foundations for Interpersonal Cooperation in Organizations. *Academy of Management Journal, 38*(1), 24–59.

Müller, R., Andersen, E. S., Kvalnes, Ø., Shao, J., Sankaran, S., Turner, J. R., . . . Gudergan, S. (2013). The Interrelationship of Governance, Trust, and Ethics in Temporary Organizations. *Project Management Journal, 44*(4), 26–44. doi:10.1002/pmj

Müller, R., Turner, J. R., Andersen, E. S., Shao, J., & Kvalnes, Ø. (2014). Ethics, Trust and Governance in Temporary Organizations. *Project Management Journal, 45*(4), 39–54.

Müller, R., Turner, J., Andersen, E. S., Shao, J., & Kvalnes, Ø. (2015). Governance and Ethics in Temporary Organizations: How Corporate Governance Influences the Temporary Organization. In *Proceedings of the IRNOP 2015 (International Research Network for Organizing by Projects) Conference*, June 22–24, 2015, London, UK.

Nooteboom, B. (1996). Trust, Opportunism and Governance: A Process and Control Model. *Organization Studies, 17*(6), 985–1010.

Ouchi, W. G. (1980). Markets, Bureaucracies and Clans. *Administrative Science Quarterly, 25*, 129–141.

Ouchi, W. G., & Johnson, J. B. (1978). Types of Organizational Control and Their Relationship to Ennotional Well Being. *Administrative Science Quarterly, 23*(2), 293–317.

Ouchi, W. G., & Maguire, M. A. (1975). Organizational Control: Two Functions. *Administrative Science Quarterly, 20*(4), 559–569.

Pinto, J. K., Slevin, D. P., & English, B. (2009). Trust in Projects: An Empirical Assessment of Owner/Contractor Relationships. *International Journal of Project Management, 27*(6), 638–648.

Schoorman, F. D., Mayer, R. C., & Davis, J. H. (2007). An Integrative Model of Organizational Trust: Past, Present, and Future. *Academy of Management Review, 32*(2), 344–354.

180 *Ralf Müller*

Turner, J. R., & Müller, R. (2004). Communication and Cooperation on Projects Between the Project Owner as Principal and the Project Manager as Agent. *European Management Journal, 21*(3), 327–336.

Wang, E. T. G., & Chen, J. H. F. (2006). The Influence of Governance Equilibrium on ERP Project Success. *Decision Support Systems, 41*(4), 708–727. doi:10.1016/j.dss.2004.10.005

12 Project Governance and Project Ethics

Ralf Müller and Øyvind Kvalnes

This chapter addresses the interaction of project governance structures and ethical issues in projects. We start conceptually, with a brief introduction to organizational ethics and their process, outcome, and character orientation. Then we outline empirical research findings on types and frequencies of ethical issues in projects, the relationship of ethical issues with different project governance paradigms, and the measures organizations take to avoid or mitigate the occurrence of ethical issues. We conclude by theorizing on the role of governance paradigms in the mix of ethical issues in projects.

Ethics

Recent corporate scandals, such as those involving Enron, WorldCom, or Volkswagen, have turned the public focus toward the ethics in organizations' conduct of business. We define ethics as a systematic approach to issues regarding what is morally right or wrong, permissible, obligatory, or forbidden in human interaction (Kvalnes, 2015, p. 11). In the context of projects in organizations, ethics offers conceptual tools and principles that allow us to analyze concrete situations, such as those of stakeholders' conflicting interests, where a prioritization of competing moral considerations is required from the decision maker.

Ethics and the related concept of morals are the Greek and Latin concepts for what is acceptable and required human behavior. However, in everyday use the terms have gradually come to signify different phenomena. Morals are personal and common beliefs about right and wrong, which individuals have adopted through upbringing and social interaction (Buchholz and Rosenthal, 1998, p. 4; Goodpaster, 1992, p. 111). Ethics is the systematic discipline of thinking about right and wrong, providing language and concepts for analyzing the moral dimensions of a situation that calls for a decision. Hence, ethics is the reflection of morals on the particularities of a given situation.

Several schools of thought exist in the realm of ethics. Among the most popular ones are *normative* and *behavioral ethics*. The former stems from philosophical, theological, and other related disciplines to develop links between

182 Ralf Müller and Øyvind Kvalnes

traditional moral philosophy and management. Normative ethics focuses on what a person or organization ought to do in a given situation, and the principles and norms to be taken into account when making a decision. Approaches to address these questions fall into three main categories of process, outcome, and character respectively:

- *Process orientation* in ethics—also known as deontology and duty ethics—build on the moral philosophy of Immanuel Kant. It emphasizes that conduct is governed through rules, maxims, norms, and principles (Kant, 1998). While Kant emphasized absolute moral duties and principles to govern conduct, Ross (1930) used the concept of *prima facie* duties to process orientation. These duties are always situation contingent and never absolute. Importance and relevance of duties vary by situations.
- *Outcome orientation* in ethics, also known as consequentialism or utilitarianism, builds on eighteenth and nineteenth century philosophical contributions from Jeremy Bentham (1970) and John Stuart Mill (2002). It defines right conduct in terms of the alternative likely to produce the best overall outcome for all stakeholders and applies cost-benefit analysis on behalf of the community of all stakeholders. Decision makers should prioritize and act with an aim to maximize the common good. In a project management setting, this means to give equal weight to the interests and preferences of all stakeholders, and to identify the alternative most likely to produce the best overall satisfaction.
- *Character orientation* focuses on moral virtues like honesty, integrity, and courage, and the ways to develop and nurture them. It stems from classical virtue ethics, as developed in antiquity by Plato (2000) and Aristotle (1984). Their ethical theories guide action to a lesser degree than deontology and utilitarianism, in that they focus on how individuals can develop a stable disposition to do the right and appropriate thing under given circumstances. Virtue ethics addresses questions of right and wrong in particular contexts indirectly, by first asking what constitutes a person of moral virtue, and then inquiring about what that person would do in those contexts. In recent decades, empirically oriented research contributions in moral and social psychology have raised doubt about the viability of the character orientation, highlighting how circumstances can be more predictive of conduct than features of the decision maker's character.

Behavioral ethics take the perspective of social psychologists and other social scientists in an attempt to determine why individuals behave unethically in the workplace. Kish-Gephart, Harrison, and Trevino (2010), in their meta-analytical study, distinguish between three areas of inquiry, which they term bad apples, bad cases, and bad barrels.

- *Bad apples* is research focused on individuals and explains, among other things, cognitive moral developments, idealism or relativism, and locus

Project Governance and Project Ethics 183

of control. Examples include Shalvi, Handgraaf, and De Dreu (2011), who showed that otherwise honest people might act unethically under certain circumstances.

- *Bad cases* is research focused on moral issues, such as Jones' (1991) moral issue construct, which explains unethical behavior in situational terms. This enables identifying how factors that are beyond a person's dispositions to act can affect their behavior.
- *Bad barrels* is research focused on the organizational environment. Popular topics include perceived ethical climate (Victor & Cullen, 1988), perceived ethical culture (Trevino, 1986; Trevino, Lengel, Bodensteiner, Gerloff, & Muir, 1990), and ethical climate's impact on individual's knowledge management participation (Tseng & Fan, 2011).

These three orientations offer important insights into why individuals engage in unethical conduct. While they are present in the general literature on ethics and management, they are mostly absent in the literature on ethics in project management. The project management literature has predominantly engaged with normative ethics (e.g., Godbold, 2007, 2008; Godbold & Turner, 1996), and could benefit from some more behavioral ethics approaches.

Moral dilemmas are a particular form of issue. These are situations where a choice has to be made between two equally undesirable or unsatisfactory options (Kvalnes, 2015). The decision maker must prioritize one moral value over another or over several others (e.g., fair treatment for some versus job security for others). The person facing a dilemma must decide which moral duty to prioritize, where "whichever action is taken it will offend an important moral value" (Maclagan, 2003, p. 23). This is different from what can be called *false dilemmas*, where a decision maker clearly perceives and knows what the right course of action will be, but he or she is tempted or ordered to do something else (Kvalnes, 2015, p. 15).

Ethics and Projects

The above discussion on process or outcome orientation resembles the discussion on governance paradigms in Chapter 4, where we showed that process or outcome orientation constitute a major dimension in the governance of projects. We will come back to the particularities of these dimensions later in this chapter. But before that we report on the types of ethical issues and dilemmas in projects.

Through several studies, where we collected data from 28 interviews and 331 responses to a worldwide survey, we investigated the types of ethical issues found in projects and in different project governance structures (see Müller et al., 2013; Müller, Turner, Andersen, Shao, & Kvalnes, 2014 for details of these studies). Through a qualitative study we identified three major categories of ethical issues, which are transparency, optimization, and relationship issues. These were confirmed in a subsequent worldwide survey, where 97% of the project managers indicated that they had ethical issues of at least one of these three categories in their last project. In the same survey, the project managers gave us feedback on other types of ethical issues, which we categorized as power and politics, illegal actions, role conflicts, and governance issues:

1. *Transparency issues* refers to situations when project managers are reluctant to report the real project performance. They do this because they fear project termination or loss of employment. Sometimes they intend to balance higher costs through reduced functionality of the product, or think they can recover the project through other, yet unknown, means over time. This category includes the well-known tactic of senior staff winning a bid but being replaced by junior staff on the actual project.

2. *Optimization issues* refers to the balance between risk and benefits. Should the project be optimized toward meeting the objectives of sponsor/company, or the supplier, project manager, or other stakeholders? This includes well-known questions like: Should we deliver as planned or with the best value for the customer? Should local safety standards be applied or those of the project's or team members' home countries?

3. *Relationship issues* refers to inappropriate or undisclosed interpersonal relationships. Examples include inappropriately close buyer–supplier relationships, where, for example, invitations and gifts are so frequent that it becomes difficult to distinguish between a gift and a bribe. Other examples include expatriates' inappropriate contact with locals in some countries.

4. *Power and political issues* refers to the enforcement of decisions or changes through power and politics. This includes cases where stakeholders use their power to replace uneasy team members, or cases where they press for hiring their relatives. Other examples include customers enforcing free-of-cost changes to a project.

5. *Illegal actions* refers to fraud, corruption, blackmail, bribery, or other illegal actions. Examples given by the project managers include steering groups requesting payments for signing off on specifications or stakeholders requesting/accepting bribes, as well as diversion of project funds to other purposes or projects.

6. *Role conflict issues* refer to actions that people are forced to do which are against their culture, religion, country's laws, or career values. This can include violation of established norms in some countries when male team members are forced to speak with female peers, or enforcing work practices not in line with peoples' religious beliefs or career ambitions.

7. *Governance issues* refers to cases of too little, inappropriate, or complete lack of involvement of governance institutions, especially when their participation is crucial for project progress. This includes cases where steering groups or customer management do not engage, or cases when senior project managers have to handle instructions from incompetent PMO members.

Project Governance and Project Ethics   185

Through analysis of the ethical issues above, we identified four ethical dilemmas that project managers are exposed to:

DILEMMA 1. There is a conflict between two equally valid ethical choices. Examples include the project manager reporting budget overruns early in the project (which implies a loss of face because of improper planning) or late in the project (a loss of face because of poor cost management). Both are equally undesirable but valid choices.

DILEMMA 2. There is a conflict between what is ethically correct and what the company policy is. Examples include inappropriately close project manager–supplier relationships, with frequent invitations to dinners, where the borderline between a gift and a bribe gets blurred in respect of the company policy.

DILEMMA 3. There is a conflict between what is ethically correct and what the law dictates. Examples include relationships of male expatriates with female locals in some countries. What is ethically correct in the expatriate's home country may be against the law in the host country.

DILEMMA 4. There is a conflict between what is legally correct and the company's policy. Examples include companies that set objectives of 100% billable work in customer projects, knowing fully well that administrative and other non-billable work must be done during the consultant's leisure time. Hence, the total amount of time spent by the individual may be in conflict with the maximum number of hours of work permitted in some countries.

These dilemmas should be avoided through a careful design of the governance structure, where the above mentioned bad apples, bad cases, and bad barrels are addressed through clearly set and acceptable standards for behavior (by both organization and individuals), avoidance of factors that negatively impact people's ethical behavior, and the development of an ethical climate and culture that fosters ethical behavior.

We analyzed the data on ethical issues in respect of the governance paradigms and their associated agency versus stewardship approaches (explained in Chapter 4). Figure 12.1 shows the distribution of ethical issues. The darker shaded triangle shows the area with a predominant agency perspective toward governance. This area is characterized by control as the main governance mechanism, implemented through process compliance and a shareholder orientation. The strongest expression of agency perspective is in the lower left quadrant, with the conformist paradigm. Most reported ethical issues in projects governed by this paradigm are transparency issues (50% of all reported issues), followed, albeit on a much smaller scale, by optimization issues (18% of all reported issues). This indicates a relationship between the agency perspectives of the governing institutions and improper reporting of project performance.

The lighter shaded triangle indicates the area with a predominantly stewardship perspective toward governance. This area is characterized by trust

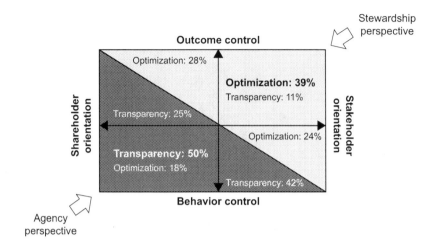

Figure 12.1 Types of Ethical Issues by Project Governance Paradigm

as the main governance mechanism, implemented through control of project accomplishments (as opposed to process compliance) and a stakeholder orientation. The upper right quadrant, the versatile artist paradigm, shows a majority of optimization issues (39%), followed by transparency issues on a smaller scale (11%). Thus, it is contrary to the conformist paradigm. This is indicative of a relationship between stewardship oriented governance and the presence of optimization issues.

Projects governed by the Flexible Economist paradigm (upper left quadrant) show a balance of transparency (25%) and optimization (28%) issues. The existence of both agency and stewardship perspectives in this paradigm, implemented through a general outcome and shareholder orientation, is indicative of trust as the main governance mechanism in circumstances of a more equal distribution of ethical issue types. Contrarily, the agile pragmatist paradigm in the lower right quadrant shows a clear dominance of transparency issues (42%), followed by optimization issues (24%). This paradigm, potentially governed from both agency and stewardship perspectives, is implemented through behavior control and stakeholder orientation. Behavior-control based paradigms, as also shown in the conformist and the agile pragmatist paradigms, are dominated by transparency issues, whereas outcome-controlled paradigms show a dominance of optimizations issues. At this point, we do not suggest any causality (such as a particular governance paradigm will 'cause' certain ethical issues); instead, we defer the discussion on causality to a section later in this chapter.

In subsequent regression analyses, we tested the systematic correlation of the top three categories of ethical issue types with the dimensions of the governance paradigm. This resulted in a statistically significant model, and

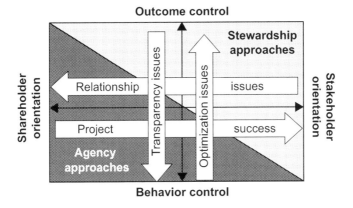

Figure 12.2 Correlations of Ethical Issues and Success with Project Governance Dimensions

thus a systematic correlation between the governance dimensions and the types of ethical issues. The results (see Figure 12.2) show that the different dimensions of the governance paradigm relate to different types of ethical issues. Transparency issues (the most reported issues) correlate with behavior control in governance. Relationship issues correlate with a shareholder orientation in governance. This indicates an increase of relationship and transparency issues in projects related to an increase in agency perspective in the governance of these projects. Hence, the stronger the agency approach, the more transparency and relationship issues can be expected.

Similarly, projects governed by outcome control face more optimization issues, and increases in stakeholder perspective in governance correlate with higher project success (see Chapter 10). Hence, stronger stewardship approaches in governance relate to reduced transparency and relationship issues and increased optimization issues and chances for project success. Again, we do not imply causality here, as it is yet unclear whether the project status and the ethical issues cause a certain type of governance or the governance causes a particular mix of project success and ethical issues.

The discussion above shows that different dimensions of governance relate to different ethical issues and success. The control dimension of governance influences, or is influenced by, the most frequent and most severe ethical issues in projects, which are transparency and optimization. The corporate governance orientation influences, or is influenced by, the relationship issues and the overall performance of the project.

Causality

The discussion in this chapter raises the question of a causal relationship between project governance (as cause, i.e., independent variable) and ethical

188 *Ralf Müller and Øyvind Kvalnes*

issues and project success (as effect, i.e., dependent variable). Hair, Babin, Money, and Samouel (2003) suggest that four conditions must be met to assume causality:

1   Time sequence—the cause must occur prior to the effect
2   Covariance—changes in the hypothesized independent variable are associated with changes in the dependent variable
3   Non-spurious associations—the relationship is not due to other variables that may affect cause and effect
4   Theoretical support—a logical explanation for the relationship.

The study design and analyses support conditions 2 and 3. However, condition 1 cannot be tested through quantitative means and requires further discussion.

Condition 1 (time sequence) may be met when organizations impose one governance structure at the outset of the project and then do not adjust their governance structures over the project life cycle. In these cases, it is reasonable to assume that all conditions for causality are met and the governance structure 'causes' the ethical issue and has an impact on project success. This view is supported by, for example, the Organization for Economic Co-operation and Development (OECD) in its report by the Business Sector Advisory Group on Corporate Governance (Millstein, Albert, Cadbury, Feddersen, & Tateisi, 1998) or Bekker and Steyn's (2008) qualitative (i.e., opinion-based) finding that project governance impacts project success.

However, governance structures may also be adjusted over the project life cycle, contingent on the project's status, the ethical issues, or other parameters. This view is supported, among others, by transaction cost economics (TCE), which suggests that governance structures vary by the specificity of the transaction's (i.e., the project's) outcome, its general risk, and its frequency (Williamson, 1979). Changes to the three dimensions of TCE can easily happen during the project life cycle. Thus, governance structures may be aligned to new circumstances in the project. In these cases, condition 1 will not be met, and we may face a situation where the circumstances within the project 'cause' a certain governance structure.

Condition 4 requires us to go back to existing literature, which showed published research on governance often assumes and tests for a causal relationship between governance and organizational success (Joslin & Müller, 2015). The stakeholder literature in general and the literature on stewardship theory (Davis, Schoorman, & Donaldson, 1997) in particular emphasize its importance for organizational success. However, alternative explanations are still possible. For example, projects with a higher risk profile are governed more from an agency perspective than those with lower risk profiles. This is supported by Klakegg, Williams, Magnussen, and Glasspool (2008), as well as Müller and Lecoeuvre (2014), who showed that larger projects, such as public investment projects, are subject to more agency perspectives in governance than smaller projects.

Project Governance and Project Ethics 189

While we cannot claim a general causality in either direction, we suggest that a limited causality, where the governance structure impacts ethical issues and success, can be assumed when the following conditions are met, in addition to conditions 2 to 4 above:

- The governance structure exists before a project is chosen
- The governance structure is independent of the project type, size, and risk
- The governance structure does not change during the course of the project.

Preparing for Ethical Issues

Organizations address the emergence or avoidance of ethical issues in projects in various ways. In one of our studies (Müller, 2014) we investigated this further and found large variance by governance paradigm (see Table 12.1 below).

Organizations with a process orientation address transparency and relationship issues by enforcing process compliance and optimization issues through policies, closed control systems, and escalation of issues to managers. Organizations with an outcome orientation in their governance are more diversified in their approaches. Those subscribing to a flexible economist paradigm address transparency and relationship issues through sporadic audits and policies, and optimization issues through training in expected behavior. The versatile artist paradigm shows the largest variety in

Table 12.1 Organizational Measures to Address Types of Ethical Issues

	Conformist	*Flexible Economist*	*Versatile Artist*	*Agile Pragmatist*
Transparency Issues	Process compliance	Sporadic audits and site visits Policies	Periodic and formal reporting with follow-up meetings Informal meetings	Process compliance
Relationship Issues			Training in business ethics 24-hour ethics hotline	
Optimization Issues	Policies 'Closed loop' control system	Training/ consulting about expected behavior	Policies Interpretation of laws	Escalation to manager Policies Interpretation of laws

measures, where transparency issues are addressed through periodic formal reporting, followed by various types of meetings. Relationship issues are addressed through training in business ethics and provision of a 24-hour hotline for reporting ethical issues. Optimization issues are addressed through policies and interpretation of local laws.

About two thirds of organizations make their project managers sign a code of ethics. A comparison with organizations not applying this practice showed no difference in the frequency of ethical issues. Cirka and Messikomer (2012) suggest overcoming this by aligning assumptions, espoused values, and artifacts in organizations in order to develop a culture in which ethics is central, visible, integrated, and enduring. They see a code of ethics as only one component of an organization's ethics program and emphasize the need to include the members of an organization in its development, so that it can become 'lived' behavior.

Other organizations make their project managers attend training in business ethics. These organizations have a significantly lower frequency in optimization issues, compared with organizations that do not provide this type of training. Training appears to pay back in terms of more clarity on how to address or avoid optimization issues.

Theorizing on the Relationship Between Project Governance and Ethical Issues in Projects

Before starting to theorize, we need to devise an underlying philosophical stance on which to build a theory, because theories should only be interpreted from the ontological perspective they were created in. We take a critical realist view, which assumes a mind independent reality (Archer, Bhaskar, Collier, Lawson, & Norrie, 1998; Bhaskar, 1975). It builds on three layers of reality, where the lowest layer provides the objective foundation of reality, named mechanics. This is achieved through the relatively objective quantitative survey studies we did on the topic. The mechanics give rise to situations within which phenomena happen. This describes the situations in which governance happens, that is, the data on governance situations and context we collected in both the questionnaire studies and the interviews. These situations give rise to people's experiences, in this case with governance and ethical issues. These are captured through the interviews we did and partly through the questionnaire. The research results described above are derived from investigations using this ontology. We continue with this ontology when we theorize in the following.

The interpretation of the results for theorizing on project governance and ethical issues is subject to a number of limitations. Most obvious is the small number of studies and the related limitation in empirical data, as well as the lack of clear indicators for causality, as described above. Therefore, we assume a limited causality (where governance impacts the occurrence of ethical issues) based on the results of a quantitative study by Joslin and Müller (2015) on the impact of project management methodologies on project success

Project Governance and Project Ethics 191

in different project governance contexts. The researchers used the analysis framework from Sharma, Durand, and Gur-Arie (1981) to test for moderation and mediation effects by project governance and found that governance is an antecedent variable, not a moderating variable. This is supported by many conceptual studies, which often perceive governance to span the entire life cycle of projects, and especially that the shareholder or stakeholder orientation should be relatively stable. We also assume the organizational control structures to be stable across projects. Hence, we use Stinchcombe's (1965) argument that "the founding characteristics imprinted at the birth of an organization [here a project] influence its subsequent behavior" (Van de Ven, 2007, p. 169). In other words, we assume "temporal precedence of the cause [project governance] occurring before the effect [ethical issues]" (Van de Ven, 2007, p. 169), contingent on the set up of project governance structures that are independent of project type, size, or other project characteristics.

Applying these assumptions to Figure 12.2 indicates that the original position on the matrix has a key impact on the particular mix of ethical issues. Steering groups that start their governance with an initial agency perspective foster a climate of control and lack of trust (which is also shown empirically in Müller et al., 2014). Thus, a position in the lower left quadrant is indicative of a high level of relationship issues, due to their correlation with shareholder orientation, and a high level of transparency issues, due to their correlation with behavior control approaches to governance. At the same time, the number of optimization issues will be relatively small because process compliance is enforced.

With an initial agency approach it will take a long time to develop trust between the project and its governors; thus governance is unlikely to change to a more stewardship type perspective in the short-term. The project will most likely be stuck in the lower left quadrant, whose transparency issues will prevent the building of trust and the associated move to more success-prone, stewardship-based governance structures. The project develops the well-known agency problems of utility-maximizing behavior of both principal and agent, which will not help in building more trust-based governance structures. The project will most likely be governed from an agency perspective throughout its life cycle.

An initial stewardship approach to governance provides for a different development. Starting in the upper right quadrant, the number of optimization issues is high, while the number of transparency and relationship issues is low. The number of optimization issues can be significantly reduced through training in business ethics. Hence, the number of ethical issues is lower and more manageable than in agency approaches. Moreover, a more trustful climate prevails between steering group and project, coupled with a higher likelihood to deliver the project successfully. As long as the trustful relationship is not broken, it is likely that governance remains in its stewardship approach. The project will continue with a higher chance of being successful.

192 *Ralf Müller and Øyvind Kvalnes*

However, the initial position may change over the course of the project. Examples may include a disappointed steering group, which lost its trust in the project manager. Here, the governance approach will move from an initial outcome control to a more behavior control, for example, from the top right to the lower left quadrant. This implies a change in attitude from stewardship to agency, which is difficult to reverse, due to reasons outlined above. Hence, the project will most likely be now governed from an agency perspective.

This resembles the first mover advantage concept in TCE, where the initial position on the matrix impacts not only the project at hand, but also the related and subsequent projects in the future. Through learning and experience with one another, and sometimes through market forces, the steering group and the project manager may move from one quadrant to another over the lifetime of the project, potentially steered by changes in mutual trust. This is especially strong in programs or series of projects where the parties work together over an extended period of time. Thus, they become more predictable for either side, and governance as well as project management becomes more stable in its approach.

Game theory reminds us of the risk with the last project in such a program or series of projects. If the parties have no plans to work together in the future, then they may opt for opportunism and use the trust that was established over a longer period for their own gains.

This explains one of the governance problems with one-off or large public investment projects. The parties to the project do not necessarily expect to work together again in the short-term, thus they have little to lose when they opt for maximizing their short-term gains at the expense of others. This is often seen in large public projects, which are therefore governed from the outset by strict agency perspectives. This approach, however, may prevent parties who are used to, and demand, more trustful work cultures and governance structures from joining the project. To that end, agency-based project governance structures may become victims of themselves by attracting only those partners that are used to work in environments where utility maximization and thinking in short-term gains prevails, while it scares off those partners that have the attitudes and trust demands that are typically correlated with successful projects.

This chapter has outlined the relationship of different project governance approaches with the types of ethical issues that can be expected within these approaches. Theorizing on the results of empirical studies provided some explanation of existing governance phenomena in failing and successful projects.

References

Archer, M. S., Bhaskar, R., Collier, A., Lawson, T., & Norrie, A. (1998). *Critical Realism: Essential Readings*. London, UK: Routledge.

Aristotle (1984). *Nicomachean Ethics*. Trans. by Hippocrates G. Apostle. Grinnell, IA: The Peripatetic Press.

Project Governance and Project Ethics 193

Bekker, M. C., & Steyn, H. (2008). The Impact of Project Governance Principles on Project Performance. In *PICMET Conference Proceedings*, July 27–31, 2008, Cape Town, South Africa (pp. 1324–1330). doi:10.1109/PICMET.2008.4599744

Bentham, J. (1970 [1789]). *An Introduction to the Principles of Morals and Legislation*. Oxford: Clarendon Press.

Bhaskar, R. (1975). *A Realist Theory of Science*. Leeds, UK: Leeds Books Ltd.

Buchholz, R. A., & Rosenthal, S. B. (1998). *Business Ethics*. Englewood Cliffs, NJ: Prentice Hall.

Cirka, C., & Messikomer, C. (2012). Behind the Facade: Aligning Artifacts, Values, and Assumptions in Assisted Living. *Business & Professional Ethics Journal*, *31*(1), 79–107.

Davis, J. H., Schoorman, F. D., & Donaldson, L. (1997). Toward a Stewardship Theory of Management. *Academy of Management Review*, *22*(1), 20–47.

Godbold, A. (2007). Managing Ethics. In J. R. Turner & S. J. Simister (Eds.), *Gower Handbook of Project Management* (4th ed., Vol. 3, pp. 838–854). Aldershot, UK: Gower Publishing.

Godbold, A. (2008). Ethics and Projects. *Proceedings of the IPMA Expert Seminar*, February 14–15, 2008, Zurich, Switzerland.

Godbold, A., & Turner, J. R. (1996). Ethical Project Management. In J. R. Turner, K. V. Grude, & L. Thurloway (Eds.), *The Project Manager as Change Agent* (pp. 170–190). Maidenhead, UK: McGraw-Hill.

Goodpaster, K. E. (1992). Business Ethics. In L. C. Becker & C. B. Becker (Eds.), *Encyclopedia of Ethics*. New York: Garland Publishing.

Hair, J. F., Babin, B., Money, A., & Samouel, P. (2003). *Essentials of Business Research Methods*. Hoboken, NJ: John Wiley & Sons Inc.

Jones, T. M. (1991). Ethical Decision Making by Individuals in Organizations: An Issue-Contingent Model. *Academy of Management Review*, *16*, 366–395.

Joslin, R., & Müller, R. (2015). Relationships between Project Methodology and Success in Different Governance Contexts. *International Journal of Project Management*, *33*(6), 1377–1392.

Kant, I (1998[1785]). *Groundwork of the Metaphysics of Morals*. New York: Cambridge University Press.

Kish-Gephart, J. J., Harrison, D. A. & Trevino, L. K. (2010). Bad Apples, Bad Cases, and Bad Barrels: Meta-Analytic Evidence About Sources of Unethical Decisions at Work. *Journal of Applied Psychology*, *95*(1), 1–31.

Klakegg, O. J., Williams, T., Magnussen, O. M., & Glasspool, H. (2008). Governance Frameworks for Public Project Development and Estimation. *Project Management Journal*, *30*(Supplement), S27–S42.

Kvalnes, O. (2015). *Moral Reasoning at Work: Rethinking Ethics in Organizations*. London: Palgrave MacMillan.

Maclagan, P. (2003). Varieties of Moral Issue and Dilemma: A Framework for the Analysis of Case Material in Business Ethics Education. *Journal of Business Ethics*, *1*, 21–32.

Mill, J. S. (2002). *Utilitarianism and On Liberty*. Oxford: Blackwell.

Millstein, I. M., Albert, M., Cadbury, A., Feddersen, D., & Tateisi, N. (1998). *Improving Competitiveness and Access to Capital in Global Markets*. Paris, France: OECD Publications.

Müller, R. (2014). Ethics and Governance in Temporary Organizations. In R. J. Klimoski, B. Dugan, C. Messikomer, & F. Chiocchio (Eds.), *Advancing Human Resource Project Management* (pp. 489–512). San Francisco, CA: Jossey-Bass, Inc.

Müller, R., Andersen, E. S., Kvalnes, Ø., Shao, J., Sankaran, S., Turner, J. R., Biesenthal, C., Walker, D. H. T., & Gudergan, S. (2013). The Interrelationship of Governance, Trust, and Ethics in Temporary Organizations. *Project Management Journal*, 44(4), 26–44. doi:10.1002/pmj

Müller, R., & Lecoeuvre, L. (2014). Operationalizing Governance Categories of Projects. *International Journal of Project Management*, 32(8), 1346–1357. doi:dx.doi.org/10.1016/ j.ijproman.2014.04.005

Müller, R., Turner, J. R., Andersen, E. S., Shao, J., & Kvalnes, Ø. (2014). Ethics, Trust and Governance in Temporary Organizations. *Project Management Journal*, 45(4), 39–54.

Plato (2000). *The Republic*. Ed. G. R. F. Ferrari, trans. Tom Griffith. Cambridge: Cambridge.

Ross, W.D. (1930). *The Right and the Good*. New York: Oxford University Press.

Shalvi, S., Handgraaf, M. J. J., & De Dreu, C. K. W. (2011). Ethical Maneuvering: Why People Avoid Both Major and Minor Lies. *British Journal of Management*, 22, S16–S27. doi:10.1111/j.1467-8551.2010.00709.x

Sharma, S., Durand, R., & Gur-Arie, O. (1981). Identification and Analysis of Moderator Variables. *Journal of Marketing Research*, 18(August), 291–300.

Stinchcombe, A. L. (1965). Social Structure and Organizations. In J. G. March (Ed.), *Handbook of Organizations* (pp. 142–193). Chicago, IL: Rand McNally.

Trevino, L. K. (1986). Ethical Decision Making in Organizations: A Person-Situation Interactionist Model. *The Academy of Management Review*, 11(3), 601. doi:10.2307/258313

Trevino, L. K., Lengel, R. H., Bodensteiner, W., Gerloff, E. A., & Muir, N. K. (1990). The Richness Imperative and Cognitive Style. *Management Communication Quarterly*, 4(2), 176–197.

Tseng, F.C. and Fan, Y.J. (2011). Exploring the Influence of Organizational Ethical Climate on Knowledge Management. *Journal of Business Ethics*, 101(2), 325–342.

Van de Ven, A. H. (2007). *Engaged Scholarship*. Oxford, UK: Oxford University Press.

Victor, B., & Cullen, J. B. (1988). The Organizational Bases of Ethical Work Climates. *Administrative Science Quarterly*, 33(1), 101. doi:10.2307/2392857

Williamson, O. E. (1979). Transaction-Cost Economics: The Governance of Contractual Relations. *Journal of Law and Economics*, 22(2), 233–261.

Part V

Cases of Organizational Project Governance

This part presents cases of organizational project governance in practice. It starts at the project level and gradually raises the perspective to the corporate level. This provides examples for project governance, governance of projects, and finally integrated organizational project governance that spans from corporate level to individual projects.

The governance of a large-scale public-benefit project is shown in Chapter 13 by describing the successful delivery of the Sugarloaf Pipeline during a period of prolonged drought in Australia. The project delivered the originally stated outcome on budget and ahead of schedule, while ensuring staff safety, community satisfaction, and the reinstatement of flora and fauna, as well as an overall environmental net gain.

The types of ethical issues found in project-based organizations and their need for governance are described in Chapter 14. The case exemplifies the issues arising from self interest versus organizational interest in decision making, and how this can be addressed through governance practices that minimize 'interface' problems at the front end of projects.

The successful transformation of Tasly Pharmaceuticals Group from a functional organization to a project-based organization is described in Chapter 15. The particular governance approach for this organizational transformation is described in detail, along with its issues and the strengths and weaknesses of such a transformation.

The authors of the prior chapters cross-referenced the cases as real life examples of governance practices.

13 The Sugarloaf Alliance Case Study

Beverley Lloyd-Walker and Derek Walker

The case study reported describes a public-benefit project delivered by an Alliance during a time of critical need. The major source of information was the book written by Smith, Anglin, and Harrison for the Alliance detailing the project from conception to delivery; other sources of information used include government-related publications, publications of Alliance team organizations, and newspaper articles. Refereed literature is used to support discussion of concepts, theories, and models.

The Sugarloaf Pipeline Alliance

The Sugarloaf Pipeline Alliance (also referred to as 'the Alliance') was formed to deliver water to a growing city during a period of prolonged drought. The Alliance partners were John Holland Group, GHD Australia, Sinclair Knight Merz, and Melbourne Water. Under pressure to ensure continued water supply, of the quality to which citizens were accustomed, to the city of Melbourne despite a severe drought that had lasted over a decade, the State government considered several alternatives. In June 2007 it was announced that a north-south pipeline would be constructed to carry water from the Goulburn River in the north east of the state to the Sugarloaf Reservoir, 70 kilometers away. It was planned to pump water from the Goulburn River into the pipeline and on to the Sugarloaf Reservoir, one of 10 reservoirs providing water to the city of Melbourne, Victoria, Australia (Melbourne Water, 2014). The intention of the project was to protect Melbourne against future water shortages that might occur in times of severe and prolonged drought. Water from the Eildon Reservoir can also be released into the Goulburn River. The Victorian government had established some time before construction of the pipeline was commissioned that the water in Lake Eildon could only 'be used in times of critical human need.' This was defined as when the total water storage for Melbourne, held within the 10 reservoirs, was at or below 30% of capacity on 30 November of any year, when approaching the lower rainfall summer months (Melbourne Water, 2015). The water in Lake Eildon is not included in Melbourne's total water storage figures; it is referred to as 'Melbourne's critical water reserve,' set aside as a supply

198 *Beverley Lloyd-Walker and Derek Walker*

available in an emergency, such as that which presented in 2007 after more than 10 years of drought, and increasing demands on that supply from a growing population. Such a water reserve, and the pipeline connecting it with a reservoir servicing Melbourne and its surrounding suburbs, would, therefore, be well placed to provide emergency water supplies in the future.

The water from the Sugarloaf Pipeline is not currently being used for Melbourne's water supply. It remains, as originally intended, as insurance against future droughts to supplement supplies "when storages are extremely low, or when needed for local fire fighting" (Melbourne Water, 2015). In 2015 predictions are that the state is about to enter another El Niño period, with low rainfall expected over the coming years, which the World Meteorological Organisation predicts could be the most powerful in 15 years (Hannam, 2015; Moncrief, 2015).

The project setting, overall project objective, and guiding ethical principles are described. Using Millstein et al's (1998) report for OECD and its four governance principles, the effectiveness of actions taken to ensure the Alliance's objectives are discussed in relation to: Transparency, Accountability, Responsibility, and Fairness. These objectives are achieved. Lockwood (2010, p. 754) suggests a seven-principle framework for "good governance for terrestrial protected areas," adding Legitimacy, Inclusiveness, Connectivity, and Resilience to Millstein et al.'s (1998) framework, including responsibility within the three common elements. These will be examined against the Alliance's stated commitment to social responsibility by being a 'good neighbor;' staff, and community, health and safety; ensuring environmental sustainability and providing an environmental 'net gain;' and protecting the cultural heritage of the area. This analysis explores the extent to which effective communication and control mechanisms were applied to achieve the stated ethical principles and thus the project objectives.

What is an alliance? And, how does it differ from other forms of collaborative engagement in project delivery? The Department of Finance and Treasury Victoria (2010, p. 9) describes project alliancing as:

> *a method of procuring . . . [where] All parties are required to work together in good faith, acting with integrity and making best-for-project decisions. Working as an integrated, collaborative team, they make unanimous decisions on all key project delivery issues. Alliance agreements are premised on joint management of risk for project delivery. All parties jointly manage that risk within the terms of an 'alliance agreement', and share the outcomes of the project.*

Walker and Lloyd-Walker (2015, p. 29–33) identify key elements of an alliance as hands-on engagement of the project owner with design and delivery partners, and a reliance on developing trust and aligning goals between project partners to form a one-team mindset. They also note (2015, p. 167) that the reason why some clients (project owners) choose an alliance project

The Sugarloaf Alliance Case Study   199

delivery mode includes a best-value motivation that may be driven by need for proactive shaping and delivery assurance of triple bottom line and corporate social responsibility project performance outcomes. The triple bottom line refers to sustainability from financial, social, and physical environment perspectives (Elkington, 1997).

The Setting

There are three levels of government in Australia: Federal, State (or Territory), and Local governments. The responsibility for water supply rests largely with the State (or Territory) governments. The State Government commissioned the project, but planning permission was required from all three levels of government for certain stages of the Sugarloaf pipeline (Barber, 2011).

Australia is often referred to as the driest continent; however Antarctica, which has only a very small temporary population of mainly researchers, does have a lower annual rainfall. By comparison, Australia's population is fast approaching 25 million. From 1996 until early 2010, the state of Victoria, with a population reaching 5.91 million in March 2015 (ABS, 2015), was in the grip of drought (National Climate Centre, 2010), whilst at the same time experiencing population growth, especially in the greater metropolitan area of Melbourne. Studies conducted prior to commissioning of the pipeline revealed that growth was expected to continue at a fast pace and that current water storage capacity was not going to be sufficient, especially with climate change predictions that included an increased likelihood of droughts in the future.

Melbourne, the capital of Victoria, now has a population of 4.4 million (Lucas, 2015), and its growth has outpaced that of any other state capital. Not only is Melbourne's population growing at a fast rate, but, when compared with the largest city in Australia—Sydney (4.8 Million; Melbourne is the second largest city)—the mismatch between population and rainfall becomes clear. Sydney's long-term average annual rainfall sits at 1276.5 mm, whilst Melbourne averages only 654.4 mm a year.

The pressure on the state government to take action to meet the growing demand for water by Melbourne residents was unrelenting. The principle of the greater social good could be applied here, but taking water from anywhere else in the state was going to both cause disruption and at least appear to be threatening the 'social good' of a smaller but important group. The project was based in an area of the state where considerable agricultural activity took place, providing produce for domestic use and export.

The Project

From the outset, the aim of the project was to ensure continuing water supply to Melbourne in times of drought, but to do so with minimum disruption to the communities through which the pipeline would pass and minimum damage to the environment it would transverse, whilst ensuring the safety of all staff involved in completing the pipeline. The stated purpose of the Sugarloaf Pipeline Alliance was "to deliver a truly remarkable water project as part of securing Victoria's sustainable future by being a high performance team and a caring neighbour to the community and the environment" (Smith et al., 2010, p. 17). The Alliance stated a clear commitment to not only protecting the environment, but to creating "an environmental 'net gain' for the region" (Smith et al., 2010, p. 130).

Clear statements about its intent were made from the outset, and actions demonstrated the level to which the Alliance leadership team was committed to the principles of fairness and accountability. Within temporary organizations, an interrelationship exists between governance, trust, and ethics (Müller et al., 2013). The case study project was completed in a rural region that contained areas of environmental sensitivity and which were protected from development. Lockwood (2010, p. 754) states, "Ethics are central to protected area governance as they underpin what is necessary and acceptable with respect to core values, rights and responsibilities." So, was the governance framework within which the Alliance operated, and were the initiatives implemented to support the strategy, in line with Millstein et al.'s (1998) and Aras's and Crowther's (2010) 'good governance' framework? And, did the Alliance include elements specific to projects within a protected area, where environmental issues and recognition of the value of retaining flora and fauna are important to the success of the project?

Project Governance

Aras and Crowther (2008, p. 434) see governance "as an environment of trust, ethics, moral values and confidence—as a synergic effort of all constituents of society—that is, the stakeholders." Project governance comprises two elements: procedural and human dimensions. The procedural dimension includes the development of structured plans and controls within governance frameworks, which provide "clearly defined processes, roles, and responsibilities" (Müller, Turner, Andersen, Shao, & Kvalnes, 2014, p. 41). The human dimension relates to the willingness of those involved to collaborate "for the good of the organization or the society as a whole" (Müller et al., 2014, p. 41). As this was a public project, providing water for a city by piping water from another area, the good of the society as a whole was a major issue. The greater good could only be achieved by the Alliance's 'business objectives' being aligned with those of all stakeholders (Ims & Pedersen, 2015). There was a need to consider the greater good of the community, residents of the state of Victoria, and the wider community in relation to protection of flora and fauna and in

The Sugarloaf Alliance Case Study   201

curbing greenhouse gas emissions, which could be held to have caused the need for the project because the drought was said to be a symptom of climate change.

There was considerable disquiet amongst the communities of the Goulburn valley, for they too were experiencing drought and the region has long been viewed as the food bowl of Victoria; indeed the north-south pipeline was referred to as part of a group of 'Food Bowl Projects' by some (e.g., Ker & Rood, 2008), a group of interlinked water projects. Good governance principles were going to be required to ensure fairness for the overall population of Victoria whilst providing a water supply that would support Melbourne's growing population. Communities affected by the physical laying of the pipelines and apprehensive about its effect on their water supply, local flora, fauna, and cultural heritage would require their concerns heard, the Alliance's consideration of those concerns explained, and total transparency in relation to communication about the project in general. The way communication with stakeholders is designed is an important issue for governance (Aakus & Bzdak, 2015). A range of environmental and heritage concerns had been identified and plans developed to address them. Groups from across the country, those with an interest in protecting the environment, conserving water resources, and reducing greenhouse gas emissions also formed part of the broad stakeholder group the Alliance needed to negotiate with. Actions that these groups might take before and during construction had the potential to delay work and increase costs. Brower and Mahajan (2013, p. 314) studied the link between stakeholder demands and corporate social performance (CSP) and concluded that:

> *firms which (1) have greater sensitivity to stakeholder needs as a result of a strategic emphasis on . . . value creation, (2) face greater diversity of stakeholder demands, and (3) encounter a greater degree of stakeholder scrutiny or risk from stakeholder action have a greater breadth of CSP in response to the stakeholder landscape that they face.*

A range of ethical issues had to be considered, planned for, and the plans implemented for the Sugarloaf Pipeline Alliance to successfully deliver the 70 kilometers of pipeline and to achieve the desired level of CSP. A large number of employees would be involved in implementing these plans, many of whom would work for subcontractors. It would be important to gain the required willingness to accept responsibility from all if the Alliance was to meet its governance objectives, and if the local community and broader society were to view the Alliance as an ethical temporary organization (Müller et al., 2014). The Alliance's actions from the beginning indicate that they were driven by their broad stakeholder group to 'be good,' thus planning and acting with the greater social good in mind to achieve a high level of corporate social performance. The governance structures in place, and the

202 *Beverley Lloyd-Walker and Derek Walker*

responses of project managers to ethical issues (Müller et al., 2014), would determine success. The matters to be addressed included:

- Community liaison and stakeholder management
  - Minimizing disruption to the community
- Minimizing greenhouse gas emissions
- Cultural heritage and the environment within the construction corridor
  - Flora, fauna, and aquatic life
  - Not only ensuring no environmental degradation remained, but providing a net environmental gain (a commitment given by the Alliance)
- Health and safety of staff and the community

Good governance has been written about and spoken of for some time, but what is good corporate governance? (Bessire, Chatelin, & Onnée, 2010, p. 38). Bessire et al. (2010, p. 48) conclude that 'good' corporate governance lies "in the quality of entrepreneurial democracy, which systematically questions the enterprise's mission and its relation to the common good." To measure the Sugarloaf Alliance's governance performance against Millstein et al.'s (1998) good governance framework, their plans and actions across a range of areas are discussed and the extent to which intentions were delivered considered against the framework. The extent to which 'the common good' drove project managers' decision making throughout the planning and construction phases will also form an important part of this analysis. Accordingly, the Sugarloaf Alliance's corporate social performance, which incorporates principles of social responsibility and social responsiveness and the policies developed and actions carried out that address the social issues of stakeholders (Bessire & Onnée, 2010) will be assessed.

Community Liaison and Stakeholder Management

From the outset, the Alliance was determined to take a proactive approach to addressing a broad range of ethical issues. The ethical considerations that drove the planning and conduct of the project included working closely with the affected communities. The Alliance recognized that the management of their relationship with the "whole stakeholder community" (Aras & Crowther, 2010, p. 467) was vital for success. Research has found that it is trust that establishes and maintains the critical stakeholder relationships that contribute to project success (Pinto, Slevin, & English, 2009). The Sugarloaf Alliance prepared a submission for consideration by the Public Relations Institute of Australia's (PRIA's) Golden Target Awards, which are designed to recognize "excellence in public relations and communication in

Australia" (Public Relations Institute of Australia, 2010). In 2010 the Alliance sought recognition under the award category 'Community Relations' and received a commendation for their community relations efforts on the Sugarloaf project. Their submission provides details of their planning, actions, and outcomes over the duration of the project, and details of their actions provided below are based on the submission document, *Transforming Negative Community Sentiment Through Positive Engagement* (Public Relations Institute of Australia, 2010). The actions detailed in the Alliance's submission demonstrate that they recognized the importance of developing strong relationships with all stakeholders.

The Alliance recognized the importance of open and transparent community consultation. The pipeline was to pass through 85 private properties, would need to cross several waterways, and presented risks to flora and fauna. In addition, the increased traffic during construction would inevitably impact traffic flows along the Melba Highway. The timing of the project, during a drought, the worst in over 100 years, presented additional challenges in communicating and negotiating with the community and other stakeholders. Concerns were also being expressed from outside the affected area, with interest groups questioning the potential impact on the immediate environment and from, for instance, emissions generated from pumping the water, and from the vehicles and machinery used during construction. Negative media reports were appearing across the state and around the country, and the project was being referred to as a topic of ongoing controversy (Dowling, 2007; Ker & Rood, 2008), with claims being made that it and other water projects were not needed (Fyfe, 2009). The issue of public sentiment was not confined to the immediate community; thus the number and type of stakeholders was numerous and complex.

The Alliance team realized that construction of the pipeline would impact many people. The building of the Sugarloaf pipeline was viewed by many in the broader Murray-Goulburn Food Bowl area as a threat to their livelihoods. Taking water away from any community in the driest (permanently inhabited) country in the world was always going to be viewed negatively; in an area where the economy depended on the ability to produce dairy products and fruit and vegetable crops, this was never going to be an easy proposition to put to the community. The initial studies acknowledged this conundrum. The Sugarloaf pipeline and other linked water projects that included upgrading of the local water distribution network to reduce irrigation water losses were designed to provide a comprehensive new water strategy for the state and part of an overall national approach to water management (Australian Government Department of the Environment, 2010; Victorian Department of Sustainability and Environment (DSE), 2004). The aim of these upgrades was to enable water savings, with the additional water being redistributed to users in the area. This needed to be effectively communicated to the affected community.

The Alliance management team realized that they were commencing the project in an environment of poor relationships with the local communities and stakeholders, and that the project was receiving negative media coverage. It was expected that protest action would take place and that this could result in costly delays, with the potential to damage the reputations of both the Government of Victoria and Melbourne Water. Communicating with the community, listening to their concerns, and responding appropriately to them was going to be vital if the project was to succeed. The Alliance team confronted what at times could be described as 'vocal community opposition;' however by the end of the project, community sentiment had changed and employment for approximately 3,000 workers had been provided by the project (Smith et al., 2010).

A strategic community relations program was developed, targeting the various different stakeholders and communities affected, which was designed to inform and to provide opportunities for consultation such that interested groups and individuals could have input into the design as well as learn more of the links between the Sugarloaf project and other water initiatives to increase water flow and availability. To build and develop goodwill, a range of benefits were delivered to the affected communities. These included donations to sporting clubs and other organizations, and information about these donations was also included in communications with the public. This was designed to enable groups to ensure that the desired environmental net gain could occur, and that sporting and other activities could be maintained into the future.

The communication strategy was designed to establish positive relations with both the local community and other stakeholders during the planning stage and throughout construction. The development of this program commenced with research into the key stakeholders and all landowners and community groups who could potentially be impacted by the project. Completed during the planning phase, the research included a social impact assessment that was used to inform decisions related to the preferred pipeline route. Information was gathered largely from face-to-face events—public information sessions, meetings with local councils in areas that the pipeline would transverse, meetings with a range of interest groups, residents, and landowners. This information was supported by a desktop review conducted of reports and publications by councils within the region, census data, and media reports. The social assessment went beyond residents and owners to identify social land uses and users.

A Project Impact Assessment (PIA) report resulted from the extensive front-end research conducted and, in line with the Alliance's commitment to transparency, was made available to the public for comment. The state government Minister for Planning convened a committee to review the report and the 104 public submissions received. This was accompanied by seven days of public hearings, and the report was also used to develop the community engagement strategy to be implemented for the life of the project.

The Sugarloaf Alliance Case Study 205

The principles focused on within the engagement strategy included (based on the Alliance's *Transforming Negative Community Sentiment Through Positive Engagement*, Golden Target Award submission):

> *Using honest and open communication; ensuring staff and subcontractors were aware of stakeholder relations objectives and procedures; consulting with landowners, the various local communities impacted, and stakeholders on issues that affected them and keeping these groups informed of project plans, progress, and likely impacts in advance; through these consultations, working collaboratively with the relevant groups to resolve issues and to follow through on actions that had been agreed. Project contact details were to be publicized widely and all queries and concerns were promptly responded to. Every attempt was to be made to investigate ways in which initiatives to improve community and stakeholder outcomes might be implemented.*

The plan was extended to include providing support for appropriate community projects and initiatives and to keeping all parties informed of project accomplishments and community involvement activities.

Such a long list of principles was going to demand a detailed implementation plan if the strategy was to be achieved. It involved use of consistent branding of the project and providing staff with relevant training on community needs and communication policies. To live up to their commitment to promptly respond to all enquiries, a 24-hour, seven-days-a-week response service was established using a free call service. This led to 1,200 calls being responded to over a 12-month period. The stakeholder database, containing 16,000 contacts, was continually updated and maintained. More than 20 community sessions were conducted and information was provided via display boards in shopping centers. Information gathered at these sessions informed design elements. Where possible, the route was varied or other changes made to address community concerns. Feedback to inform changes was also gained from stakeholder advisory groups that met regularly and provided input into issues related to the environment and traffic management.

Meetings, face-to-face or by telephone, were held with the 85 landowners, with more than 3,000 calls being made to impacted landowners over the planning and construction phases of the project. All landowners received an information pack that provided aerial photographs of their land detailing the proposed pipeline easement and supporting structures. This pack provided specific information on compensation for each landowner and included key contact details. The effectiveness of this comprehensive communication plan was demonstrated by only two of the 85 landowners denying access to their properties. The Alliance's willingness to treat landowners with respect, to accept responsibility for returning their property to its original state, and their clear and transparent communication informing landowners of the impact of the construction on their land and progress throughout the project were rewarded. Letters of commendation were received in relation to the standard of their reinstatement efforts.

Site tours were organized for industry and community groups, and articles were submitted to local newspapers providing updates on the project's progress. Prior notice was provided of activities, for instance planned changes to traffic flow were advised via email. In addition to landowners and residents, schools and businesses were also included in this communication loop, and to ensure that all were aware of changes, newspaper advertisements and door knocking efforts supplemented emails and public information sessions.

Staff became involved in the communities by attending festivals, for instance, and when, near completion of the project, the area under construction was devastated by the worst bushfires ever experienced in Australia (the Black Saturday Bushfires, when 173 lives were lost across the state on one day; 120 of those lives were lost across the wider pipeline route area), 122 employees of the Alliance worked, under the direction of the local fire authority, to provide 24-hour assistance to the community and the firefighters. Temporary organizations, such as projects, confront additional challenges in developing trust due to their short-term relationship with other parties, in particular stakeholders, but establishing trust is important for project success (Munns, 1995). Choosing an alliance as the delivery mechanism supported development of strong trust between the Alliance members; however, the trust of the local and wider community was also required. Stakeholder oriented governance (Müller et al., 2014) would be required to achieve the desired higher levels of trust. Indeed, a high level of trust could be of non-financial value to this project, given the possibility of demonstrations interrupting work (Smyth et al., 2010). Avoiding delays was of importance to this project.

Demonstrating a commitment to the community during their time of great need helped Alliance staff gain a deeper understanding of the community and their concerns. The community appreciated the assistance provided and stronger relationships developed through this. Over time, media reports provided several positive stories acknowledging the Alliance's contribution to the local community. Their commitment to working with the community to minimize disruption was also acknowledged. Discussions with local schools led to construction works near schools being completed during school holidays to avoid the possible negative effects of noise and dust on students' learning and health. Feedback from the community even led to changes in the color of a pump station roof and the landscape design surrounding the station.

The Alliance's efforts in relation to community liaison and stakeholder management demonstrate Millsein et al.'s (1998) and Aras's and Crowther's (2010, p. 268) "four principles of good corporate governance" of: Transparency, Accountability, Responsibility, and Fairness. All stakeholders were kept informed via a range of media. Two-way communication occurred and changes were made to the project planning and delivery based on feedback. The Alliance accepted responsibility for protecting the community's interests and demonstrated a willingness to respect the community's rights, for instance by completing works near schools only when students were not in attendance. By aligning the strategic community relations program with the project's strategy, despite the potential for considerable disruption to works, the project was completed five months ahead of schedule and on budget (Smith et al., 2010).

Demonstrated Concern for the Community

In addition to rearranging schedules to avoid inconveniencing school students, the Alliance took a range of actions, and met the cost of these, that were for the benefit of the region impacted by construction and the broader community. These actions included efforts to reduce greenhouse emissions; protect the cultural heritage and environment of the construction corridor; demonstrate concern for 'neighbors' by minimizing dust, noise, and vibration; develop waste management and offset management plans; and conduct water quality monitoring.

Greenhouse Gas Emissions

Environmental management activities for the duration of the project focused on management of the Alliance's greenhouse footprint. Early research had identified energy supply and emissions as an issue for concern. Because the project was required "to secure Melbourne's water supplies against the impact of climate change," a review led to the view that it was "doubly important that energy for the project come from renewable sources" (Environment Victoria, 2008a, p. 2). In response to these recommendations, an assessment of the likely sources of greenhouse gases was conducted, and it revealed that they would come mainly from fuel and energy use during construction. Accordingly, the Alliance ensured that plant, equipment, and vehicles hired were newer models with lower emission ratings. Within the Alliance's offices, green electricity was used, and where possible local suppliers that would have shorter distances to cover to deliver supplies became the preferred providers. Additionally, suppliers were asked to use only that packaging required to protect items during transit, reducing the amount of packaging that had to be disposed of. By disposing of soil from the project in a local disused quarry, "tens of thousands of litres of fuel over the next best alternatives" was achieved (Smith et al., 2010, p. 146).

Completion of the north-south Pipeline by the Sugarloaf Pipeline Alliance included a commitment to using renewable energy to provide ongoing greenhouse gas emission reductions for the life of the pipeline. The Alliance met this commitment. The pipeline is powered entirely by renewable energy, including incorporation within the design of capacity to generate energy when passing

208   *Beverley Lloyd-Walker and Derek Walker*

through a hydroelectricity plant as it enters the Sugarloaf Reservoir (Melbourne Water, 2015). This could be viewed as both addressing concerns of interest groups (e.g., Friends of the Earth, 2009) and providing an ongoing net environmental gain.

Some community groups had been critical of the potential for the north-south pipeline to increase the already high level of greenhouse gases generated in Australia. The Alliance accepted the challenge to include initiatives to address these concerns. They viewed it as their responsibility to build these changes into the design. They viewed this as an ethical, fair, and responsible way to act, and the Alliance met the related costs.

Cultural Heritage and the Environment
Within the Construction Corridor

To support their proactive approach, the Alliance employed a "team of environmental and cultural heritage specialists" (Smith et al., 2010, p. 130). Based on the recommendation of the heritage specialists, actions taken included: changing the route of the pipeline, consulting with government agencies, and engaging with the communities affected by the construction of the pipeline.

Protecting the cultural heritage of the region included the involvement of Aboriginal community leaders who worked with the Alliance archaeologists to locate places of cultural significance, and 46 sites were identified. Actions to address the need to preserve these sites included altering the planned pipeline route. Aboriginal artefacts were collected and protected and scarred trees retained by changes to plans. Historical Society members were understandably interested in having any excavated artefacts preserved; hence the Alliance invited members of the Society to observe the excavation. In line with the commitment to return a net gain, the archaeological knowledge gained from the excavation has "contributed greatly to understanding of Aboriginal occupation in the region" (Smith et al., 2010, p. 156). Working with local groups proved beneficial to both the Alliance and the community.

Other cultural heritage sites included retention of old homesteads, and, as part of the exploratory work carried out, remains of buildings destroyed by past fires were 'rediscovered,' including a water well that had been used by a destroyed hotel. The Alliance management team committed to protecting the cultural heritage of the area, and this included gathering information on sites at their various community meetings. Additionally, by responding to all queries, they were able to learn of sensitive areas and take responsibility for organizing Alliance staff and community groups to gather and arrange for protection of artefacts. The Sugarloaf Alliance took responsibility for ensuring the cultural heritage of the area. Their actions led to the community acknowledging that not only was protection provided, but actions led to sites and artefacts that had been lost over time being rediscovered, and thus the project led to a net gain in cultural heritage for the areas the pipeline crossed.

The Sugarloaf Alliance Case Study   209

Flora and Fauna

Overall, the Alliance took actions to ensure a proactive approach to all issues identified during the assessment process, including protection of flora and fauna, biosecurity, and protection of aquatic species. Potential habitat loss was acknowledged in the original documentation, and was noted by concerned groups as possibly adversely affecting fauna in the region (Environment Victoria, 2008a). Aquatic species were also identified by an environmental interest group because the Goulburn River "is home to several Environment Protection and Biodiversity Conservation (EPBC) listed fish species, including Murray Cod, Trout Cod and Macquarie Perch" (Environment Victoria, 2008a, p. 1). The Sugarloaf Alliance developed plans to address all these concerns and acted on them.

The Alliance's commitment to preservation of the flora and fauna was demonstrated by efforts taken to ensure that "every body of water" (nearly 100), "hollow tree and log was observed for at least one evening" (Smith et al., 2010, p. 133) by the Alliance's team of zoologists. Additionally "the Alliance took a proactive approach to minimising damage to flora along the construction corridor" (Smith et al., 2010, p. 131). Recognizing that the construction activity would have an impact on the local flora and fauna, the Alliance developed a range of initiatives to mitigate the effects on the environment, including "a 'habitat slab replacement' trial" (Smith et al., 2010, p. 140). EPBC listed species, two fauna and one flora, were located in the area affected by the construction of the pipeline. They were the striped legless lizard, golden sun moth, a critically endangered species, and the matted flax-lily (Melbourne Water, 2014). The 2013–14 Annual Report to the Federal Department of Environment on the Sugarloaf Pipeline Project found that the management of these species and all others listed by the EPBC were continuing to be managed according to the Environmental Management Strategy, which had been endorsed by both the State and Federal Governments (Melbourne Water, 2014).

The state government required that an Environmental Management Plan (EMP) be approved by the relevant Minister, and the Commonwealth government's approval was required for some stages of the pipeline. The various EMPs produced addressed a range of construction scenarios and measures that would be taken to address each, and contained a total of 18 environmental programs. These programs were designed to address a comprehensive range of issues which included: air quality, biosecurity, contaminated land, erosion and sediment, fauna, fires, slope stability, greenhouse gas, ground water, hazardous substances, noise and vibration, cultural heritage, pest animals, reinstatement, vegetation, waste, waterway, and weed management (Smith et al., 2010). The EMPs produced guided project management processes, and these were communicated to all alliance staff involved in activities to which the EMP related.

With a commitment to an overall environmental net gain, offset management was important. The Alliance purchased areas of similar vegetation to

210 *Beverley Lloyd-Walker and Derek Walker*

that which had to be cleared for the pipeline, ensuring continued availability of natural habitat for many species, including the endangered golden sun moth and striped legless lizard.

A proactive approach was taken to addressing the concerns of landowners who were well aware of the potential risk of disease transmission if soil was moved from one property to another. These risks would impact the landowners' livelihoods. For instance, the commitment to biosecurity led to the development of strict biosecurity protocols that impacted on all site workers. Biosecurity management involved all workers' boots being treated every day to protect both agricultural crops, such as grapes, and animal production within the grazing districts. The protocols established included retaining any topsoil removed within the property from which it was taken and ensuring all earthmoving equipment underwent thorough cleaning to avoid moving infected soil from one property to another (Smith et al., 2010).

Minimizing Adverse Construction Impacts

Because construction was taking place close to residential areas, including schools and historic buildings, monitoring of construction noise and vibration occurred to ensure that it was within legislated levels. In particular, work outside normal construction hours was carefully monitored. In some areas, the lack of noise from other sources, especially of an evening, required low level noise limits. To ensure this happened, work schedules were changed to ensure only work that could be completed within the agreed levels occurred after hours. Vibration levels were maintained well within limits throughout the construction period.

Given the rural setting of the pipeline works, minimizing waste and finding ways to reuse materials was important. Recycling bins were used and innovative ways of encouraging their correct use included the 'Waste Wise Games,' which included incentives such as free lunches (Smith et al., 2010). On completion of the project, to ensure original commitments were met, innovative ways of disposing of leftover items were used. Again, these could be called providing a 'net gain,' as the Alliance donated materials. Some of these were of particular use to organizations, such as sporting clubs, schools, and councils, as they included silt fencing, plastic water tanks, and timber. Indeed, the efforts were rewarded with a Silver Waste Wise certificate from Sustainability Victoria.

Because the pipeline involved crossing waterways, and in recognition of the dwindling water supply situation, the Alliance developed protocols to protect both water quality and aquatic life. Water quality monitoring occurred regularly and included checking the impact on stream wildlife. Any concerns expressed by landowners along the pipeline route were addressed by the installation of further sediment controls, at the expense of the Alliance.

The Sugarloaf Alliance Case Study   211

Health and Safety of Staff and the Community

The Sugarloaf Pipeline Alliance committed to a "vision of 'no harm,' aiming to set a new industry benchmark for occupational health and safety" (Smith et al., 2010, p. 160). Accordingly, safety principles were introduced for employees and all contractors. Potential hazard identification was an important part of their health and safety procedures. The plans stated initiatives in relation to the safety, welfare, and future supply of water for all communities affected, not just the population of Melbourne.

Keeping the level of awareness high throughout the project, whilst laying pipes at record speed, was a challenge; complacency was not tolerated. Behavioral change initiatives, such as "the 'Think Five Stay Alive' campaign" (Smith et al., 2010, p. 160), which encouraged staff to assess potential risks before commencing tasks, were introduced to support the stated vision.

In addition to programs to address potential physical risks, staff were also confronted by members of the public, some of whom "weren't shy to voice their opinions" (Smith et al., 2010, p. 161) when activities slowed their travel along the Melba Highway, for instance. At times this constituted abuse. Such events led to strengthened efforts to further improve their traffic management efforts (an example of stakeholder demands driving Corporate Social Performance?). The result? The Alliance Project Manager proudly stated that "there were zero lost time injuries" (Cranston in Smith et al., 2010, p. 13), a remarkable outcome for a project of the size and scale of Sugarloaf, with more than two million hours of work completed. The Alliance's vision was achieved; the project's safety records show incident rates below the industry average.

In areas where the pipeline corridor came close to residential areas and vineyards, for instance in the Yarra Valley, efforts were taken to minimize dust, which may have had a negative impact on the health and comfort of residents and may have adversely affected grape production. Regular air quality monitoring occurred, concentrating especially on sensitive areas such as vineyards and wetlands, as well as homes, schools, and medical facilities. The Alliance employed an agricultural consultant to monitor grapevines located close to the pipeline corridor to ensure that dust was being sufficiently minimized to avoid damage to the vines and their fruit. Given the extremely dry conditions over the years leading up to the construction of the pipeline, the Alliance confronted a challenging task. Their strategy for dust minimization was implemented by on site workers abiding by strict speed limits and by dampening of dusty areas, but with the water shortage, which had led to the need for the pipeline, the Alliance had to consider where the water for dust suppression might be obtained. To address this issue, sedimentation ponds were created to collect rainwater for this purpose and thus avoid taking water from dwindling town water supplies along the construction corridor (Smith et al., 2010).

212 *Beverley Lloyd-Walker and Derek Walker*

Concluding Discussion

A range of theories and frameworks were cited, and the outcome of the case study, the Sugarloaf Pipeline Alliance project, will now be discussed (analyzed) against these theories and frameworks.

Lockwood's (2010, p. 754) seven principles of good governance relate specifically to the land, and he refers to his governance framework as being developed "for terrestrial protected areas." The first of Lockwood's (2010, p. 758) seven principles is *Legitimacy*, which is "a key factor in the ethical acceptability of governance arrangement." It is about the organization's authority, "conferred by law or democratic mandate" or "earned through the acceptance of stakeholders," and includes "the integrity and commitment with which authority is exercised." The Sugarloaf Pipeline Alliance had authority to construct the pipeline. They had a right to enter private land when required and could divert traffic, but they also had to abide by environmental and community-related requirements placed on them. The project evaluation process found that all laws and all requirements set out in the Project Impact Assessment statement to protect the environment had been followed. Stakeholder acceptance was demonstrated by the letters of commendation received from landowners, and other community members, when the project was drawing to a close (Smith et al., 2010). According to Müller et al. (2014), good project governance in relation to their human dimension would measure the level of willingness to collaborate both for the good of the project and, given the Alliance's stated objectives, the good of society as a whole. Positive feedback from groups originally very negative toward the project confirmed that efforts to address stakeholder needs had occurred and were successful. Public meetings, the provision of a contact phone number, and speedy response to queries, phone calls, and visits to landowners, combined with actions taken to address concerns, demonstrated a willingness to collaborate. This benefited the project, as did the initiatives taken to ensure the greenhouse gas reductions during construction, and for the life of the pipeline, society in general.

Examining the project planning and conduct against the first of Millstein et al.'s (1998a) and Aras's and Crowther's (2010) four good governance framework principles, *Transparency*, it is necessary to consider the extent to which project management processes were first established, then actioned through the project's life. Lockwood sees transparency as being grounded in ethics that respect the right of all stakeholders "to know about matters that affect them" (2010, p. 759) and which includes having visible decision-making processes and clear communication of reasoning behind those decisions. Stakeholders should have access to performance reporting so that they may track "achievements against management plan objectives" (Lockwood, 2010, p. 759).

Internally, for the project strategy to be achieved it would be necessary therefore for all those involved in completing the various activities across all

The Sugarloaf Alliance Case Study   213

stages of the project to follow those aspects of the overall plan relevant to their tasks. Obviously, a range of contractors and subcontractors would be involved in such a large and widely spread project, so documenting and communicating objectives would be vital for transparency to be demonstrated.

The Alliance developed a clear purpose and provided reasons for the project and the approach being taken to its completion. The overall strategic plan was provided by the Alliance leadership team. This was communicated to all staff, and cascaded through supervisors and contractors to all people working on the project. It was acknowledged that "the success of the Sugarloaf Pipeline Alliance relied on the quality of its people, governance and leadership. The Alliance leadership team, effectively the 'board', comprising executives from all the Alliance partners, provided the project with its overarching strategic direction" (Smith et al., 2010, p. 21).

A Project Impact Assessment (PIA) report was prepared and approval granted to commence the project. Public hearings were held and submissions received. Decisions, for instance, choosing the pipeline route, were made based on the PIA and feedback from the public. The next step was to develop a series of Environmental Management Plans (EMPs) for approval by the various levels of government, with a total of 17 EMPs being developed. These plans contained detailed design drawings to support compliance. Each EMP contained 18 environmental programs including issues such as air quality, biosecurity, fauna, fires, greenhouse gas, ground water, noise, and vibration (Smith et al., 2010). Next came the Plan of Environmental Controls (PECs), supported by aerial maps covering the pipeline corridor. Again these were detailed and contained checkpoints that included threatened flora, potential fauna habitat zones, and details of traffic management works required for access. Site Environment Plans (SEPs) summarized requirements for each of the 17 EMPs, listing key management measures and who was responsible for each item. Site specific Work Activity Packs (WAPs) were created—in total 129—covering all work to be completed, and included checklists, details of work processes and construction method statements, the site specific PEC and SEP, and the WAPs directly linked back to the strategic plan, detailing all environmental considerations and related activities. Comprehensive governance and compliance plans were developed and Deb Cowley managed the process that she said entailed ensuring compliance, governance, and completion and thus "making sure we're doing it right" (Cowley quoted in Smith et al., 2010, p. 126). Müller et al. (2014) identified two dimensions of project governance: procedural and human. For the Alliance to have met the requirements of good governance within the procedural dimension, they would need to have developed structured plans and controls to make clear all the processes, roles, and responsibilities. This occurred, and the plans were found to have been adhered to.

Evidence that the plans were effectively communicated across and cascaded down the organization was provided by John Drury, the Alliance's senior electrical engineer. His comments also confirmed a close working

214 *Beverley Lloyd-Walker and Derek Walker*

relationship between several stakeholders. He stated "we worked in a process where all people were kept informed . . . vendors and suppliers . . . designers and site management. Working with so many different organisations could have gone badly, but it didn't. All problems were found, resolved, clarified and action plans initiated" (Smith et al., 2010, p. 105).

The Alliance's vision was communicated to the wider community via face-to-face meetings, shopping center displays, and meetings with community and stakeholder advisory groups. In excess of 30 fact sheets were developed and distributed widely relating to matters such as environmental management, cultural heritage, and reinstatement. Emails were used to advise users about planned changes to traffic flow, and schools and local businesses were provided with information specific to their needs. Community members were provided the opportunity to ask questions, were provided with reasoning behind decisions made, but were also heard, and changes were made to plans where appropriate. The opportunity was provided for stakeholders to participate in the planning of the pipeline construction and "to influence decision making processes and actions" (Lockwood, 2010, p. 760). This fits with Lockwood's fourth principle, that of *Inclusiveness*, where effective governance means having policies and structures to support contributions by stakeholders. Landowners were visited, phoned, and provided with information packs detailing the planned pipeline route and its potential impact on their property. Again, they were able to seek explanations and were able to request changes; most of these could be incorporated via changes to the original plans. Door knocking efforts and site visit invitations also helped to ensure that all people could know how the construction would affect them. Performance reporting about the progress of the project was provided via local newspaper articles as well as presentations to councils and industry and community groups and other media outlets.

Open communication of the planned pipeline route led to a clear understanding of the tasks to be performed. Processes were established, modified to address stakeholder concerns, and new processes communicated to support action. The commitment to achieve better than average occupational health and safety (OH&S) standards was supported by training of all employees involved on the project, and daily emails kept awareness levels high and provided a forum for feedback and continuous improvement of OH&S processes, and, with linked training and communication, improved safety behavior occurred. The 'Think Five, Stay Alive' campaign updated the OH&S processes, and these changes to processes were supported by supervisors that ensured workers stopped to assess risks before commencing work (Smith et al., 2010).

Objectives or goals may be easily stated, but ensuring that the strategy is enacted by linking the goals of each of the stages of the project to the overall strategic goals requires monitoring to ensure that objectives are achieved. This relates to Millstein et al.'s (1998) and Aras's and Crowther's (2010) *Accountability* principle, where accountabilities are assigned for all aspects of the project and what is to be delivered, what each project manager is accountable for, is clear. According to Lockwood (2010, p. 759), *Accountability* within governance systems that involve protected areas, as for this case study, is about "allocation and acceptance of responsibility for decisions and actions; the extent to which a governing body is answerable to its constituency" and to which it "is answerable to 'higher level' authorities; and allocation of responsibilities to those institutional levels that best match the scale of issues and values being addressed." The constituency to which the Alliance was answerable was broad: the Federal, State, and several Local government authorities, landowners whose properties would be directly impacted, and other residents, business, the road users, schools, and other public facilities located in the area, the broader population of the state of Victoria, and interest groups representing at times global concerns.

The driving goal of being a caring neighbor, with the concerns for people, the environment, and heritage of the area, meant that all decision making needed to be made with this vision in mind if the Alliance's strategy was to be achieved. Considerable delegation of authority was going to be required because the work was spread along a 70-kilometer construction corridor. With work spread across a broad rural area, with areas of public land, protected areas, and private properties that would need to be entered and work carried out on them, heading up operations across the various stages of the pipeline would need to meet the Alliance's specific objectives to support achievement of the projects goals. Clear details of responsibilities and expected outcomes would be required, with those managing each stage having been given the power to make decisions to achieve their goals. With overall project management possibly located some distance away, the leadership team would need to place trust in the ability of the project manager of each stage to take responsibility for their contribution to the overall project. Largely, this occurred through induction programs for all contractors and their employees entering the project at various stages, and with the information cascaded from the project strategy through the Environmental Management Plans (EMPs), Plan of Environmental Controls (PECs), Site Environmental Plans (SEPs), and, in particular, the detailed Work Activity Packs (WAPs) for each parcel of work.

The Alliance's statements about their concern for the environment, the communities of the area, and the residents of Melbourne who would benefit from the water in times of need, were expressed in a variety of ways, including 'being a caring neighbor,' and actioned through the tasks and responsibilities detailed in the WAPs. *Responsibility,* according to Aras and Crowther (2010), entails having sufficient trust in others to hand on power to them so that they might achieve their objectives; for the Alliance this would be as set out in the relevant WAP. In addition to responsibility for delivering stage outcomes, project managers would require the decision making power required to execute the organization's strategy. The Occupational Health and Safety (OH&S) Manager committed to the project vision of 'no harm.' The trust and responsibility placed with him provided him the freedom to develop a new approach to managing OH&S to achieve the 'no harm' vision. He created a confidential hotline so that Alliance workers could report safety ideas, concerns, and incidents. This was rolled out across the Alliance, and was used by Alliance staff and subcontractors, resulting in a change in safety behaviors and the OH&S culture. This assisted the Alliance to achieve its objective as well as below industry average incidents and a record of no lost time injuries (Smith et al., 2010).

If being judged as a caring neighbor was important, and project stage managers were to be judged on the extent to which the 'neighbors' in their area perceived them to be caring, they would require the autonomy and authority to modify plans to achieve this objective. This would represent the *Fairness* principle within Millstein et al.'s (1998) and Aras's and Crowther's (2010) good governance framework. Lockwood (2010, p. 760) also sees the *Fairness* principle within governance as important and as incorporating giving attention and respect to stakeholders' views and involving "respect between higher and lower levels of authorities" within the organization. It addresses issues such as consistent and unbiased decision making; recognizing the rights of all, with due respect given to the rights of indigenous people within the affected area; and acknowledging "the intrinsic value of nature."

For the Alliance's stated objectives to be delivered, and for good governance to be perceived to have occurred, therefore, all project managers, those responsible and accountable for the various components of the project, would need to make decisions which supported achieving the greater common good. Efforts taken to reduce noise, vibration, and dust, to minimize disruption to traffic flow, and to protect the environment indicate an ethical approach to project delivery that included fairness. Stakeholders expressed concern for wildlife that was addressed by installing a wombat gate that enabled wombats to be moved to a safe area during construction. Landowners did not want pests or plant diseases transported from one property to another. Those responsible for work on private property adopted strict biosecurity protocols which, though time consuming, dispelled landowners' concerns. The project director was quoted as saying, "I'm especially proud of the way pipeline employees worked with landowners and agricultural specialists to reinstate paddocks, alleviating understandable anxieties. Our people have worked at a consistently high standard to overcome all sorts of uncertainties and challenges along the way" (Melbourne Water Corporation, 2009, p. 1). Public meetings were held, newsletters were published advising progress and planned work, and feedback was listened to and, where appropriate, respect for the relevant stakeholders' views was addressed by changes to the project plan.

Lockwood (2010, p. 760) includes the principle of *Resilience* in his framework, which involves ensuring "the right balance" is found "between flexibility and security;" building new knowledge "into decision making and implementation;" being aware of and managing threats as well as opportunities and associated risks, and reflecting on performance of individuals,

The Sugarloaf Alliance Case Study 217

the organization, and systems. Research conducted prior to the commencement of the project revealed the threat of disruptive actions by concerned groups, with the potential to delay work. The communication plan, actioned before work began and continued throughout the project, addressed this risk. Changes made to plans demonstrated flexibility, and the building in of new knowledge from meetings, feedback, and learning through the construction process fed into these changes to plans.

Lockwood's principles of good governance also include *Principle and Connectivity,* which includes "effective coordination within and between levels of protected area governance" (2010, p. 761). The linking of plans related to protecting flora, fauna, and cultural heritage, as well as the project communication plan, provided a coordinated approach to governance across all sensitive areas along the construction corridor. It supported a coordinated approach across levels of operation. Overall, ethical project management will include ensuring compliance with any requirements placed on the project by authorities. The EBPCs outlined these requirements and the extent to which the Alliance complied with requirements continues to be monitored. In 2014 it was found that the Sugarloaf Pipeline Alliance had complied with all EBPCs and that the client, Melbourne Water, was continuing to ensure compliance (Melbourne Water, 2014). Monitoring continues, and the 2014 report to the Federal Government stated that the "Sugarloaf Pipeline Alliance and Melbourne Water have implemented actions and adhered to the conditions placed on the Project by the then Federal Minister for the Environment, Heritage and Arts" (Melbourne Water, 2014, p. 36).

Brower and Mahajan (2013) predicted that stakeholders could drive good corporate social performance. From the outset the Alliance's strategic planning, and procedures to support implementation and guide practice throughout the project, indicated they had a high level of sensitivity to their stakeholders' needs. They stated a desire to be a caring neighbor. Their goal was to deliver a remarkable water project, one that would ensure Victoria's sustainable future, whilst protecting the environment. This indicated a driving desire to value creation, Brower and Mahajan's (2013) first element to support corporate social performance as a response to stakeholder demands. The Alliance faced a broad and diverse group of stakeholders (Brower and Mahajan's element 2), and they faced scrutiny by governments, residents, interest groups, and the media. Indeed the Alliance confronted the risk of action that could jeopardize the timely progress of the project from community or interest groups (element 3). According to Brower and Mahajan (2013), the Alliance's response to CSP would be spread across a wider range of actions, relating to the broad and complex range of issues they faced from stakeholders.

Extensive research and preparation was carried out before commencing construction of the pipeline. Progress was halted if community feedback or the Alliance's own continuous monitoring efforts indicated that the established principles and stated goals would not be achieved. Despite this, or

218 *Beverley Lloyd-Walker and Derek Walker*

perhaps because of it, the Sugarloaf Alliance was one of two major pipeline projects completed to provide water to the city of Melbourne. Both were delivered via alliances that have been described by the Managing Director of Melbourne Water as incredibly successful, "under budget and ahead of schedule" (Skinner quoted in Smith et al., 2010, p. 10).

The Alliance allowed input from the community into their plans, thus providing full transparency and the opportunity for interest groups to influence design. In 2010, the Sugarloaf Pipeline Alliance team was recognized by the Alliancing Association of Australasia, winning the Team Excellence award (GHD.com/Australia, 2010). The choice of "a progressive alliance model" (Smith et al., 2010, p. 17) may well have been a contributing factor to the high level negotiation skills applied during the project, and the creative solutions that were found to support successful completion of the project, whilst ensuring a net gain to the environment and community. Two members of the alliance management team commented on what they felt had been the most significant achievement of the Sugarloaf Alliance, stating: "The Alliance encouraged innovation throughout the life of the project. Innovations ranged from simple ideas such as gates to protect wombats, to new techniques to improve pipelaying speed and safety" (Smith et al., 2010, p. 22). The process of agreeing and committing to guiding principles at the beginning of the project that an alliance approach supports, combined with a 'best for project' culture, appears to have contributed to the success of this project. At the same time, this high level commitment culture (rather than the good of any one alliance member organization over that of other member organizations) supported the establishment of and implementation of initiatives to ensure delivery of the project governance principles.

The Sugarloaf Alliance delivered the original stated outcome on budget and ahead of schedule, whilst ensuring the safety of staff, satisfaction of affected communities, reinstatement of flora and fauna, and an overall environmental net gain. The project's outcome continues to support provision of the better good to the society and will do so into the future. The criticisms that the project received in relation to removing water from the 'food bowl,' the construction having an adverse impact on the environment, and pumping of the water adding to increased greenhouse gas emissions have largely been addressed. Currently the water is not being taken from the Goulburn River, and pumping is thus not required. However, along with weather conditions not requiring the emergency water supply to be called on in recent years, the use of hydro and other 'green' sources of energy have allayed the greenhouse emission concerns. Practices during construction ensured that the environment was not adversely affected and the related project that renewed pipes within the Goulburn irrigation system has provided net savings in water for the benefit of local communities, supporting continued food production. Some groups do still question the government's actions in commissioning the project (see, for instance, Friends of the Earth, 2011), but the project governance principles applied reduced public opposition and have provided positive outcomes, securing Victoria's sustainable future by providing an 'insurance' against future droughts for Melbourne's, and the state's, growing population.

References

Aakus, M., & Bzdak, M. (2015). Stakeholder Engagement as Communication Design Practice. *Journal of Public Affairs*, *15*(2), 188–200.

ABS. (2015). *Australian Demographic Statistics*.

Aras, G., & Crowther, D. (2008). Governance and Sustainability: An Investigation into the Relationship between Corporate Governance and Corporate Sustainability. *Management Decision*, *46*(3), 433–448.

Aras, G., & Crowther, D. (2010). Corporate Social Responsibility: A Broader View of Corporate Governance. In G. Aras & D. Crowther (Eds.), *A Handbook of Corporate Governance and Social Responsibility* (pp. 265–280). Farnham, UK: Gower Publishing Limited.

Australian Government Department of the Environment, W., Heritage and the Arts. (2010). *Securing Our Water Future*.

Barber, J. R. (2011). Sugarloaf Pipeline Landslide Risk Management and Planning Approvals. *Australian Geometrics*, *46*(2), 163–174.

Bessire, D., Chatelin, C., & Onnée, S. (2010). What is 'Good' Corporate Governance? In G. Aras & D. Crowther (Eds.), *A Handbook of Corporate Governance and Social Responsibility* (pp. 37–50). Farnham, UK: Gower Publishing Ltd.

Bessire, D., & Onnée, S. (2010). Assessing Corporate Social Performance: Strategies of Legitimation and Conflicting Ideologies. *Critical Perspective on Accounting*, *21*(6), 445–467.

Brower, J., & Mahajan, V. (2013). Driven to be Good: A Stakeholder Theory Perspective on the Drivers of Corporate Social Performance. *Journal of Business Ethics*, *117*, 313–331.

Department of Finance and Treasury Victoria. (2010). *The Practitioners' Guide to Alliance Contracting*. Melbourne: Department of Treasury and Finance, Victoria.

Dowling, J. (2007). Taboo Water Plan in Pipeling. *The Age*.

Elkington, J. (1997). *Cannibals with Forks*. London, UK: Capstone Publishing.

Environment Victoria. (2008a). Environment Victoria Submission to Project Impact Assessment of the Sugarload Pipeline Proposal.

Friends of the Earth. (2009). Pipeline Threatens Endangered Species and Our Struggling Rivers. *Media Release*.

Friends of the Earth. (2011). Letter in the Weekly Times. *The North South Pipeline*. Retrieved from http://www.melbourne.foe.org.au/the_north_south_pipeline_mel bourne_it_s_time_to_take_a_stand

Fyfe, M. (2009). Water Project 'Not Needed'. *The Sydney Morning Herald*.

GHD.com/Australia. (2010). GHD Sugarloaf Award. Retrieved September 29, 2015, from http://www.ghd.com/global/about-us/news/media-lounge-2010/ghd-sugarloaf-award/

Hannam, P. (2015). Bureau of Meteorology Declares El Nino Event in Australia. *The Sydney Morning Herald*.

Ims, K. J., & Pedersen, L. J. T. (Eds.). (2015). *Business and the Greater Good: Rethinking Business Ethics in an Age of Crisis*. Cheltenham, UK: Edward Elgar Publishing Limited.

Ker, P., & Rood, D. (2008). Full Review to Guide Murray-Darling Water Deals. *The Age.*

Lockwood, M. (2010). Good Governance for Terrestrial Protected Areas: A Framework, Principles and Performance Outcomes. *Journal of Environmental Management, 91*(3), 754–766.

Lucas, C. (2015). Australian cities boom as Melbourne closes in on Sydney. *The Age.*

Melbourne Water. (2014). Annual Report to the Federal Department of Environment. *Sugarloaf Pipeline Project.*

Melbourne Water. (2015). What We Do: North-South Pipeline. Retrieved September 2, 2015, from http://www.melbournewater.com.au/whatwedo/supply-water/reservoirs/Pages/water-storage-reservoirs.asp

Melbourne Water Corporation. (2009). *Sustainability Report: A Review of Melbourne Water's Performance in 2008/2009.*

Millstein, I. M., Albert, M., Cadbury, A., Feddersen, D., & Tateisi, N. (1998). *Improving Competitiveness and Access to Capital in Global Markets.* Paris, France: OECD Publications.

Moncrief, M. (2015). Inside the Desalination Plant—Your Guided Tour. *The Age.*

Müller, R., Andersen, E. S., Kvalnes, Ø., Shao, J., Sankaran, S., Turner, J. R., Biesenthal, C., Walker, D. H. T., & Gudergan, S. (2013). The Interrelationship of Governance, Trust and Ethics in Temporary Organisations. *Project Management Journal, 45*(4), 39–54.

Müller, R., Turner, J. R., Andersen, E. S., Shao, J., & Kvalnes, Ø. (2014). Ethics, Trust, and Governance in Temporary Organizations. *Project Management Journal, 45*(4), 39–54.

Munns, A. K. (1995). Potential Influence of Trust on the Successful Completion of a Project. *International Journal of Project Management, 13*(1), 19–24.

National Climate Centre. (2010). Australia's Wettest September on Record But It Is Not Enough to Clear Long-Term Rainfall Deficits. *Special Climate Statement, 22.* National Climate Centre, Bureau of Meteorology, Australian Government, Melbourne, p. 10.

Pinto, J. K., Slevin, D. P., & English, B. (2009). Trust in Projects: An Empirical Assessment of Owner/Contractor Relationships. *International Journal of Project Management, 27*(6), 638–648.

Public Relations Institute of Australia. (2010). Golden Target Awards. Retrieved September 2, 2015, 2014, from http://www.pria.com.au/evensawards/golden-target-awards

Smith, S., Anglin, T., & Harrison, K. (2010). *Sugarloaf Pipeline: A Pipe in Time.* Melbourne, Victoria: Sugarloaf Pipeline Alliance.

Smyth, H., Gustafsson, M., & Ganskau, E. (2010). The Value of Trust in Project Business. *International Journal of Project Management, 28*(2), 117–129.

Victorian Department of Sustainability and Environment (DSE). (2004). *Securing Our Water Future Together: Victorian Government White Paper.*

Walker, D. H. T., & Lloyd-Walker, B. M. (2015). *Collaborative Project Procurement Arrangements.* Newtown Square, PA: Project Management Institute.

14 Governance at the Front-End

Managing the Clash of Objectives in Project Organizations

Shankar Sankaran and Christopher Biesenthal

This chapter describes two case studies conducted in Australia to investigate ethical issues that occurred in two project organizations. The issues were primarily a result of internal conflicts, as each party tried to protect its own interests or was concerned about how decisions taken by them in the interest of the organization might affect them personally. The authors propose that such conflicts could be minimized if the organizations adapted their governance practices to minimize 'interface' problems.

Introduction

While working on a collaborative project investigating the Interrelationship of Governance, Trust, and Ethics in Temporary Organizations with Ralf Müller, the two authors of this chapter carried out two case studies in Australia. In these studies they came across ethical issues that arose internally within organizations or between an organization and its principal due to clash of objectives. The two case studies described in this chapter analyze the issues that arise at the front-end of projects in these organizations where decisions made can have an impact on the overall success of the project. The issues that arise between sales departments who sell a project and the implementers of the project (usually the engineers or software developers) are a problem well known to practitioners who work in organizations that carry out projects. Surprisingly, a review of the literature shows that this 'interface' problem is not discussed well in the project management literature. Our case studies highlight this interface problem and the ethical issues that arise from it.

The chapter is structured as follows. After a brief review of the literature on ethical issues in projects and the impact of problems at the front-end of projects, we present a framework that we use to analyze the cases. We then present the two cases. We start with the ethical dilemmas faced in each case study, followed by a structured analysis of the cases using four key characteristics of good project governance discussed in the framework that we proposed. We then discuss other issues that arose in the case studies that contributed to ethical concerns. Finally, we discuss our findings from

222 *Shankar Sankaran and Christopher Biesenthal*

the case studies and relate them to the literature reviewed. We conclude by suggesting that incorporating governance of interface issues in project-based organizations can help overcome internal ethical issues in projects to help them be more successful.

Ethics in the Project Management Literature

The concept of ethics and how it applies to the field of project management is a highly under-researched topic in the literature despite the increasing importance of moral, behavioral, and political correctness of the modern business environment. Moreover, the concepts of ethics in project management can be approached from multiple angles, stemming from different underlying academic disciplines (Müller et al., 2013). The field of normative ethics constitutes the majority of research work being done in this area (Godbold, 2007, 2008; Godbold & Turner, 1996) and is concerned with linking traditional moral philosophy and the management of projects. More precisely, normative ethics deals with the high-level nature of ethics to ensure that the organizational processes in place are just, fair, and reasonable, do not violate human rights, and their outcomes are equally ethical (Müller et al., 2013). This type of ethics sets the ethical frame in which project work is being delivered, and can thus be closely linked to the topic of project governance, as governance "is ultimately concerned with creating the conditions for ordered rule and collective action" (Stoker, 1998, p. 155) within the project context. In other words, project governance is concerned with the normative nature of project work that defines the value system and organizational processes that enable projects to achieve their objectives (Müller, 2009, p. 4). Good project governance should facilitate ethical practices at multiple levels of the organization, and thus ethical behavior. However, this is not always the case, as the case studies show.

Ethical behavior is closely related to ethical decision making, as any decision can have a significant impact on the organization and its stakeholders, in regards to health, safety, consumer satisfaction, profitability, etc. (Trevino, 1986). At times, project managers (i.e., decision makers) face situations where a particular decision creates an ethical tension between two moral principles (e.g., private gain vs. the public good, sustainability vs. profit), where obeying one would transgress the other. In this chapter, we describe such ethical tensions as ethical dilemmas. These situations often reflect a choice between an ethical and an unethical decision, such as a decision that is taken in one's self-interest, which violates a moral principle of the organization (or the individual). Despite the fact that organizational decisions cannot always be classified as right or wrong, ethical dilemmas and unethical decisions are common occurrences in our daily business life.

Behavioral ethics is driven by questions regarding why individuals behave unethically in the workplace (Müller et al., 2013). Social scientists occupy this area of ethics, but there is a lack of research on aspects of ethics in the field of project management. Unethical behavior has different drivers, and Kish-Gephart et al. (2010) distinguish between three specific drivers that are based at the organizational level, namely, *bad apples*, *bad cases*, and *bad barrels*. *Bad apples* reflect the individual level of unethical behavior, stating that individuals may act unethically (or cheat) based on their cognitive moral development, underlying idealism, or demographic factor, e.g., age or education (Müller et al., 2013; Shalvi et al., 2011). *Bad cases* describe the situational nature of unethical behavior, where unethical actions can be triggered by moral dilemmas at the workplace and cultivated by the scale of consequences, social consensus, probability of effect, and temporal immediacy (Müller et al., 2013). *Bad barrels* explain the organizational-level drivers of unethical behavior of the individual, which can be described as the ethical culture of the organization (Trevino, 1986, 1990) or ethical climate of the workplace (Victor & Cullen, 1988), often manifested in codes of conduct (or not). In conclusion, all three behavioral orientations provide valid clarifications about why individuals engage in unethical actions.

But what is ethical behavior in the first place? In its most generic form, ethics can be described as 'being good' or 'doing the right thing' based on the values of the our society; ethical behavior is acting in accordance with the underlying rules of our modern society. This includes the acceptance of national and local cultural values, workplace norms, and best practices, as well as having an understanding of what it means to do the 'right thing.' However, these values and rules that drive ethical behavior are riddled with ambiguities, interpretations, and inconsistencies, based on cultural, organizational, and individual differences and perspectives. Some authors even argue that ethical behavior does not exist in business or project management (Walker & Lloyd-Walker, 2014). Donaldson (2008) takes an even stronger stance in regards to the topic of ethics in management, arguing that teaching it can be ineffective and counterproductive. Adopting ethical behavior is therefore not as straightforward as it may seem and is more than just 'doing the right thing,' especially in a business environment where financial profits are often the main driver of human behavior. To get a more balanced understanding of ethical behavior, project managers need to consider the wider stakeholder community and "balance contractual, morality and relativist perspectives when performing project work" (Walker & Lloyd-Walker, 2014, p. 568).

Traditional project management assumes that individuals in organizations act unethically in a self-interested fashion to maximize their own profits and returns. The most dominant example of this is the influence that Agency Theory has on our understanding of corporate or project governance, where traditional governance structures of organizations are developed around the idea that individuals merely act in their own interest and therefore have to be controlled and monitored closely (Eisenhardt, 1989). Traditional theories therefore fail to provide a rich and contextual picture of ethics in the project management area, and even foster bad management practice (Ghoshal,

224 *Shankar Sankaran and Christopher Biesenthal*

2005). One of the main shortcomings of traditional project management theories is their ability to link behavioral ethics to normative ethics (Müller et al., 2013). This chapter will therefore follow Loo (2002) and explore ethical dilemmas in the project environment or, more precisely, a situation that describes a mental conflict between moral imperatives. Our cases focus on the front-end of projects, as it provides a fertile ground for ethical dilemmas.

The Front-End of Projects

Morris (2013) and Williams and Samset (2010) have highlighted the importance of paying more attention to the front-end of projects to improve project success. Morris (2013) argues that studies on success factors of projects have emphasized the importance of the development of the front-end definition and the key role of the owner/sponsor taking a holistic, big picture perspective on projects. He also points out that 'interface management' in projects is not a well-researched topic. Williams and Samset (2010) state that "the initial choice of project concept" is also critical and could have the "largest impact on long-term success and failure" (p. 38). They point to the increasing importance of "quality at entry," and describe a World Bank survey which found that projects that are better identified, prepared, and appraised have four times the success rate of those that have not paid attention to the front-end.

Williams and Samset (2010) discuss front-end issues of projects generally from an external perspective (i.e., when projects are decided upon) in public sector projects before being authorized. However they do not touch upon interface issues that occur when projects are handed over within an organization, which is the focus of our case studies. We argue that front-end governance of internal project transfer between parties that negotiate a project order from an organization and transfer them internally to another part of the organization responsible for implementing the project is also critical to project success.

One organization, where one of the authors was employed in the engineering department, often faced 'interface problems' due to sales under-quoting projects. The engineers were given 48 hours, after a project was handed over to them from sales, to report to top management on realistic performance criteria for the project (time, cost, and quality). Any increase in internal costs or resource allocation to achieve the promised target was agreed to between the engineering department and the top management. While it was too late to reject the project, such a review helped the organization to get a true picture of the situation. This also helped avoid further internal conflicts during the execution of the project, as management then asked sales and engineering to cooperate and recover costs when the project was executed.

While interface issues between the front and back end of an organization have not been discussed extensively in the project management literature, they have been discussed in the (industrial) marketing literature. Keaveney

(2008) described the "marketer–engineer" conflict in high technology companies and found that such "blame games" have a high proportion of personal attributions and relationship conflicts in contrast with task conflicts reported in earlier marketing literature. Shaw and Shaw (1998) have suggested physically co-locating the two departments (marketing and engineering) and provide marketing training to engineers as a way of minimizing the conflict between engineers and marketers. Griffin and Hauser (1992), who analyzed patterns of communication between marketing, engineering, and manufacturing in new product development, found that greater communication between parties can help the development to be successful. Blomquist and Wilson (2007) conducted an exploratory study of project marketing and project management functions in four firms in different industries— engineering, shipbuilding, telecommunications, and IT—and suggest that projects that have a high amount of uncertainty will require close interactions with the customer from both the project marketing and project management functions. This seems to highlight that uncertainty may be a factor that has an impact on the relationship between front-end selling/marketing and project management.

Managing uncertainty in projects is a topic that is often discussed in the project management literature. Atkinson et al. (2006) suggest that, as projects take on 'softer' characteristics, such as when goals and objectives are ambiguous, trust between parties plays a part in uncertainty management. Smyth et al. (2010) investigated the value of trust in project business, and found that trust is socially constructed and can assist in making better business decisions while handling projects. One of the prominent factors that became evident during the investigation of the Interrelationship of Governance, Trust, and Ethics in Temporary Organizations was trust in situations involving ethics. The following 'good governance' framework was therefore used to analyze and make sense of the cases.

Framework Used for Analysis of Interviews

Aras and Crowther (2009) developed a 'good governance' framework that incorporates fundamental ethical concepts and provides a richer and more comprehensive picture of ethics in project governance. The framework establishes four principles that constitute sustainable (and ethical) project governance, namely, transparency, accountability, responsibility, and fairness (Aras & Crowther, 2009). Transparency is concerned with the level of visibility and clarity around organizational processes and goals. The following questions are examples of some transparency issues: is there an established project management process in place and do managers know about it? Are the goals of the project clear to all stakeholders involved in the project? The notion of accountability deals with the organization's ability to ensure that the objectives are achieved, intra-organizational objectives are aligned (i.e., strategic goals with project performance), and clear

226 *Shankar Sankaran and Christopher Biesenthal*

accountabilities are assigned. Responsibility refers to the establishment of work tasks, which includes handing over power and having trust in people to meet the objectives. The concept of fairness in Aras's and Crowther's (2009) model describes the ethical execution of the organizational practices in place and whether the organizational objectives and performance measures are reasonable and achievable.

In summary, the above-described model of good governance has four underlying principles. These principles will be used to analyze the cases in this chapter and to explore how the ethical issues occurred at the front-end of projects and within the existing governance structure of the project.

Case Study 1—Spatial

Spatial is a management consultant that provides advice to organizations on people, place, and performance at 12 locations around the world. In Australia, they provide consultancy services for commercial buildings, including advice on effective utilization of space in offices. The recent increase in mobility due to technology has created some new opportunities for Spatial. The organization undertakes small projects worth A\$20K for advice to large projects worth thousands of dollars that include a longer engagement to manage change within organizations.

We interviewed both the project owner and project manager (PM) of a Spatial project, but most of our discussions are based on the interview with the project manager, as the project owner was not involved deeply in the project we were studying although affected by it.

When we visited Spatial they were going through an organizational transition due to being acquired by a large international organization, 'Big Guy.' The ethical issues associated with this case mainly involved the front-end of the takeover project. One of the staff of Spatial, the PM, was the main link between Big Guy and Spatial, and became involved in the front-end of the changes that will occur due to the takeover.

Several ethical issues due to this takeover project arose for the PM:

First, several people working at Spatial were likely to be retrenched due to the takeover, including the PM. So the first ethical dilemma was between his self-interest and the company's interest. He had worked very hard for Spatial for several years, including taking a pay cut during the global financial crisis, and faced the prospect of being retrenched. This put him in an untenable situation.

> *So it's a clear ethical issue of—for me—self-interest versus company interest. Because clearly I'm here working as part of the company and working very hard to do that, then not knowing of course where I will go or what will happen after that.*

The second dilemma that the PM faced was professional in nature. One of the processes involved in the takeover project was carrying out a due

Governance at the Front-End 227

diligence of Spatial's finances. The PM was also a professionally accredited accountant and this caused tension, as he had to meet professional obligations that could prove detrimental to him.

> *Because clearly you have—professionally I have to operate within that scope or I lose my designation, but it's really interesting to me because it's the first time it's been a personal, personal, ethical issue.*

The third dilemma was being unable to respond to queries by his colleagues who wanted to know what was going to happen to them. As a project manager he had to keep things confidential while at the same time he had worked with several people in the company for a long time and had developed close relationships with them.

> *I mean day to day you're still ethical because it's what's best for company and there are people here that obviously you have professional relationships with and you want to make sure that they're okay.*

On analyzing the interviews using the four principles of good governance, the following issues were revealed.

Transparency

The PM became aware that communication from Big Guy was being funneled through one individual on a daily basis to him in a controlled manner without divulging a lot of detail, which frustrated him.

> *We certainly have not had a conversation about the governance structure in relation to ethics. We've certainly not received documentation on how we're to be operating in that space.*

Lack of clear communication also contributed to transparency issues by not enabling the PM to explain what was going on in the transition period to people in Spatial who were going to be affected by it.

> *So, for instance, they've said a week ago, well we'll have to start to have conversations about what we're going to tell our employees. I said well that's great, because I started telling employees two months ago every week what's happening, so if you want to start to have a conversation you're about two months too late because I've been doing it for two months.*

Accountability

While accountability was enforced by the organization through steering committees or governance structures, the interviews did not reveal such

228 *Shankar Sankaran and Christopher Biesenthal*

issues. However, we could observe that the PM felt that he was accountable to provide valid information to Big Guy from a professional point of view.

Responsibility and Fairness

There were no issues that could be classified under this theme from the interviews.

The interviews also yielded evidence that Spatial had several procedures that were meant to establish appropriate project governance, which did not always work as intended.

One of the procedures that came up was the reporting structure that the PM was asked to follow.

> *I mean, I guess it's who I report to directly in terms of that isn't it? So it's a bit of a complicated structure because it depends on who you're talking to. I mean, essentially I report—I've got a co-lead who's a member of our new project and then we report up into the transition team, which is a [overseas] based team.*

The second was the lack of apparent processes to deal with Spatial during the transition.

> *It's interesting, not necessarily the best managed process, and this is a company that does mergers and acquisitions all the time. I mean they do it all the time, so you'd think that they would have processes for that interim period.*

Another theme that is of interest to the topics covered in this book is 'Trust.' There was certainly a lack of trust from Spatial's PM on the intentions of Big Guy.

> *I mean, you're right, maybe that's—I'm sceptical and I have no trust at this point. . . . I wish I trusted them, maybe I can trust—maybe in a month, you come back, and I've got another job with them and I trust them.*

The way communication was organized did not contribute to establishing trust between the two firms.

> *You can't just actually pick up the phone and have a conversation. They'll send four emails, they'll invite 10 people to the conversation, you actually all get on so you've got 10 people and everyone's just talking on the phone. You don't know the voices so you don't know the people that you're talking to, so the calls we've had like that, it's really difficult to establish that trust because you don't have a one-on-one— you don't even have a one-on-one dialogue.*

Governance at the Front-End 229

From the comments made by the PM on processes, communication, and trust, Big Guy seemed to rely more on behavioral control rather than outcome control in terms of governance over the acquisition project.

Case Study 2—Connectivity

The second case study that was carried out in Australia was an IT solutions provider whose main products were to assist supporting computer networks in organizations. We met both the project owner or sponsor and the project manager. They were handling more than 50 projects and there were close to 25 project managers and administrators and program managers.

The main ethical dilemmas that were faced by Connectivity were primarily with the sales team, who sold projects to customers without understanding the full technical aspects of the project and without validating the solution with the technical experts who had to implement them. This resulted in the technical side having to spend more money to address gaps, which was not in the overall interests of Connectivity.

One of the ethical dilemmas faced by the project owner was how to protect the project team from being unsuccessful due to the mistakes made at the front-end of the project at the sales phase.

> *I want to [do] well by [my] organization, but I also don't want to throw my team into a positioning or a project whereby they're not going to be successful from the very beginning.*

Another dilemma that arose in the organizations was due to different ways in which the sales and project teams were rewarded. While the sales team enjoyed individual rewards, the project teams were rewarded for collective outcome, which is further supported by the following statement:

> *We're structured differently. The sales team are incentivized and they are commission based. My team isn't. We get a bonus at the end of the year, based on performance. So a number of things—company performance, individual performance and then they . . . individual performance is made up of a grade and then that's a percentage of the bonus application.*

The issues related to governance and ethics also arose out of conflict between the objectives of the parties involved. One conflict was due to their different interests in the project.

> *But I have had ethical situations in the sense that—or conflict—with other stakeholders within [XXXX]. So most primarily sales team, where they are promising or engaging with end customers, without really understanding the full aspect of the project, and they're promising on things that won't happen.*

230 *Shankar Sankaran and Christopher Biesenthal*

The conflict resulted in the project team being unable to plan properly.

> *So the account managers often have a grow plan or an account planning strategy. But the service sales team, they try to align with them as much as possible, but they pretty much take whatever comes in the door. From our perspective, in terms of planning, it's a little more difficult.*

The situation made it difficult for the project manager to stay up to date with the project.

> *Although I may push back as a manager because I come from professional organizations, the sales might commit on our behalf. Therefore, we're behind the eight ball; we're not setting ourselves up for success. We're always catching [up] we're [actually] chasing ourselves for the whole time.*

There was also apparent lack of knowledge of the importance of project managers and appreciation of their roles.

> *This is one of our constant battles, because we often are saying this to our management team or saying this to sales, is that—and partially is due to uneducation and ignorance. Part of the difficulty is parts of the business don't understand the value of a project manager. They see them as glorified administrators or secretaries. They don't understand that they manage risk, they manage stakeholders and we're having to educate all the time. Even when we educate, that value proposition is still undervalued.*

Each party viewed its own success differently, which affected the success of the project.

> *We have clear dependencies and we have a clear outline as to how we deliver this. In order to get to the price point place they want to do that. So their success is not our success. Their success is the sale. Unfortunately, that's a conversation that we always have with them. Not always, we have often. I mean, we've improved over the last three years, but that's the type of conversation we've had.*

On analyzing the interviews in Case Study 2 using the four principles of good governance, the following issues were revealed.

Transparency

One of the issues that was raised by the project owner was the lack of transparency between the sales team and the project team during the selling phase, which caused repercussions down stream.

> *They unintentionally try to sell something to the customer that is not feasible to achieve by the delivery team. Once the sale is made, the customer*

Governance at the Front-End   231

is passed onto the delivery team and the sales team's job is done for this particular client. The delivery team, then, has to manage the expectations and readjust the promised service.

While the customer saw the organization as one entity, unaware of the internal issues, the sales and project departments saw themselves as separate.

The customers are not aware of the internal problems and structural discrepancies of the company. They see it as one entity that delivers a product.

The project manager felt that while informal discussions helped in making issues transparent between sales and projects, it was not always formalized later.

There will be some informal discussions over the coffee, or they're discussing things. You will not make every discussion . . . formal, but, what I'm saying is, if you discuss a certain aspect or some item, you will bring it to the formal meeting as well and get everybody to understand it as well. Sure, you will make progress and you will keep moving, but you will inform everybody in a formal way that this work has been discussed and [give them] a heads up.

The issues that occurred between the sales and project teams were not confined to the front-end and continued during the project. Often, to maintain good relationship with the customer, the sales teams agreed to some changes without consulting or informing the project team during the implementation.

They often engage with the customer without letting the project manager know. Sometimes, they make promises [on our behalf] and the project manager is the last person to find out, which is not the right way that we work. It's not part of the methodology, it's not part of the agreement, it's not part of the governance structure.

Accountability

While project managers were held accountable for delivering on time, the organization was flexible if the customer relationship allowed the company to negotiate delays. The project owner felt that the organization was trying to improve accountability of project managers. It was not always possible to comply with all the customer's requirements.

We don't always get that right, because the customer's not willing to comply at times. So I think that's something that—I mean, I don't know if you're looking specifically at governance as something that often is missed on large projects, for whatever reason. But we are trying, as an organization, to do that better . . . highly complex, high-risk projects.

Responsibility and Fairness

There were no issues conveyed during the interviews that could be classified under these themes.

The interviews showed that Connectivity used procedures to manage issues related to governance and implementation of projects. The project manager explained how the company's ethics policy helped to minimize ethical issues.

He kept emphasizing the company's well-defined ethics policy and structures that are in place. He even mentioned that he reads them every year so that he can say "yes, I have read and understood what the corporate policy is on the ethics and being currently [used] in the business."

At times, we felt that the project manager was cautious in his replies and wanted to indicate to us that he toed the company's line.

However, some flexibility to discuss when ethical dilemmas, such as accepting gifts, arose was explained during the interviews. Both the project owner and project manager mentioned the appropriateness of acceptance of gifts from stakeholders during the project.

> *There are ways to talk to our HR and the legals that, in our present situation, what should be done in this particular—if there has to be some way around, but there's a very well-defined policy.*

Procedures also came in handy when projects became more complex, giving rise to unusual situations. The project manager felt positive about the guidance that can be obtained from policies.

> *The more complex a project is, the more important it is to have a detailed project management plan (PMP) in place. The PMP defines the rules and responsibilities of the people who are involved and it will also define the steering committee, who is representing who—what the reporting structure [is] and how the project is set up to ensure that all of that [had to be done] will be done.*

This was reiterated by the project owner, who confirmed that the company ensured that employees read and understand the company's policies about accepting gifts.

> *I'm 10 years with [Connectivity], every year I have to refresh on that and say that, yes, I have read and understood what the corporate policy*

Governance at the Front-End 233

is on the ethics and being currently used in the business. We've got a very strict process and the guidelines, what sort of gift can we accept and—if the client can give me a gift or something and whether I can accept.

However, despite the existence of clear policies and rules, the company remains somewhat flexible around the issue.

Flexibility was also evident in the way governance was managed in projects.

Some projects will structure that we need to have bi-weekly steering committee, where all the stakeholders or their delegate need to be there to make the decisions and they're more formal. In many projects there are only one or two stakeholders or they are well aware and they do not want to be hands on, so the steering committee meeting or the [board] meeting may be once in a month. So we work out with the customer on what is the best and how they want to handle it as well and you structure the steering committee accordingly.

There was some evidence of outcome control through the procedures on the project management side of the organization.

We don't have individual compensation for individual projects. Our overall compensation and company bonus and the employee bonus does factor in the customer satisfaction overall, so we'll have a target of the customer satisfaction across the globe, not just one project.

The project owner also had the power to manage issues arising between project managers and sales teams.

On situations like that, I actually have an internal meeting or with the individual stakeholders and address the situation at hand. I would bring in the project manager and the team at all stages. Pretty much the project manager, the buck stops there. They are the person that's responsible for [the project], and they know that. When the sales teams do not align to that, then we have to ask them to align to that.

The other dilemma was that the reward systems favored individual effort in sales while it rewarded collective effort in projects. One idea that the project owners proposed to remedy issues arising between sales and projects was to put them in the same organization, which is also suggested in the literature.

We support the sales team in that, but they are what we call a service sales team, and they are separate to our organization. So that is one—it would be an area of improvement in our organization. We often comment that that team should be with the professional services team, so that we would get early engagement with our customers. So eventually when the statement of work hits our table, we are fully aware and fully engaged. It's not like a catch up.

Following are some observations made regarding issues that influenced trust within the organization.

Both the project manager and owner confirmed that trust was high in the firm, but it appeared that there was lack of trust between the sales and project teams, which has been covered earlier.

In terms of communication, the project teams and project owner seemed to have good communication. When there was a resource conflict this was communicated ahead well.

We avoid that situation with regular update and all that, so the project manager will be aware upfront, oddly enough, that this is not going to be met.

Although trust issues were not explained during the interviews, it was obvious that the trust between sales and projects was quite low, which resulted in the project owner trying to establish behavioral control by organizing meetings, but these do not seem to have worked effectively so far.

Discussion

Both organizations faced ethical dilemmas or tensions during their projects. In Spatial, most of these were personal to the project manager, whereas in Connectivity they arose between teams who faced a clash of objectives. The ethical dilemmas in Spatial are probably representative of issues across departments or of managers working in a large organization that has just taken over a smaller firm with a close-knit culture where there is frequent fact-to-face communication between employees. The project manager and the employees of Spatial felt disenchanted with the way they were being treated after serving the company for several years and through a global financial crisis. In Connectivity, the reward systems perpetuated the ethical issues, with each department being concerned about their own interests, which had a detrimental effect on their projects and the organization.

Both cases exhibited issues due to lack of transparency and related to accountability. However, in both cases the interviews did not explicitly reveal any issues of responsibility and fairness, but these were latent in other concerns expressed, such as the ongoing tension between the sales team and project team.

In Spatial, the transparency issues arose mainly due to restricted communication, which suggests a 'we will tell you only what you need to know' approach. Truilli and Floridi (2009, p. 111) proposed a definition of the ethical nature of information transparency, not as an ethical principle in itself, but as a pro-ethical condition, that is, an operation that becomes ethically 'enabling' when the disclosed information is considered in a relationship of 'dependence' or 'regulation.' The accountability issue focused on the PM's own sense of responsibility to maintain his professional integrity.

In Connectivity, the transparency issues arose from not being open about what the sales team members were telling the customers without consulting with the project department. This seemed more like 'protecting the turf,' which results in the 'interface problems' mentioned by Morris (2013). The organization is also responsible for creating this issue by setting up the rewards systems that do not support collaboration. The organization did attempt to improve accountability issues, but there was room for further improvement.

In both cases, the organizations seem to be using 'procedures' (or behavioral control) to minimize conflicts that lead to ethical issues rather than relying on trust (outcome control). This agrees with the findings of Müller et al. (2015, p. 18) that a "TO [temporary organization] governance uses control and not trust as a governance mechanism to manage the frequency of ethical issues in TOs." This was also evident from the lack of 'trust' expressed during the interviews at Spatial and Connectivity.

Referring back to the literature review presented earlier in the chapter, Müller (2009) proposes that project governance helps to decide the value system and organizational processes that enable projects to achieve their objectives. From the two case studies, it is apparent that while the two organizations have governance measures instituted in their procedures, this is not helping to resolve the 'interface' issues in the projects examined. The PM at Spatial complained that the processes used by Big Guy were unclear in practice. In Connectivity, the value system prevalent due to the different reward systems does not encourage collaboration, which, in turn, affects the achievement of organizational objectives.

The two organizations believed firmly in minimizing ethical issues and in the sanctity of project governance, so the issues that resulted in ethical issues occurred due to situational instances where ethical dilemmas are triggered by moral dilemmas in the workplace (Kish-Gephart et al., 2010).

Conclusions

The 'interface' problems that resulted in the ethical issues at the front-end of projects in the cases studied point to the lack of consideration in project governance to internal issues within project-based organizations. We urge more practice-based studies in this aspect of project governance.

The literature shows that when uncertainty is present in projects, more trust between the parties involved in delivering a project is desirable and can lead to better decisions. So organizations, like Connectivity, which can achieve

236 Shankar Sankaran and Christopher Biesenthal

efficiency in delivering 'less uncertain' projects by dividing the responsibility, should consider more flexible structures and processes when the projects become more complex (uncertain and ambiguous). It was clear from the conversations we had with Connectivity's managers that the sales department only realized their incentives after a project was delivered, which frustrated them when projects were delayed due to inherent complexity. It therefore makes sense for the sales and project departments to work together at the front-end for mutual benefit.

The organizations studied also seem to rely on behavioral control of ethical issues using procedures and policies. While having policies is important, they could also include aspects of outcome control to provide their managers some flexibility, within bounds, to enhance collaboration.

Acknowledgements: We thank Professor Siegfried Gudergan for his contribution to the case study interviews when they were originally conducted for the research project titled 'Interrelationship of Governance, Trust and Ethics in Temporary Organizations' led by Professor Ralf Müller.

References

Aras, G., & Crowther, D. (2009). Corporate Governance and Corporate Social Responsibility in Context. In G. Aras, & D. Growther (Eds.), *Global Perspectives on Corporate Governance and Social Responsibility* (pp. 1–41). Aldershot, UK: Gower.

Atkinson, R., Crawford, L., & Ward, S. (2006). Fundamental Uncertainties in Projects and the Scope of Project Management. *International Journal of Project Management, 24*, 687–698.

Blomquist, T., & Wilson, T. L. (2007). Project Marketing in Multi-Project Organizations: A Comparison of IS/IT and Engineering Firms. *Industrial Marketing Management, 36*, 206–218.

Donaldson, L. (2008). Ethics Problems and Problems with Ethics: Toward a Pro-Management Theory. *Journal of Business Ethics, 78*, 299–311.

Eisenhardt, K. (1989). Agency Theory: An Assessment and Review. *Academy of Management Review, 14*(1), 57–74.

Ghoshal, S. (2005). Bad Management Theories are Destroying Good Management Practices. *Academy of Management Learning and Education, 4*(1), 75–91.

Godbold, A. (2007). Managing Ethics. In J. R. Turner, & S. J. Simister (Eds.), *Gower Handbook of Project Management* (4th ed., Vol. 3, pp. 838–854). Aldershot, UK: Gower.

Godbold, A. (2008). Ethics and Projects. *Proceedings of the IPMA Expert Seminar*, February 14–15, 2008, Zurich, Switzerland.

Godbold, A., & Turner, J. R. (1996). Ethical Project Management. In J. R. Turner, K. V. Grude, & L. Thurloway (Eds.), *The Project Manager as Change Agent* (pp. 170–190). Maidenhead, UK: McGraw-Hill.

Griffin, A., & Hauser, J. R. (1992). Patterns of Communication Among Marketing, Engineering and Manufacturing—A Comparison Between Two Product Teams. *Management Science, 38*(3), 360–373.

Keaveney, S. M. (2008). The Blame Game: An Attribution Theory Approach to Marketer-Engineer Conflict in High-Technology Companies. *Industrial Marketing Management, 37*, 633–683.

Kish-Gephart, J. J., Harrison, D. A., & Trevino, L. K. (2010). Bad Apples, Bad Cases, and Bad Barrels: Meta-Analytic Evidence About Sources of Unethical Decisions at Work. *Journal of Applied Psychology, 95*(1), 1–31.

Loo, R. (2002). Tackling Ethical Dilemmas in Project Management Using Vignettes. *International Journal of Project Management, 20*, 489–495.

Morris, P. W. (2013). *Reconstructing Project Management.* Chichester, UK: John Wiley & Sons.

Müller, R. (2009). *Project Governance.* Aldershot, UK: Gower.

Müller, R., Andersen, E. S., Kvalnes, O., Shao, J., Sankaran, S., Rodney, Turner J., Biesenthal, C., Walker, D. H. T., & Gudergan, S. (2013). The Interrelationship of Governance, Trust, and Ethics in Temporary Organizations. *Project Management Journal, 44*(4), 26–44.

Müller, R., Turner, J., Andersen, E. S., Shao, J., & Kvalnes, Ø. (2015). Governance and Ethics in Temporary Organizations: How Corporate Governance Influences the Temporary Organization. In *Proceedings of the IRNOP 2015 (International Research Network for Organizing by Projects) Conference.* June 22-24, 2015, London, UK.

Shalvi, S., Handgraaf, M. J. J., & De Dreu, K. W. (2011). Ethical Manoeu- Vring: Why People Avoid Both Major and Minor Lies. *British Journal of Management, 22*, 16–27.

Shaw, V., & Shaw, C. T. (1998). Conflicts Between Engineers and Marketeers: The Engineer's Perspective. *Industrial Marketing Management, 27*, 279–291.

Smyth, H., Gustaffson, M., & Ganaasku, E. (2010). The Value of Trust in Project Business. *International Journal of Project Management, 28*, 117–129.

Stoker, G. (1998). Governance as Theory: Five Propositions. *International Social Science Journal, 50*(155), 17–28.

Trevino, L. K. (1986). Ethical Decision Making in Organizations: A Person-Situation Interactionist Model. *Academy of Management Review, 11*, 601–617.

Trevino, L. K. (1990). A Cultural Perspective on Changing and Developing Organizational Ethics. In R. Woodman, & W. Passmore (Eds.), *Research in Organizational Change and Development* (Vol. 4, pp. 195–230). Greenwich, CT: JAI Press.

Truilli, M., & Floridi, M. (2009). The Ethics of Information Transparency. *Ethics in Information Technology, 11*, 105–112.

Victor, B., & Cullen, J. B. (1988). The Organizational Bases of Ethical Work Climates. *Administrative Science Quarterly, 33*, 101–124.

Walker, D., & Lloyd-Walker, B. (2014). Client-Side Project Management Capabilities: Dealing with Ethical Dilemmas. *International Journal of Managing Projects in Business, 7*(4), 566–589.

Williams, T., & Samset, K. (2010). Issues in Front-End Decision Making on Projects. *Project Management Journal, 41*, 38–49.

15 Governance and Governmentality at Tasly Pharmaceuticals

Dan Li

This chapter describes the transformation of Tasly Pharmaceutical Group from a functional organization to a project-based organization. The case shows how conflicts between functional departments and project departments were dealt with through project governance, and how roles and functions were balanced by means of a project management office.

Introduction

Tasly Holding Group was established in 1994 in Tianjin, China. The Tasly Pharmaceutical Group held its initial public offering (stock code: 600535) on August 8, 2002. As a modern manufacturer of Chinese traditional medicine, it began with a single product, the compound Danshen dropping pill, in 1994. After ten years of rapid expansion, the company, which specialized in modern Chinese medicine, also had pharmaceutical chemistry and biological pharmacy as its secondary businesses.

From 2002 onwards, Tasly advocated and promoted project management as a way to link the different profitable parts of the organization by the means of project administration. This new governance removed obstacles in communication and cooperation, and provided obvious economical and coordination benefits for the company. For this, the company received several awards, including first prize in the Innovative Category of the British Chamber of Commerce in China Entrepreneurship and Innovation Awards in 2005, the International Project Management Association International Excellence Award in 2006, and was in the Forbes 2014 Best Top 50 listed companies in the Asia-Pacific region.

What is Project Management?

Because of the increasing pace of change, companies are paying more attention to governance of innovation activities and one-off works in most management practices. This involves dealing with challenges in coordination and the management of resources in different departments in order to coordinate the completion of joint tasks. Here, traditionally, the management

Governance and Governmentality at Tasly Pharmaceuticals 239

style does not meet the demands for high efficiency and rapid development in companies. Hence, the integration of single projects, works, and events into a modern model of scientific governance is significant for the whole company.

Along with the increased business, the company's organizational structure changed gradually in specialization and functions, such as the gradual differentiation of levels and formation of twelve departments and three stock traded organizations in a hierarchical structure. Vertical differentiation gradually evolved into eight levels from the general manager to the front-line workers. The rapid expansion resulted in problems of complexity and uncertainty, a long chain of command, decrease in innovation, lack of responsibility, increase in execution costs, and a failure to respond in a timely manner to market demands. Even though the company solved the problem of ownership and organizational structure, deficiencies still existed in matters of corporate governance. In addition, conflicts between the organizational structure and management strategy became the main obstacle in the sustainable development of the company.

With this background, Tasly adopted a project-driven governance structure (internally referred to as project management) for the daily management of the company. In other words, this governance approach aimed to separate project-related tasks from operational tasks into temporary tasks with clear targets and budgets. Through use of techniques and measures provided by project management (i.e., the governance structure), as well as better interdepartmental cooperation, project objectives were accomplished more effectively and efficiently.

The Process of Project Governance in Tasly

Test and Explore

From 1995 to 2000, Tasly's average growth rate reached 80%, mainly driven by two key products. As a fast growing Chinese medicine enterprise, Tasly faced the twin challenge of simultaneously guaranteeing the quality and quantity of the drugs demanded by the market and launching new products quickly.

Traditional functional patterns in companies emphasize fixed relationships between employees and their supervisors, which included modes of communication with fixed vertical links. At the same time, work was organized in the form of routine tasks, which were focused on discharge of functions and finishing of tasks and plans. Contrarily, the newly introduced project way of working emphasizes the breakdown of boundaries between departments and pays attention to interdepartmental cooperation and governance of projects as one-off, unrepeated, independent, and differentiated tasks.

For Tasly, which was facing an urgent need for delivery speed and a strong increase in orders, traditional management measures seemed inappropriate for coping with the scale of expansion and frequent changes in a hypercompetitive market. As a result, the project way of working was first introduced on a trial basis in 2001 for the launch of a new product. Through optimization of resources, combined with integration of tasks, the time to market for this new product was one year shorter when compared with similar developments in the former functional organization.

Because of this, the project group began to expand the project management structure throughout the enterprise by consciously defining some important tasks as projects. Additionally, the company founded an organization to guide and manage related internal project-related works as well as necessary education and training in project management for employees. This organization later became the Project Management Office (PMO).

The key to solving problems in project management is to set up an organization that provides support, methods, policies, and guidance across the company.

Figure 15.1 shows that the PMO is a matrix organization. It consists of two major groups, an expert group for project management and its continuous improvement, and a project information management group for information collection and distribution. The virtual PMO is made up of line managers from different departments and levels in the organizational hierarchy (e.g., directors, department managers, and their deputies), and the PMO members fulfill a dual role by simultaneously serving in the line and the PMO function.

In the beginning, the PMO acted as advocate and leader to implement the concept of project management (i.e., governance) by studying related successful cases and communicating them to employees and managers. Publicity for the project way of working originated at the top level in the organizational hierarchy, and the PMO acted as a bridge between the functional system and new project system in order to integrate, exchange, and balance toward establishing values and concepts of project management in the company.

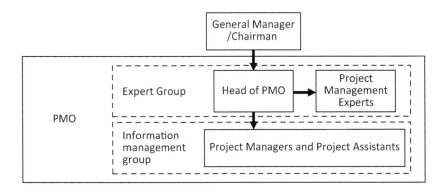

Figure 15.1 The Project Management Office

Governance and Governmentality at Tasly Pharmaceuticals   241

For a company deeply rooted in flow-based operations, the first step of project management was not to reform the whole organization, but to clarify and select some projects as pilots for this new way of working. During this period, project management was extensive and non-standard, but it was a good way to introduce the concept. Success was measured in terms of employees paying attention to and being interested in the concept of project management.

To improve understanding of and familiarity with the new practices of project management, as well as to speed up the influential projects in the company, Tasly encouraged stuff members to use project measures and tools to solve problems in their daily work. By these means, many tasks were done as projects and the number of projects increased quickly. Additionally, in order to keep up the employees' enthusiasm, the company took measures for people to easily become knowledgeable in and be recognized for their involvement in projects. Hence, staff members studied new kinds of knowledge, learned new techniques, and used new working methods, through which lots of talented new project managers emerged.

However, this phenomenon did not last very long. The reason for this was that the employees had no guidance for selecting between project and operational tasks in their daily work. Many conflicts arose out of this, including conflicts about short-term goals, cross-utilization of resources, and ambiguity in performance appraisals, especially between employees from functional groups that worked in daily operations and those in project groups that worked in projects, and the associated governance structure. In the original functional organization structure, the division of labor was clear-cut, but the structure and duties became confused after project management was established.

In change management, we cannot succeed in a hurry. The approach was meant to bring about the change quickly, but it also brought about failure quickly, as there was no strong theoretical base that informed the change and little guidance for the staff. In the beginning stage of project management, one of the biggest challenges faced by the company was that no matter how comprehensive the designed system, it would remain a paper document if there was no cautious implementation in controlled situations for the eradication of doubt and resistance.

Operation and Execution

Through a long introductory phase and associated acceptance over time, project management became popular and a trend in the company. Through continuous exploration and improvement, the rules and regulations were settled. Meanwhile, the employees' enthusiasm and motivation grew steadily. While employees were encouraged to deepen their understanding of how parts of operations could be transformed into projects, the focus of administration was more on how to improve the management level and appraisal

242   *Dan Li*

standard. During this period, the company emphasized the gradual under-standing of project and process management in project management. With the improvement of the processes for project approval, examination, and acceptance of projects, the company took measures such as open-door enrolling in projects. Through these means, the recognition and understand-ing of the project way of working grew gradually, despite different kinds of pressures. As a result of this phase, employees had a realistic and deep understanding of the project management structure.

After the initial confusing period in project execution came to an end, the project management team (i.e., the PMO) started the company-wide implementation. In their role as the backbone and part of the permanent organization structure, the PMO faced lots of problems in establishing the project management structure and process. The main mission of the PMO was to keep up smooth operations by governing projects and programs from a company-wide perspective. Here the PMO played the role of rule maker in order to gradually establish a complete project governance and management system.

One of the priorities was the establishment of a professional training and internal project management certification examination. The training program was internally developed and included four levels: primary, jun-ior, senior, and advanced. Employees were enrolled in the different levels depending on their existing knowledge and their particular situation at work. Employees who passed the intermediate level had a chance to partici-pate in the internal certification qualification for project managers at Tasly. Those who passed the internal certification had a chance to be enrolled for external certification by international professional organizations for project managers, such as the International Project Manager Professional (IPMP) certification and the Project Management Professional (PMP) certification.

Through the above-mentioned measures, the company approached the change toward the project way of doing work from three different angles. The first was top-down, with the company's strategic projects; the second was projects identified as one-off tasks with clear targets, requirements, budgets, and procedures in products research, technical innovation, and management improvement; and the third was bottom-up projects identified through total progressive movement (TPM).

TPM is an important part of the project management system and a tool to reduce costs, increase efficiency, improve management, and enhance com-petitiveness of companies. TPM aims to motivate employees to participate in management improvement, to train employees in critical thinking skills and problem-solving ability, and to guide the company to develop a culture of responsibility.

In order to better integrate innovation and to boost activities and project consciousness of employees, the company systematically adopted TPM. Lots of good practices were not enforced by managers, but were a direct result of the feedback received by the different management levels. According to a

Governance and Governmentality at Tasly Pharmaceuticals 243

proposal's benefit, creation, practicability, and other elements, the company created corresponding standards for grading projects and set up six different levels of incentives as well as regulations for best proposals' reporting. Through these measures, employees felt respected, valued, and responsible when they participated in project activities. Technological improvements and management activities became clearer, and the standard of work and corporate culture became more vigorous.

In addition, projects were categorized into three levels: company, department, and team levels, referred to as levels A, B, and C respectively.

The management of projects required the balancing of goals, actions, resources, and motivation of staff. For example, project managers were granted rights to mobilize resources, but also had to be responsible for results. However, these approaches were in conflict with their prior duties and traditional management measures in the functional departments, which led to conflict and fuzziness. For example, in cases where operational plans were not integrated with project plans, the different departments started to work independently and in an uncoordinated way with projects. Double reporting patterns added additional pressures, collisions, and dilemmas in each department.

Employees exposed to the change toward the project way of working went through development stages similar to Tuckman's (1965) sequential model of four stages in team development, which are: forming, storming, norming, and performing. For example, initial experience from working in projects often caused confusion. Meanwhile, another problem was how to deal with collisions between functional managers and project managers. Other issues that needed to be addressed simultaneously were resource prioritization in production tasks, process optimizing, and rules formulation.

A lot of projects needed to be done at the same time. According to the enterprise's actual resources, the PMO adjusts different projects' starting time, scope, and completion time, and can even decide to discontinue them. At this stage, through established and improved procedures and regulations for project management, lots of one-off tasks were completed as projects, which improved the timely and speedy attainment of targets. Slowly but surely the project administration approaches started to pervade the company through various regulations and combined with different rules and regulations in the operations, examination, and motivation. And this became the new mode of working in the company.

Improvement and Optimization

Tasly cooperated with Nankai University of China to do a survey on "the psychological environment of project administration within companies." In terms of problems identified through the survey, the PMO carried out a major revision, combination, and simplification of the project documents. Meanwhile, the company rolled out the new approaches for planning,

244 Dan Li

control, and assessment, as well as for standards in managing multiple projects and individual projects. By providing training in project manager software skills to motivate project members, simplifying project management procedures, improving project communication, and permitting reporting in three different versions—study version, normal version, and simplified version—the organization allowed for the flexible management of projects. Other measures included defining the different duties and roles in project administration, strengthening guidance from project managers and supervisors, and providing the professional role of the specialist in the PMO. Last but not least, remuneration systems and awards were aligned and synchronized with projects with the objective of saving capital for the company.

Through this, project management began to transform from the standard to the elastic phase. The company adopted a matrix structure that relied on flexible institutions to match situational requirements and employees' abilities. Further, the company upgraded communication and reporting systems in project management and implemented one-page management reporting in C level projects. Gradually, management became professional and formed a culture of projects in the company.

In 2006, Tasly was honored with the IPMA Silver Award. This significant award is not only a recognition of project administration in the project management field, but also a strong affirmation of the Chinese management ability and level from the international project management field. Further, this award is a record of the innovation history and growth of Tasly.

Deep in the Heart

After five to eight years, project management had pervaded the entire organization, and had gained acceptance from top management to general staff. Activities such as strategy development, annual budgeting, work review, and brand communication were all related to project management. The concept of project management had trickled down into the consciousness of the company and became a most important element of the company's culture. Meanwhile, teamwork in functional departments had become a part of daily work. Having a brand new organization structure embedded in the original highly integrated process-oriented structure advanced the capability of providing high quality products and services and becoming more efficient and effective.

During every stage in the implementation of the project administration, the PMO set up quantitative objectives. It also paid attention to assessment at any moment in time, such as the calculation and appraisal of input and output ratios of different kinds of projects, both periodically and financially, in order to provide a reference for the next project. Project meetings were used to check and assess the degree to which these objectives were met, and to grasp the degree of employees' familiarity with project management. This was aided through Tasly's internal project manager certification

Governance and Governmentality at Tasly Pharmaceuticals 245

program, and allowed the PMO and management to evaluate the implementation of training objectives. Regular meetings allowed for assessing the degree of maturity and application level of project management to learn about the changes in opinions about the project information system. All this helped to form an excellent atmosphere for work and from which to remain competitive.

Project management in Tasly could be summed up in eight steps:

Step 1: The Project Committee is made up of functional managers, professional project staff members, and top management. It consists of two branches, which are project experts and the PMO. The Project Committee and the PMO are responsible for the evaluation, assessment, monitoring, and inspection of projects.

Step 2: Departments submit a work list according to the annual work plan, select tasks based on cost, time, scope, and cross-sectoral work, set them up as a project, and then hand them over to the PMO.

Step 3: The PMO organizes meetings, and the project committee selects those projects that are necessary and valuable to implement. And then, depending on their origin, importance, and complexity, it schedules the projects.

Step 4: The committee approves the application of projects, signs a formal contract with relevant project managers, and reviews the project plan supplied by the project manager. The project plan includes objectives, WBS (Work Breakdown Structure), group members, duration, delivery, responsibility matrix, resources, and standards of a particular project.

Step 5: The PMO controls and coordinates the implementation of project items and provides assistance for project managers to manage the whole process of the projects.

Step 6: The project manager, in accordance with the procedures, documents the requirements to manage the whole project and contacts the PMO for the required support. Technology tools are used according to the project plan, budget, schedule, milestones, changes, reporting, etc.

Step 7: The PMO holds meetings to coordinate or evaluate projects, mediate conflict, and provide necessary suggestions for improvements. At the same time, the PMO could also require projects to cease, integrate, or be postponed depending on the current situation, and organize expert committees to make an assessment of the completed projects.

Step 8: Organize an annual project review and reward meeting, feed 5%–10% of the project profit back to outstanding project team members by recognizing top performing employees, and send them to certification and management trainings.

In a word, the PMO executes functions at two levels. At the corporate or strategy level, the PMO controls project performance, develops project

246 *Dan Li*

management competencies and methodologies, and is involved in multi-project management, strategic management, and organizational learning. At the daily, operational level, the PMO provides support, methods, procedures, systems, and policies for project management across the company.

With regards to project governance, the PMO has the following five responsibilities:

1 Ensure that the project objectives comply with the company's overall strategy.
2 Ensure continuous improvement of the project management system.
3 Track project progress, allocate resources, provide problem-solving support, and create an effective multi-projects information system.
4 Cultivate talents and provide training, certification, and guidance of related works.
5 Help create the soft assets of the company, such as accumulated experience, template development, and knowledge management, as well as file management of projects. These assets provide the necessary information and guidance for a new project manager.

Evaluating the Influence of Project Governance

Positive Effects

Traditional manufacturing companies have their own characteristics, and generally find it difficult to change to the project way of working. Traditional governance relies on the four principles of transparency, accountability, responsibility, and fairness (Aras & Crowther, 2010). However, there are some inherent shortcomings in traditional management, and project management could help fill these gaps to some extent.

Transparency: In flow-based manufacturing companies, the whole organization is divided into a variety of units, and the organization puts more time and cost into coordinating and balancing the different interests of the various departments. In contrast, project governance forms a matrix structure in the company, and the different departments are empowered to manage their own daily routines. In addition, a project organization keeps the original line structure, together with different functional groups, to become a common project group in the organization. The origin of projects includes top-down projects and bottom-up projects. For employees, tasks that needed to be managed through eight different management levels now just need one or two management levels. So managers in the company have a holistic view of their objectives and are not limited by a single department's goals.

Responsibility: In traditional organizations, detailed tasks are assigned to employees during a certain time, and this model has high executive efficiency. However, ambiguity often appears when project work interferes with functional work. Such work is separated in project organizations, with

Governance and Governmentality at Tasly Pharmaceuticals   247

professions supervised and managed by projects, ensuring quality of completion. However, in a project organization, these tasks will be recognized as projects that a particular manager will take responsibility for, with necessary deputies in other departments in order to finish the promised tasks on schedule. In the past decade, we have successfully completed nearly 600 projects and solved several operational problems along the way.

Fairness: Jobs in traditional organizations are related to functional work. Communication in a department is mainly about a certain type of knowledge, and companies with a traditional functional structure prefer to employ professional talents of certain fields. In a project organization, because of cross-departmental collaboration, employees have a chance to learn about subjects in other fields, fostering a company-wide view, which is an opportunity for employees to engage in interdisciplinarity. In Tasly, general managers and high-level managers in the pharmaceutical area are internally promoted to managerial positions, while managers in other areas, such as hospitals and nursing homes, are hired from outside.

Accountability: Staff in traditional hierarchical structures rely on job descriptions to do their work, and are responsible for their own procedures and results. Their performance is judged by their line managers, who rely on some index of operation by others. In project structures, rights and liabilities are held by the project managers, and then fed back to the employees.

Over several years, project governance has been of great value for Tasly in three aspects: efficiency, benefits, and results.

With regard to efficiency, improvements are obvious in production, delivery of orders, and effective use of working hours. For example, the production phase of the main product was reduced from 28 days to 15 days, and the time taken to process an international order decreased from 45 days to 18 days. With regard to benefits, through the increase in the rate of production of the finished product, and reduced consumption of energy and packing materials, the company saves about 60 million RMB. And as for results, employees could be a member of projects or a leader in other projects; through this permeable management pattern and exchangeable resource platform, employees could challenge their assumptions. Finally, creative enthusiasm and active execution have been increased for the employees, and good relationships and cooperation formed in the company.

Negative Effects

Every coin has two sides. Project work improves the abilities, creativity, and cooperation of employees. However, there are still some problems through project management.

On one hand, projects lead to heavy workload and work pressure for employees. In traditional companies, managers and employees work at their own jobs individually. For example, with every employee having an eight hour workday, if the project work increases, ordinary employees will think

248 *Dan Li*

that they need to finish functional work and project work in that time frame, and find it hard to control the variety of work within the same time. After some time, they even become unwilling to join projects. These bad experiences decrease employees' enthusiasm to a large extent. For this reason, they need to balance the functional work and project work well.

At the same time, because of drawbacks in the promotion and remuneration system, feedback on work is sometimes not equal to the employees' efforts. Through projects, the ability of employees improves, but income and salary remain the same. Moreover, the prospects of promotion are limited, and this easily leads to dissatisfaction with the gap between the amount of effort and the remuneration.

On the other hand, functional work and project work also compete for common resources. Functional management pursues standards and efficiency, and staff just work on their own objectives. However, project management pursues results. Because members in project teams come from different functional departments, they are led by functional managers as well as project managers simultaneously. When facing problems and conflicts, they get confused and have no idea how to go about dealing with them. In addition, projects are related to job performance, and performance in projects will be evaluated at a high level. For managers, deciding how to allocate different resources and how to balance the competing demands of functional work and project work present significant challenges.

In sum, how to minimize negative impacts from project administration remains a challenge for companies that rely on the project way of working. This needs to be addressed through proper governance and governmentality.

References

Aras, G., & Crowther, D. (2010). Corporate Social Responsibility: A Broader View of Corporate Governance. In G. Aras & D. Crowther (Eds.), *A Handbook of Corporate Governance and Social Responsibility* (pp. 265–280). Farnham, UK: Gower Publishing Limited.

Tuckman, B. W. (1965). Developmental Sequence in Small Groups. *Psychological Bulletin*, 63(6), 384–399.

Index

accountability and responsibility 37, 52, 63–4, 73, 75, 78, 102, 111, 124
Adler, T. R. 33
agency theory 2, 28, 30, 31, 32, 39, 60, 173, 223
agile 2, 43, 108, 155, 166, 169n1, 176
agile pragmatist paradigm 43, 176, 177, 186
alignment: organizational enablers 82
Allen, W. T. 28
Alliancing Association of Australasia 218
Andersen, E. S. 58, 59, 61, 131
APM *see* Association for Project Management
Aras, G. 15, 200, 206, 212, 214, 215, 216, 225, 226
Aristotle 182
asset specificity 32–3
Association for Project Management (APM) 16; *Guide to Governance of Project Management* 3–4, 5
Atkinson, R. 225
Aubry, M. 54, 57, 98, 119
authoritarian governmentality 82, 114, 115
autonomous character 23, 112, 117, 142–3
autonomy and self-responsibility of project managers 80, 97, 98, 111–2, 120, 125
Ayoob, M. 116

Bachmann, R. 174
Bagel Metaphor 57
Barthes, R. 21
Barton, S. L. 33
behavior control 22, 41, 42, 43, 82, 115, 118, 176, 177, 178, 186, 187, 191, 192

behavioral ethics 181, 182–3, 222, 224
Bentham, J. 182
Bessire, D. 202
Biesenthal, C. 2
biosecurity 210, 216
Black Saturday Bushfires 206
Blomquist, T. 28, 53, 225
board-level governance of projects 18
board of directors 52
Brady, T. 121
Broker-Steward Model 53
Brower, J. 201, 217
Brown, S. 176
Bruzelius, N. 134, 136
business alignment 109–10
Business Sector Advisory Group on Corporate Governance 3, 14, 188

Capability Maturity Model Integration 168
causality 187–90
Chen, J. H. F. 163
Chicago School of Law and Economics 27
chief executive officer (CEO) 12, 16, 55, 93, 109; context-driven evolvement of enablers 97–8
Christensen, T. 136
Cirka, C. 190
Clarke, T. 13, 40; *Theories of Corporate Governance* 27
Clases, C. 174
common good for society 132, 133, 134, 182, 202, 216
conformist paradigm 42–3, 44, 178, 185, 186

250 *Index*

Connectivity case study 229–34; accountability 233–4; responsibility and fairness 232–4; transparency 230–1
context-driven evolvement of enablers 97–8
control as governance mechanism 8, 118, 124, 176–7, 178; clan 176
convergent methodologies 108
Cooke-Davies, T. 121
corporate-level governance 2, 12
corporate social performance 201, 202, 211, 217
Cowley, D. 213
Crawford, L. 58
Crowther, D. 15, 200, 206, 212, 214, 215, 216, 225, 226
cultural-cognitive elements 79, 80

Davis, J. H. 31, 118, 119, 173, 174
Dean, M. 113–4
decision making 40, 58, 61, 62, 110, 114, 115, 117–18, 132, 133, 144–8, 175, 215
De Dreu, K. W. 183
Department of Finance and Treasury Victoria 198
Donaldson, T. 40, 41, 167
Donaldson, L. 13, 30, 40, 119, 188, 223
Drury, J. 213
Durand, R. 191
Dusters, G. 83
Dvir, D. 160

Eildon Reservoir 197
Eisenhardt, K. M. 41, 42, 118, 176, 223
embeddedness 2, 91, 92–3, 94, 95–6, 97, 99, 101, 102; social 89; structural 89
emergent methodologies 108
employee role 117
enablers, organizational see organizational enablers
enabling mechanisms 90, 93, 96, 99, 102; governance orientation 13, 27, 40, 90, 92, 93, 94, 95, 96, 102, 167, 169, 187; incentives structure 90, 94; institutionalization 42, 90, 92, 93, 94, 96, 99, 100, 102, 110, 125; meeting structure 90, 92, 93, 94, 95–6, 99, 102; professionalism 90, 92, 93, 94, 95, 101, 102;

review structure 90, 92, 94, 95, 96, 102
English, B. 175
Enron 181
entrepreneur role 117
environmental management 207, 214
Environmental Management Plan 209, 213, 215
Environmental Management Strategy 209
Ericsson, 162
ethics 181–92; bad apples 182–3, 185, 223; bad barrels 183, 185, 223; bad cases 183, 185, 223; behavioral 181, 182–3, 222, 224; causality 187–9; character orientation 182; false dilemmas 183, 185; governance issues 184; illegal actions 184; morals 176, 181–3, 222–3, 224, 235; normative 181–2, 183, 222, 224; optimization issues 184, 185, 186, 187, 189, 190, 191; outcome orientation 182; power and political issues 184; preparing for ethical issues 189–90; process orientation 182; project management literature 222–4; and projects 183–7; relationship issues 184, 187, 189, 190, 191; role conflict issues 184; theorizing on relationship between project governance and ethical issues in projects 190–2; transparency issues 184, 185, 186, 187, 190, 191
extreme programming 166, 169n3

fairness 16, 64–5, 228–9, 232–4
false dilemmas 183, 185
Farjoun, M. 83
Fayol, H. 6
financial objectives 41
flexibility 90; organizational enablers 80–1
Flyvbjerg, B. 134, 136
Food Bowl Projects 201, 218; Murray-Goulburn 203
Franck, E. 31
front-end of projects 224–5; Connectivity 229–14; framework for analysis of interviews 225–6; Spatial 226–9

Gemünden, H. G. 160
General Electric 6

GHD Australia 197
Glasspool, H. 188
Global Competitiveness Index 135
global financial crisis 146, 226, 234
good governance 15–16; accountability
15; fairness 16; responsibility 15;
transparency 15
governance: positioning 3–6
governance, organizational project
11–23; comparison of corporate-
level and project-level governance
practices 16–20; concept 7, 11,
12–14, 21; governmentality 20–3;
principles of good governance
15–16; processes 13; relationship 13;
system of controls 12–13; temporary
organizations 11–2
governance institutions 51–65, 119–20;
accountability and responsibility
63–4; board of directors 52;
governance principles 62–5; fairness
64–5; other project governance
groups 62; portfolio management
and program management 52–4;
project management offices 54–7;
project owner and sponsor 58–60;
project steering groups 60–2;
transparency 62–3
governance models: governmentality-
based models 37–8; layered models
39; nested models 38–9; process
models 36–7
governance-of-project flexibility 90
governance orientation 13, 27, 40,
90, 92, 93, 94, 95, 96, 102, 167,
169, 187
governance paradigms 40–6;
adherence to job description 41;
agile pragmatist 43, 176, 177, 186;
behavior control 22, 41, 42, 43, 82,
115, 118, 176, 177, 178, 186, 187,
191, 192; compliance expectations
42; conformist 42–3, 44, 178, 185,
186; decision making 40; financial
objectives 41; legitimacy 41; level
of control 41; long-term objectives
41; outcome control 40, 41, 42,
43, 44, 46, 60, 114, 115, 176, 177,
186, 187, 192, 229, 233, 235, 236;
process versus outcome orientation
41; remuneration 41; role of
support institutions 42; shareholder
orientation 28, 29, 40, 42, 43, 44,
95, 96, 166, 177, 178, 185, 186,

187, 191; stakeholder orientation 40,
42, 43, 44, 46, 90, 166, 167, 169,
177, 186, 191; versatile artist 43, 44,
177, 178, 186, 189
governance principles 3, 5, 6, 7, 8, 13,
16, 18–20, 27, 37, 38, 41, 51, 108,
114, 124, 198, 201, 218; corporate
72, 73, 75, 78, 94, 95, 96, 102–3,
110, 111; governance institution
62–5
governance theories 27–33;
agency theory 30; shareholder
theory 27–8; stakeholder theory
28–30; stewardship theory
31–2; transaction cost
economics 32–3
governmentality: approach 114;
authoritarian 82, 114, 115;
definition 20–1; liberal 78,
114; mechanism 118–19;
neoliberal 22, 23, 74, 78, 97,
115, 152; precepts 115–16;
sovereignty 116–18
governmentality-based models 37–8;
hard factors 37–8; soft factors 38
Griffin, A. 225
growth-driven evolvement of enablers
98–100
Gur-Arie, O. 191

Hair, J. F. 91, 188
Handgraaf, M. J. J. 183
hard factors 37–8
Harrison, D. A. 182, 197
Hauser, J. R. 225
Helm, J. 59
Hernandez, M. 31, 40
Hodgson, D. 121
Hoegl, M. 160
Hough, G. 160
Hult, G. T. 91
Human Development Index 135
hybrids of programs and portfolio
thinking 54

incentives structure 90, 94
independent projects 53, 54
infrastructure 71–2, 78, 79, 80, 90,
91–2, 117–18, 125, 133, 136, 142,
144, 152, 166; communication 117;
media 95, 96
institutionalization 42, 90, 92, 93,
94, 96, 99, 100, 102, 110, 125
institutional theory 79–80, 164

252 Index

ISO: Draft Standard 4–5; Standard for Project, Programme and Portfolio Management—Guidance on Governance 4

Jensen, M. C. 13, 28, 30, 40, 41
Jensen, A. F. 131
John Holland Group 197
Joslin, R.: causality 190; comprehensive methodology 163; 'methodology elements' 162; mixed-methods study 165, 166; quasi-moderator 167
Jugdev, K. 160
Jungwirth, C. 31

Katerberg, R. 33
Keaveney, S. M. 224–5
Keegan, A. 53
Khan, K. 161, 167
Kish-Gephart, J. J. 182, 223
Klakegg, O. J. 71, 75, 76, 140–2, 150, 188

Larcker, D. 63
layered models 39
Lechler, T. 160
Lecoeuvre, L. 40, 167, 188
legitimacy 41
Leitner, D. 83
Lewis, M. 31
liberal approaches 22, 74, 114, 116
liberal governmentality 78, 114; see also neoliberal governmentality
Liu, L. 83
Lipovetsky, S. 160
Lloyd-Walker, B. M. 198
Lockwood, M. 198, 200, 212, 214, 215, 216, 217
long-term objectives 41, 53
Luhman, N. 174
Lundin, R. A. 12, 120, 121

Magnussen, O. M. 188
Mahajan, V. 201, 217
management principles 5–6
maturity-driven evolvement of enablers 101–2
Mayer, R. C. 174
Maylor, H. 121
measurement dimensions 40, 41, 101
Meckling, W. H. 28
meeting structure 90, 92, 93, 94, 95–6, 99, 102
Melbourne Water 197, 204, 217, 218

Messikomer, C. 190
Michigan Supreme Court 27
Midler, C. 120, 121
Mill, J. S. 182
Millstein, I. M. 198, 200, 202, 204, 216
Millstein Report 14, 15
morals 176, 181–3, 222–3, 224, 235
Morris, P. W. 160, 224, 235
Müller, R.: causality 190; comprehensive methodology 163; context-driven evolvement 97; factor analysis 89; governance models 164; governance paradigms 40, 167, 169; growth of organizations 54; interrelationship of governance, trust, and ethics in temporary organizations 221, 235; layered governance model 39; low-trust structures 175; 'methodology elements' 162; mixed-methods study 165, 166; organizational enablers 71, 79, 83, 97; portfolio managers 28; private sector practices 107; project business 53; project owners and managers relationships 59; steer groups 191; subjectivity on project access 160
Murray-Webster, R. 83

Naciri, A. 29
Nankai University 243
National Bank 136
neoliberal governmentality 22, 23, 74, 78, 97, 115, 152
neoliberalism 21, 22–3, 74, 78, 82, 92, 94, 97, 114, 115, 122, 124–5, 152
nested models 38–9
new public management 131, 140
Nordberg, D. 63
normative elements 79–80
Nooteboom, B. 118
Norway public projects: comparison with other countries 141; concept research program 145; context and background 135–7; cost control on portfolio level 145–6; cultural aspects 148–51; decision making on major projects 144–8; governance framework 137–9; governance framework for major public projects 135–41; practices 142–4; project governance in autonomous public agencies 142–3; projects subject to the model 145; stakeholder

Index 253

management 144; systematic approach to projects in the earliest phases 147–8; what the framework is—and what it is not 140–1
Norwegian Public Roads administration 140–1

OECD *see* Organization for Economic Co-operation and Development
Office of Government Commerce 60, 108, 162
open systems thinking 113, 124
organizational enabler factors: embeddedness 2, 89, 91, 92–3, 94, 95–6, 97, 99, 101, 102; governmentality 90; governance-of-project flexibility 90; leadership 89; project-governance flexibility 90
organizational enablers, strategic 88–103; context-driven evolvement 97–8; contribution to four corporate governance principles 102–3; evolvement of enablers for governance and governmentality in organizations 97–102; factors 89–90; growth-driven evolvement 98–100; impact on governance success 91–3; impact on project success 91; maturity-driven evolvement 101–2; mechanisms 90–1; organization-wide enablers for governance 88–93; preliminary theory of organizational enablers for governance 93–7
organizational enablers, tactical 69–84; alignment 82; concept 69–71; cultural-cognitive elements 79, 80; discursive abilities 70; discursive abilities factors 72; elements 70–1; factors 69–70; flexibility 80–1; for governance of projects 72–4; for governmentality 74–7; institutional theory 79–80, 164; mechanisms 70; nature 77–8; normative elements 79–80; process facilitators 70; for project governance 71–2; regulative elements 79, 80; role of project-related in wider organizational context 78–84; stability 81–2; 'thinking in projects' 74, 80; variety 77–8
Organization for Economic Co-operation and Development (OECD) 3, 14, 119, 136, 188, 198

outcome control 40, 41, 42, 43, 44, 46, 60, 114, 115, 176, 177, 186, 187, 192, 229, 233, 235, 236
owner or business change manger; process models 37

"Peace of Westphalia" 116
Pellegrinelli, S. 83
Pemsel, S. 71, 89, 107
Pinto, J.K. 160, 175
Plan of Environmental Controls 213, 215
Plato 182
PMI *see* Project Management Institute
portfolio management and program management 52–4
portfolios of projects 18, 51, 53, 62, 72, 73, 90
precepts 115–16, 123, 124, 125; organizational values 116; process 116; project 116
predictive methodologies 108
Preston, L. E. 40, 41, 167
Prince 2 60, 61, 108, 162, 176
private sector practices 107–25; governmentality 114–20; private 107–13; profiling governance and governmentality 122–4; projectification 120–1; relationship between strategic and tactical 124–5; strategic 113; tactical 107–13
process models 36–7; owner or business change manager 37; project manager 37; sponsor 37; steward 37
professionalism 90, 92, 93, 94, 95, 101, 102
programs of projects 53, 81
project governance 71–2, 93–7
project-governance flexibility 90
projectification 120–1, 122; dimensions to assess 121
Project Impact Assessment 204, 212, 213
project management: history 1–3
Project Management Institute (PMI) 69, 166–7; Body of Knowledge V5 162; Organization Project Management Maturity Model (OPM3) 16, 168; Practice Guide for Governance of Portfolios, Programs, and Projects 4, 5
project management methodologies 18, 22, 43, 71, 78, 79, 80, 93, 98, 107–9, 190–1; standardization 111; transparency 115

254 *Index*

project management offices (PMOs) 54–7, 109; Bagel Metaphor 57; functions 54–5; roles 57
project managers; autonomy and self-responsibility of project managers 80, 97, 98, 111–2, 120, 125; process models 37; role 117
ProjectNorway 150
project owner and sponsor 30, 51, 58–60, 129, 198–9, 226, 229, 233
project steering groups 18, 39, 51, 52–3, 58, 60–2, 109–10, 184, 192; accountability 15, 16; shareholder-oriented governance 40
project success 159–78; criteria 160; dimensions 161–2; factors 160–1; governance's direct impact 166–9; governance's indirect impact 163–6; methodology 162–3; relationship with governance 163–9
project thinking 112–13, 120, 121
public projects 129–53; characteristics of private and public sector and their projects 131–5; cultural aspects of Norwegian public sector 148–51; Norway and governance framework for major public projects 135–41; Norwegian decision making on major projects 144–8; Norwegian public projects practices 142–4; overview of recent developments 129–31
Public Relations Institute of Australia 202–3; *Transforming Negative Community Sentiment Through Positive Engagement* 203, 205

Rattsø, J. 136
Reagan, R. 131
regulative elements 79, 80
relationship-based governance 134–5
Remington, K. 59
remuneration 41, 95, 103, 244, 248
Renault 120
responsibility 37, 52, 73, 75, 78, 111, 124; accountability 63–4; autonomy and self-responsibility of project managers 80, 97, 98, 111–2, 120, 125; fairness 228–9, 232–4; good governance 15
return on investment 27, 40, 42, 43
review structure 90, 92, 94, 95, 96, 102
Ringle, C.M. 91

Rose, N. 22
Rothengatter, W. 134, 136
Rowlinson, S. 37
rule-based approaches 16

Sadowski, B.M. 83
Sadowski-Rasters, G. 83
Samset, K. 134, 136, 137, 141, 145, 224
Sarstedt, M. 91
Scherer, R.F. 33
Schoorman, F.D. 174
SCRUM 2, 108, 166, 169n2, 176, 177
Segon, M. 37
Shalvi, S. 183
Shao, J. 71, 89, 97, 102
shareholder orientation 28, 29, 40, 42, 43, 44, 95, 96, 166, 177, 178, 185, 186, 187, 191
shareholder theory 27–8, 40
Sharma, S. 191
Shaw, C.T. 225
Shaw, V. 225
Shearman and Sterling 16
Shenhar, A. 80, 160
Silver Waste Wise 210
Sinclair Knight Merz 197
Site Environmental Plans 213, 215
Slevin, D.P. 160, 175
Smith, A.: *The Wealth of Nations* 30
Smith, S. 197
Smyth, H. 225
Söderholm, A.12
soft factors 38
Sørensen, R. 136
sovereignty 116–18; definition 116; entrepreneur role 117; employee role 117; infrastructure 117–18; project manager role 117
Spatial case study 226–9; accountability 227–8; responsibility and fairness 228–9; transparency 227
sponsor 30, 51, 58–60, 129, 198–9, 226, 229, 233; process models 37
stability: organizational enablers 81–2
stakeholder orientation 40, 42, 43, 44, 46, 90, 166, 167, 169, 177, 186, 191
stakeholder theory 28–30, 40
standardization 110–1
steering groups 18, 39, 51, 52–3, 58, 60–2, 109–10, 184, 192; accountability 15, 16; shareholder-oriented governance 40

stewardship theory 30, 31–2, 37, 39, 169, 173, 188
strategic organizational enablers 88–103; context-driven evolvement 97–8; contribution to four corporate governance principles 102–3; evolvement of enablers for governance and governmentality in organizations 97–102; factors 89–90; growth-driven evolvement 98–100; impact on governance success 91–3; impact on project success 91; maturity-driven evolvement 101–2; mechanisms 90–1; organization-wide enablers for governance 88–93; preliminary theory of organizational enablers for governance 93–7
strategic practices 113, 124
structure-based governance 134–5
success, project see project success
Sugarloaf Pipeline Alliance 134, 197–218; community liaison and stakeholder management 202–7; cultural heritage and the environment within construction corridor 208; demonstrated concern for community 207–12; flora and fauna 209–10; greenhouse gas emissions 207–8; health and safety of staff and community 211; minimizing adverse construction impacts 210; project 199–200; project governance 200–2; setting 199; 'Think Five Stay Alive' campaign 211, 214
Sundarmurthy, C. 31

tactical organizational enablers 69–84; alignment 82; concept 69–71; cultural-cognitive elements 79, 80; discursive abilities 70; discursive abilities factors 72; elements 70–1; factors 69–70; flexibility 80–1; for governance of projects 72–4; for governmentality 74–7; institutional theory 79–80, 164; mechanisms 70; nature 77–8; normative elements 79–80; process facilitators 70; for project governance 71–2; regulative elements 79, 80; role of project-related in wider organizational context 78–84; stability 81–2; 'thinking in projects' 74, 80; variety 77–8

tactical practices 107–13; autonomy and self-responsibility of project managers 111–2; business alignment 109–10; open systems thinking 113; PMOs 109; project management methodologies 107–9; project thinking 112–13; relationship between strategic and tactical 124–5; standardization 110; steering groups 109–10
Tasly Pharmaceuticals 52, 238–48; evaluating influence of project governance 246–8; process of project governance 239–46; project management 238–9; total progressive movement 242
Tayan, B. 63
temporary organizations 11–12, 15, 16, 17, 74, 89, 117, 121, 163, 173, 200, 201, 206, 235
Thatcher, M. 131
Tishler, A. 160
Too, E. G. 5, 38
transaction cost economics 31, 32–3, 39, 164, 188
transition 120
transparency 15, 18, 37–8, 39, 54–5, 62–3, 72, 73, 75, 95, 96, 102, 108, 109, 110, 111, 115, 124, 152, 184, 185–7, 189–90, 191, 212–13, 225, 227, 230–1, 234–5, 246
Trevino, L. K. 182
trust as governance mechanism 39, 119, 123, 163, 173–6, 186, 235; system 173, 174, 175
Turner, J. R.: ambidexterity 83; Broker-Steward Model 53; low-trust structures 175; project-oriented organization 100; process models 36; project owners and managers relationships 59; shareholder theory 28; sovereignty 117; success criteria 160; system trust 175; value-creating in society 131

UK: Listing Authority Combined Code 4

versatile artist paradigm 43, 44, 177, 178, 186, 189
Volden, G. H. 136, 137, 142, 145
Volkswagen 181

256   Index

Walker, D.H.T. 37, 198
Wang, A. 97, 107
Wang, E.T.G. 163
waterfall model 166, 170n4
Weaver, P. 5, 38
Wehner, T. 174
Welde, M. 136, 145
Whist, E. 136
Wilden, R. 2

Williams, 28, 36, 53, 59, 188
Williamson, O.E. 32, 33
Wilson, T.L. 225
Work Activity Packs 213, 215
World Bank 58, 224
WorldCom 181

Zhai, L. 97, 107